3rd Edition Extra

with business skills lessons and self-assessment

Pre-intermediate

MARKET LEADER

Business English Course Book

with MyEnglishLab

David Cotton   David Falvey   Simon Kent

FT Publishing

FINANCIAL TIMES

GLOBAL SCALE
of English

Contents

Introduction

What is *Market Leader*, and who is it for?

Market Leader is a multi-level business English course for businesspeople and students of business English. It has been developed in association with the *Financial Times*, one of the leading sources of business information in the world. It consists of 12 units based on topics of great interest to everyone involved in international business.

This third edition of the Pre-intermediate level features completely updated content and a significantly enhanced range of authentic resource material, reflecting the latest trends in the business world. If you are in business, the course will greatly improve your ability to communicate in English in a wide range of business situations. If you are a student of business, the course will develop the communication skills you need to succeed in business and will enlarge your knowledge of the business world. Everybody studying this course will become more fluent and confident in using the language of business and should increase their career prospects.

The authors

David Falvey (left) has over 25 years' teaching and managerial experience in the UK, Japan and Hong Kong. He has also worked as a teacher trainer at the British Council in Tokyo, and was Head of the English Language Centre and Principal Lecturer at London Metropolitan University.

David Cotton (centre) has over 45 years' experience teaching and training in EFL, ESP and English for Business, and is the author of numerous business English titles, including *Agenda*, *World of Business*, *International Business Topics* and *Keys to Management*. He is also one of the authors of the best-selling *Business Class*. He was previously a Senior Lecturer at London Metropolitan University.

Simon Kent (right) has over 25 years' teaching experience, including three years as an in-company trainer in Berlin at the time of German reunification. He has spent the majority of his career to date in higher education in the UK where he has taught on and directed programmes of business, general and academic English.

What is in the units?

STARTING UP

You are offered a variety of interesting activities in which you discuss the topic of the unit and exchange ideas about it.

VOCABULARY

You will learn important new words and phrases which you can use when you carry out the tasks in the unit. You can find definitions and examples, and listen to the pronunciation of new vocabulary in the i-Glossary feature on the DVD-ROM. The DVD-ROM also contains practice exercises. A good business dictionary, such as the *Longman Business English Dictionary*, will also help you to increase your business vocabulary.

READING

You will read authentic articles on a variety of topics from the *Financial Times* and other newspapers and books on business. You will develop your reading skills and learn essential business vocabulary. You will also be able to discuss the ideas and issues in the articles.

LISTENING

You will hear authentic interviews with businesspeople and a variety of scripted recordings. You will develop listening skills such as listening for information and note-taking. You can also watch the interviews and find further practice exercises on the DVD-ROM.

LANGUAGE REVIEW

This section focuses on common problem areas at Pre-intermediate level. You will become more accurate in your use of language. Each unit contains a Language review box which provides a review of key grammar items. A Grammar reference section can be found at the back of the book and on the DVD-ROM. The DVD-ROM also provides extra grammar practice.

SKILLS

You will develop essential business communication skills, such as making presentations, taking part in meetings, negotiating, telephoning and using English in social situations. Each Skills section contains a Useful language box, which provides you with the language you need to carry out the realistic business tasks in the book. The DVD-ROM supplements the Course Book with additional activities.

CASE STUDY

The Case studies are linked to the business topics of each unit. They are based on realistic business problems or situations and allow you to use the language and communication skills you have developed while working through the unit. They give you the opportunity to practise your speaking skills in realistic business situations. Each Case study ends with a writing task. After you've finished the Case study, you can watch a consultant discussing the issues it raises on the DVD-ROM.

WORKING ACROSS CULTURES

These four units focus on different aspects of international communication. They help to raise your awareness of potential problems or misunderstandings that may arise when doing business with people from different cultures.

REVISION UNITS

Market Leader Pre-intermediate third edition also contains four revision units, each based on material covered in the preceding three Course Book units. Each revision unit is designed so that it can be completed in one session or on a unit-by-unit basis.

EXTRA BUSINESS SKILLS

The new Business Skills lessons offer the learner a task-based, integrated skills approach to the development of core business skills such as Presentations, Negotiations, Meetings, and Small Talk. These lessons appear at the end of every three units and incorporate performance review, suggestions for professional development and goal setting. They are based on the Global Scale of English Learning Objectives for Professional English. These objectives are signposted at the top of each new lesson in the Student's book and the carefully scaffolded activities are crafted around each objective, creating a clear sense of direction and progression in a learning environment where learners can reflect on their achievement at the end of the lesson.

1 Careers

'Many people quit looking for work when they find a job.'
Steven Wright, US comedian

STARTING UP

A **Discuss these questions.**

1 How ambitious are you?

2 Do you have a career plan? Where do you want to be in 10 years' time?

3 Which of the following would you prefer to do?

  a) work for one company during your career

  b) work for several different companies

  c) work for yourself

B **Look at these activities (1–7). In pairs, match each activity to its corresponding area of work (a–g). Which of these areas do you work in or would you like to work in? Why?**

1 making/manufacturing things

2 being in charge of people and running the organisation

3 selling products or services

4 dealing with clients/consumers

5 working with figures

6 dealing with employees and training

7 investigating and testing

a) Sales and Marketing

b) Finance

c) Management

d) Human Resources (HR)

e) Production

f) Research and Development (R&D)

g) Customer Service

C What should you do to get ahead in your career? Choose the four most important tips from this list. Compare your ideas in a group and try to agree on a final choice.

1 Change companies often.
2 Use charm with your superiors.
3 Attend all meetings.
4 Go to your company's social functions.
5 Be energetic and enthusiastic at all times.
6 Be the last to leave work every day.
7 Find an experienced person to give you help and advice.
8 Study for extra qualifications in your free time.

VOCABULARY
Career moves

A These phrases (1–6) all include the word *career*. Match each of them to its correct meaning (a–f). Use a dictionary to help you.

1 career move
2 career break
3 career plan
4 career opportunities
5 career path
6 career ladder

a) chances to start/improve your career
b) ideas you have for your future career
c) an action you take to progress in your career
d) a period of time away from your job to, for example, look after your children
e) a series of levels or steps in your working life
f) the direction your working life takes

B ◄)) CD1.1–1.3 Listen to three people talking about their careers. Which person is at the beginning, in the middle and at the end of their career?

C ◄)) CD1.1–1.3 Listen again. Which of the phrases with *career* in Exercise A does each person use? Which of the experiences do you think are common?

D Complete the sentences below with the verbs in the box. Use a dictionary to help you.

| climb | decide | ~~have~~ | make | offer | take |

1 Employees in large multinationals *have* excellent career opportunities if they are willing to travel.
2 Some people .... a career break to do something adventurous like sailing round the world or going trekking in India.
3 One way to .... a career move is to join a small but rapidly growing company.
4 Certain companies .... career opportunities to the long-term unemployed or to people without formal qualifications.
5 Ambitious people often .... on a career plan while they are still at university.
6 In some industries, it can take a long time to .... the career ladder.

E Look at these groups of words. Cross out the noun or noun phrase in each group which doesn't go with the verb in *italics*.

1 *make* a fortune / progress / a living / ~~a training course~~
2 *get* progress / a promotion / a bonus / fired (AmE) / the sack (BrE)
3 *earn* commission / a part-time job / money / 40,000 per year
4 *do* part-time work / a mistake / a nine-to-five job / your best
5 *take* a pension / an opportunity / time off / early retirement
6 *work* flexitime / anti-social hours / overtime / an office job

F **Complete each of these sentences with the appropriate form of a word partnership from Exercise E.**

1 In banking, you can .... with the big bonuses and retire at 35.

2 When you ...., you can arrange your own schedule, so this is very convenient when you have children.

3 People who work in sales often have the opportunity to .... on top of a basic salary.

4 Luke is ambitious and does not want to be a sales assistant all his life. In fact, he hopes to .... and become Assistant Manager very soon.

5 Many students .... when they are at university because it fits in with their studies.

6 Goran is 59, but he does not want to .... In fact, he is taking on more work!

*See the **DVD-ROM** for the i-Glossary.*

READING

Be aware of your online image

A **Discuss these questions in pairs.**

1 What social-networking sites do you a) know, and b) use?

2 Why do you use them?

B **Scan the article below quickly and answer these questions.**

1 What percentage of employers research candidates online?

2 Which social-networking sites are mentioned?

3 Who do Peter Cullen and Farhan Yasin work for?

by Andy Bloxham

Jobseekers have been warned that their Facebook profile could damage their employment prospects, after a study found that seven in 10 employers now research candidates online.

According to new figures released by Microsoft, checks on Facebook and Twitter are now as important in the job-selection process as a CV or interview.

The survey, which questioned human-resource managers at the top 100 companies in the UK, the US, Germany and France, found that 70 per cent admitted to rejecting a candidate because of their online behaviour.

But HR bosses also said that a strong image online could actually help job hunters to land their dream job. Peter Cullen, of Microsoft, said: "Your online reputation is not something to be scared of, it's something to be proactively managed. These days, it's essential that web users cultivate the kind of online reputation that they would want an employer to see."

Facebook *faux pas* include drunken photographs, bad language and messages complaining about work.

Farhan Yasin, of online recruitment network Careerbuilder.co.uk, said: "Social networking is a great way to make connections with job opportunities and promote your personal brand across the Internet. People really need to make sure they are using this resource to their advantage, by conveying a professional image."

But Mr Yasin cautioned job seekers to be aware of their online image even after landing the perfect job, after their own research found that 28 per cent of employers had fired staff for content found on their social-networking profile. He added, "A huge number of employers have taken action against staff for writing negative comments about the company or another employee on their social-networking page."

adapted from the *Telegraph*

C Read the article again and choose the best headline (a, b or c).

a) Complaining about your job could lose you your job

b) Facebook profile 'could damage job prospects'

c) Ambition is key to a successful career

D According to the article, how can social-networking sites make or break your career?

E In pairs, write a short list of things you should *not* do on your social-networking pages. You can include your own ideas.

F Should staff be allowed to use social-networking sites during the working day? Discuss.

LISTENING

Changing jobs

A ◀)) CD1.4 **Melissa Foux is the Finance Director of CSC Media Limited, a television company. Listen to the first part of the interview and answer these questions.**

1 How does she describe her current company?

2 What was her previous job?

3 Why is it easy to move from sector to sector in the finance world?

B ◀)) CD1.5 **Listen to the second part and complete this extract.**

When I was a student, although I was studying ....[1], I thought I would like to do something ....[2] afterwards, and I actually did a summer ....[3] with one of the big ....[4] firms, which was an excellent way to get an ....[5] of what the job would be like. I started off as an auditor, and it was through that ....[6] that I got my first job.

Melissa Foux

C ◀)) CD1.6 **Melissa is asked if she has had any good advice during her career. Listen to the third part and number these points in the order in which she mentions them.**

a) maintain clarity

b) be able to see the key point and the key decision you have to make

c) do not overcomplicate things

D ◀)) CD1.7 **Listen to the final part and decide which was the interviewer's question (a, b or c).**

a) What is the most interesting question you have been asked at interview?

b) What is the key difference between people who work in finance and those who work in research?

c) How would you advise people who are starting their careers?

Watch the interview on the DVD-ROM.

E **In groups, discuss these questions.**

1 What do you hope to do in the future in your career?

2 Do you think there is an ideal career for you? What is it? Why?

3 What is the best advice you have been given during your career or your studies?

**Modals 1:
ability, requests
and offers**

Modal verbs are very common in English. Match these functions (a–c) to the examples (1–3).

a) making an offer   b) describing ability   c) making a request

1 **Can** you help me?
  Could you say that again, please?

2 **Can** I help you?
  Would you like a cup of coffee?

3 I **can** speak Polish and Russian.
  She **could** read and write before she was three.

➡ *Grammar reference* page 141

A **Rearrange the words to make questions from a job interview. Then decide whether each question is a) making a request, b) making an offer, or c) asking about ability.**

1 get / you / can / I / a drink / ?

  Can I get you a drink? (b)

2 e-mail address / your / confirm / I / could / ?

3 can / you / spreadsheets / use / ?

4 speak / languages / any other / you / can / ?

5 about / tell / you / job / us / your present / more / could / ?

6 tell / your current salary / me / you / could / ?

7 would you / as soon as possible / your decision / let us know / ?

8 start / you / when / can / ?

9 like / tea / some more / you / would / ?

B **Match the questions in Exercise A (1–9) to these interviewee's answers (a–i).**

a) It's €60,000 a year.

b) Not very well, but I'm doing a course next week.

c) I can let you know next week.

d) Thank you. A cup of tea, please.

e) The address is correct, but I've got a new mobile number.

f) I'd love some. Thank you.

g) Well, I'm currently supervising an HR project.

h) Yes, I can speak Korean and Japanese.

i) My notice period is two months.

C **Work in pairs. Student A is an interviewer and Student B is an interviewee.**

Student A: Follow the instructions below.
Student B: Answer the questions truthfully.

Then switch roles.

Student A	

• Offer tea or coffee.
• Find out Student B's ability to:
  1 speak any languages;
  2 use Excel, PowerPoint or Publisher;
  3 drive.
	• Ask Student B:
	  1 to tell you about themselves;
	  2 for the best number to contact them on tomorrow;
	  3 to repeat the number;
	  4 if they would like to work abroad;
	  5 if there are any hours they wouldn't be able to work.

Telephoning: making contact

A What kinds of phone calls do you make in English? What useful telephone expressions do you know?

B ◀)) CD1.8–1.10 Listen to three phone calls and answer these questions.

1 What is the purpose of each call?   2 Do the callers know each other?

C ◀)) CD1.8 Listen to the first call again. Complete the expressions on the right so they have the same meaning as the ones on the left.

1 Can I talk to ...?   I'd _like_ to _speak_ to ...

2 Just a moment ...   Thank you. ....

3 I'll connect you.   I'll ....

4 Am I speaking to Corina Molenaar?   Hello. .... Corina Molenaar?

5 Yes, it's me.   ....

6 The reason I'm calling is ...   Yes, I'm .... your advert ...

7 Can I have your name and address?   ....
                                              your name and address, please?

D ◀)) CD1.9 Listen to the second call again and complete this extract.

A: Hello. _Could_ _I_ _speak_[1] to Giovanna, please?

B: ....[2] she's not here at the moment. Can I ....[3] a ....[4]?

A: Yes, please. ....[5] Johan from Intec. ....[6] you ....[7] her I won't be able to ....[8] the training course on Saturday? She can ....[9] me ....[10] if there's a problem. I'm ....[11] 0191 498 0051.

E ◀)) CD1.10 Listen to the third call again. Choose the phrases the speakers use.

Matt: Hello, Matt speaking.
Karl: Hi, Matt. Karl here.
Matt: Oh, hello, Karl. How are *things / you*[1]?
Karl: Fine, thanks. Listen, just a quick *word / question*[2].
Matt: Yeah, go ahead.
Karl: Do you think you could *give me / let me have*[3] the other number for Workplace Solutions? I can't get through to them. Their phone's always *busy / engaged*[4].
Matt: I've got it *here / right in front of me*[5]. It's 020 9756 4237.
Karl: Sorry, I didn't *hear / catch*[6] the last part. Did you say 4227?
Matt: No, it's 4237.
Karl: OK. Thanks. Bye.
Matt: *No problem / Don't mention it*[7]. Bye.

F Study the Useful language box below. Then role-play the phone calls.

Student A: Turn to page 132.   Student B: Turn to page 136.

USEFUL LANGUAGE

MAKING CALLS

Could I speak to Carmela Cantani, please?
Yes, this is Erika Mueller from KMV.
Is this the sales/finance/marketing department?
I'm calling about ...
Could you transfer me to the IT department, please?
Could you tell him/her that I called?
Could you ask him/her to call me back?
Can I leave a message, please?

RECEIVING CALLS

Who's calling, please?
Could you tell me what it's about?
I'll put you through.
Can you hold?
He seems to be with someone right now. Can I get him to call you?
I'm afraid there's no answer. Can I take a message?
I'm sorry, there's no answer. I can transfer you to his/her voice mail.

11

1

Case study

YOU*JUICE*

An international drinks company needs a dynamic new director to build its Latin American sales

Background

YouJuice Inc., based in Monterrey, Mexico, sells ready-to-drink juices all over the world. It was originally a Mexican company, but it is now owned by a large US corporation. YouJuice is currently looking for a Sales and Marketing Director for its sales facilities in Brazil, Argentina and Colombia.

Recently, sales results have been poor. Overall, sales revenue was 35% below target. The reasons are:

- Sales staff are not highly motivated, and staff turnover is high.
- The Sales Managers say that the low sales are due to strong competition in this segment of the market.
- The previous director had no clear strategy for developing sales.
- Not enough market research has been done, and the customer database does not produce reliable results.

A new appointment

There are three candidates for the position of Sales and Marketing Director. They all work for YouJuice in either Mexico or one of the foreign subsidiaries. The new director will be based in São Paulo, Brazil. Here is an extract from the job description for the position.

The successful candidate will be responsible for:
- increasing sales and developing marketing strategies
- coordinating the work of the sales teams so that they are more motivated and effective
- carrying out market research to improve customer numbers.

The successful candidate will be:
- a strong personality with leadership qualities
- energetic, dynamic, and enthusiastic.

He/She will have:
- a good academic background and relevant work experience
- organizational and interpersonal skills
- numeracy skills and analytical ability
- good linguistic ability.

The position will involve frequent travel in the three countries.

Profiles of the candidates

Read the essential information about each candidate. Then listen to the interview extracts.

🔊 **CD1.11, 1.12** Juana Ramos
Sanderson

🔊 **CD1.13, 1.14** Chantal Lefevre

🔊 **CD1.15, 1.16** Jeff

Juana Ramos
Mexican, aged 30
Married, two
children (seven and
nine years old)

Education
- University degree
  in Economics
- Studying for a
  Master's degree in Marketing (distance
  learning)

Experience
- Has worked for YouJuice since leaving
  university.
- Worked in market research for one year,
  then in sales.
- Has a good knowledge of computing;
  numerate.

Achievements
Top sales representative in the last five years

Languages
Fluent Spanish and Italian; good standard
of English; intermediate Portuguese

Interviewer's comments
A strong, charismatic personality. Very
competitive. Not afraid to speak her mind,
even if it upsets colleagues. A good sense
of humor. Wants to advance in her career
as quickly as possible. Intelligence test (IQ):
very high. Is she diplomatic? Interpersonal
skills?

Chantal Lefevre
Swiss, aged 41
Divorced, one child
(five years old)

Education
- University degree
  in Business
  Administration
- Diploma in Marketing

Experience
- Two years' market research, then over
  15 years' sales and marketing in various
  companies, including one year in Spain
  and six years in Portugal.
- Joined YouJuice three years ago as sales
  representative in Switzerland. Very hard-
  working. Has done an excellent job and
  earned large bonuses each year.

Achievements
A good sales record in all her previous
positions

Languages
Fluent Portuguese; intermediate Spanish;
excellent English

Interviewer's comments
A quiet, modest person, but very eager to
progress in her career. Answered questions
directly and honestly. A sociable person.
She's chief organizer of her local tennis club.
Believes that the new director should involve
staff in all decisions. Intelligence test (IQ):
average. Leadership qualities? Decisive?

Jeff Sanderson
American, aged 54
Single

Education
- University degree
  in Sociology
- Master's in
  Business
  Administration
  (MBA) from
  Harvard Business School

Experience
Joined YouJuice 20 years ago. Has always
worked in sales. In the last five years, Sales
Manager (France and Italy).

Achievements
Has increased sales by 8% in the five-year
period

Languages
Fluent English and Portuguese; Spanish:
good reading skills, needs to improve his
oral ability

Interviewer's comments
A serious person. Respected by his staff.
Has a strong sense of responsibility. 'I am
a company man.' Not very creative. Believes
new ideas should come from staff. Some
staff say he's a workaholic and difficult
to get to know. Very interested in South
American cultures. Intelligence test (IQ):
above average. Why does he really want
the job? Energetic enough?

Task

1 Work in groups. You are members of the interviewing team. Discuss
the strengths and weaknesses of each candidate. Decide who to
select for the vacant position. Note down the reasons for your choice.

2 Meet as one group. Discuss your choices. Decide who should fill the
vacant position.

*Watch the Case
study commentary
on the DVD-ROM.*

Writing

Complete this e-mail from the head of the interviewing team to Claudia López,
Regional Director of YouJuice. Write about at least three strengths of the candidate
you have chosen. Explain how these strengths relate to the job description.

To:	Regional Director
From:	Head, interviewing team
Subject:	Appointment of Sales and Marketing Director (Brazil, Argentina, Colombia)

Dear Claudia

We recently interviewed three candidates for this position.
We have decided to appoint …
I will briefly describe the candidate's strengths and explain the reasons for our decision.

 Writing file page 126

UNIT

2 | Companies

'Corporations are not things. They are the people who run them.'
Charles Handy, Irish management guru

OVERVIEW

VOCABULARY
Describing
companies

LISTENING
A successful
company

READING
Two different
organisations

LANGUAGE REVIEW
Present simple and
present continuous

SKILLS
Presenting your
company

CASE STUDY
Dino Conti Ice
Cream

STARTING UP **A** **Which of these companies do you or would you like to work for?**

1 a family-owned company

2 a multinational company

3 your own company (be self-employed)

B **Can you name a company in each of these business sectors? Is there one that you would like to work for?**

- Telecommunications/Media
- Banking and finance
- Food and drink
- Engineering
- Transport
- Retailing
- Pharmaceuticals/Chemicals
- Manufacturing
- Another service industry
- Construction
- IT/Electronics
- Tourism

VOCABULARY
**Describing
companies**

A **Complete the chart on the next page with the information in the box below. Then write sentences about the companies.**

example: *Cisco Systems is an American company which supplies
Internet equipment.*

| American Express   container-ship operator   fashion/retail   Finnish |
| Japanese   Korean   Nokia   oil and gas   pharmaceuticals   Toyota |

14

Company	Main activity	Nationality
Cisco Systems	Internet-equipment supplier	American
...........¹	Car manufacturer	...........²
Inditex	...........³	Spanish
...........⁴	Travel and financial services provider	American
Roche	...........⁵	Swiss
Samsung	Electronic-goods maker	...........⁶
...........⁷	Telecommunications	...........⁸
Hapag–Lloyd	...........⁹	German
Petrobras	...........¹⁰	Brazilian

B **Complete the sentences below with the words and phrases in the box.**

> head office   market share   net profit   parent company
> share price   subsidiary   ~~turnover~~   workforce

1 The amount of money a company receives from sales in a particular period is called its *turnover*.

2 The money a company makes after taking away its costs and tax is its ....

3 A company which owns another company is called a ....

4 The employees in a particular country or business are called the ....

5 The percentage of sales a company has in a particular market is its ....

6 The main building or location of a large organisation is its ....

7 The cost of a company's shares is its ....

8 A company which is more than 50% owned by another company is called a ....

C **Complete this extract from a company report with appropriate words or phrases from the box in Exercise B.**

> **Financial performance**
>
> I am pleased to say the *parent company*¹ has continued its excellent performance. We are changing, growing and doing well at a difficult time for the industry. ....² was €57.2 million, an increase of 15% on last year, and ....³ rose by 5% to €6.4 million.
>
> We are a highly competitive business. We have increased our ....⁴ to 20%. Consequently, our ....⁵ has risen and is now at an all-time high of €9.6.
>
> Increased production and strong demand have had a positive effect on our cashflow, so we are able to finance a number of new projects. We have successfully moved to our new ....⁶ in central London. We are now planning to start full production at the recently opened Spanish ....⁷ in October.
>
> Finally, thanks once again to our loyal and dedicated ....⁸. Our employees will always be our most valuable asset.

D 🔊 CD1.17 **Listen to the CEO reading from the company report and check your answers to Exercise C.**

E **Now talk in the same way about your own company or one you know well. Which other companies in your country are doing well / not doing well at the moment?**

See the DVD-ROM for the i-Glossary.

LISTENING
A successful company

Susan Barratt

A ◀)) CD1.18 **Listen to the first part of an interview with Susan Barratt, the Chief Executive Officer of Nature's Way Foods, and correct the six mistakes in this paragraph.**

Nature's Way Foods is a drinks-manufacturing company based on the east coast of Ireland. They put chilled product, the majority of which is milk and cheese, into various types of packaging for the major retailers and various food-service companies in Ireland.

B ◀)) CD1.19 **Listen to the second part, where Susan talks about the reasons for the company's success, and complete these notes with one word in each gap.**

First reason for success: the ....^{1}

- Health – desire to eat healthy ....^{2}
- Convenience – ....^{3}-poor
- Sustainability – low level of food ....^{4}
- Indulgence – diet Monday to Friday, but have several pieces of cake on Friday night

Second reason for success: the way they ....^{5} the business

- High-............^{6} business
- Produce hundreds of ....^{7} of units
- Need to be very ....^{8} in the way they produce them
- Invested heavily in ....^{9} and processes

C ◀)) CD1.20 **Listen to the third part and answer these questions.**

1 What two things has Susan enjoyed the most when running a company?

2 What does she not enjoy about running a company?

D ◀)) CD1.21 **Listen to the final part and complete this extract.**

I've learned a lot of lessons from the companies I've worked for. I think the key thing is that you have to make sure your ....^{1} in the organisation are engaged with the organisation and have a clear ....^{2} of what that organisation is trying to ....^{3}.

If you can get that clarity of ....^{4} and ....^{5} from the people within the organisation, then that will help move the business forward in itself.

*Watch the interview on the **DVD-ROM**.*

E **Discuss this question in pairs.**

Would you like to run your own company? Why? / Why not?

READING
Two different organisations

A **'Companies should be owned by their employees.' Discuss.**

B **Work in pairs. As you read, make a note of the key points about your company in the chart below.**

Student A: Read Article 1 on the opposite page.
Student B: Read Article 2 on the opposite page.

Tata	John Lewis
India's biggest company	Owned by its employees

Article 1

India: Tata's search for a new CEO

by Joe Leahy in Mumbai

Mr Tata, Chairman of India's biggest company, is expected to retire – yet again – in two years. But this time things look different. The group appears ready to move on, formally announcing last month that it has set up a special committee to look for a new CEO.

Instead of simply choosing the most obvious successor, the group has said it will consider all candidates for India's biggest corporate job. In a country where companies are often controlled by influential families, the idea of an outsider, particularly a foreigner, controlling a group of Tata's size and reputation is revolutionary.

At risk is more than the future of the Tata Group, though this is very important to the national economy. With its 100 subsidiaries – including India's biggest private-sector steel company, its biggest information-technology outsourcing company and its biggest automotive producer – it is also the country's first true multinational, with 65 per cent of its $71bn in revenue generated overseas.

Analysts question whether Tata can create an example for corporate India of orderly transition from family leadership to professional management. "There's a feeling if an outsider, especially a foreigner, took over a group as complex as Tata, it would be disastrous," says a banker who knows the company.

However, some critics argue that introducing professionals would help to break down a reputation for weak management in large, family-run companies.

Article 2

Is John Lewis the best company in Britain to work for?

by Jon Henley

It is owned by its employees – or partners – who have a say in how it is run and receive a share of the profits. Surely this is the way every organisation should be run?

It's just before opening time on bonus day at John Lewis and, boy, are we excited. Up and down the country, the 69,000 people who work for the nation's favourite retailer are gathered, impatient. A specially chosen staff member opens an envelope and reads out a number. Fifteen per cent. It's the percentage of their salary that each John Lewis employee takes home as that year's bonus.

If a product is on sale in a John Lewis store, you know you can trust it. Plus you can be sure you'll be served by someone who really knows what they're talking about and, most unusually of all, is eager to help.

Unlike other high-street names, John Lewis is owned by its employees, each of whom has a say in its running and a share in its profits. This is Britain's largest example of worker co-ownership. Its purpose is "the happiness of all its members, through their worthwhile and satisfying employment in a successful business".

"It's a good company to work for," says Pedro, a Waitrose* chef. "I didn't realise how good until I joined." Employer–employee relations at John Lewis, says Nicola McRoberts, "are completely different. They want you to be happy."

A veteran of five years, Kirsty Reilly, in womenswear, speaks of the "passion and commitment" that come from "being engaged, because you have a shared interest in making sure it works, for you and for the people you work with."

*A supermarket chain, part of the John Lewis group

adapted from the *Guardian*

C After reading, ask your partner what they have learned about Tata / John Lewis. Add the new information to your chart in Exercise B.

D Compare and contrast the two companies.

example: Tata is an Indian company, but John Lewis is a British company.

E Discuss these questions.

1 What are the good and bad points of bringing in someone from outside to run a family-owned business?

2 Do you know of any company like John Lewis in your country? If so, how successful is it?

Present simple and present continuous

Complete the rules below with these phrases.

a) ~~factual information~~
b) future arrangements
c) routine activities and habits
d) temporary situations

We use the present simple to:
* give *factual information*[1]
  *Tata **produces** cars.*

* talk about...........[2]
  *I usually **arrive** at the office at eight o'clock.*

Some verbs are almost always used in the present simple rather than the present continuous, for example *like, want, know, need*.

We use the present continuous to:
* describe...........[3]
  *She**'s staying** in Mumbai till the end of the week.*

* talk about...........[4]
  *What **are** you **doing** on Tuesday afternoon?*

➡ *Grammar reference page 142*

A **Complete these sentences with either the present simple or the present continuous form of the verbs in brackets.**

1 We normally ...*hold*... (*hold*) our sales conference in Mumbai, but this year we .... (*hold*) it in Delhi.

2 Although we .... (*use*) our own sales representative at the moment, we generally .... (*use*) agents in China.

3 Tatsuo .... (*work*) for a financial magazine. At the moment, he .... (*write*) an article on insider trading.

4 Usually our Sales Director .... (*deal*) with important customers, but I .... (*deal*) with all enquiries while she is on holiday.

5 I .... (*come*) from Poland, but at the moment I .... (*live*) in Germany.

6 John Lewis .... (*want*) to continue with expansion this year.

B **Complete the job advertisement below with either the present simple or the present continuous form of the verbs in the box.**

~~be~~ consider employ have grow look need offer offer prepare

Sales Manager

■ We ...*are*...[1] one of the largest mobile-phone retailers in Europe.
■ We ....[2] independent and impartial advice on mobile phones.
■ We ....[3] more than 800 stores in 10 countries, and we ....[4] fast.
■ We ....[5] over 3,000 workers. Currently, we ....[6] the next stage in our development, and we ....[7] for major growth outside Europe.
■ We ....[8] for people who are reliable, confident and enthusiastic. We ....[9] experienced people who want to work for an expanding company.
■ We ....[10] a competitive salary and private health insurance. We are willing to reward staff with attractive performance-based bonuses.

Ring 020 7946 0008 for an information pack.

C **Work in pairs.**

Student A: Turn to page 134.   Student B: Turn to page 136.

SKILLS
Presenting your company

A What sort of presentations have you given? How did you feel?

B 🔊 CD1.22 Listen to the beginning of a presentation by Robert Pullin, Director of Human Resources at DCV Fashions, and answer these questions.

1 What is the main aim of the presenter?

2 What kind of audience is he probably addressing?

C 🔊 CD1.22 Listen again and complete this paragraph.

..............[1], I'll give you some basic information about DCV Fashions. ....[2], I'll explain why we've been so successful in the fashion industry. ....[3], I'll tell you about our mission statement. This describes what we're all about, why we're in business. And ....[4], I'll explain how we communicate with people through our advertising and promotion.

D In pairs, practise giving an introduction to your own company or one which you know well.

DCV Fashions

Head office	..............[1]
Products	..............[2]
Turnover (last year)	..............[3]
Profits (last year)	..............[4]
Reasons for success	..............[5]
Advertising and promotion	..............[6]

E 🔊 CD1.23 Listen to the rest of the presentation. Work in pairs and complete the information on the left. If necessary, listen again.

F Number these phrases which introduce different sections of the presentation in the order in which they appear.

a) Moving on now to our mission ... ☐

b) Finally, a word about ... ☐

c) Thanks very much for listening ... ☐

d) OK, some basic facts ... ☐

e) What's the key to our success? ☐

G Choose one of these topics.

- Think about your company or a company you know. Study the Useful language box below, and use the headings in the chart in Exercise E to help you prepare a presentation about it.

- Use the facts provided on page 133 to make a presentation about Moda International Fashion Group (MIFG).

Work in pairs. Make your presentation and answer your partner's questions. Your audience is a group of young people from a fashion college.

USEFUL LANGUAGE

INTRODUCING YOURSELF

Hello everyone, my name's Robert Pullin. I'm Director of Human Resources at DCV Fashions.

Good morning, I'm Robert Pullin, Director of Human Resources, DCV Fashions.

STATING YOUR AIM

My purpose today is to talk to you about our company.

Today, I'd like to talk about our new projects.

OUTLINING THE PRESENTATION

First, I'll give you some basic information.

Next, I'll talk about our products.

Then, I'll discuss the reasons for our success.

Finally, I'll tell you about our advertising and marketing.

INTRODUCING NEW INFORMATION

Here are some basic facts.

Here are some key facts about our company.

CHANGING TO A NEW SECTION OF THE TALK

Moving on now to our mission.

OK/Right. What about our distribution system?

ENDING THE PRESENTATION

Thanks very much for listening to my presentation.

Thanks for coming to my talk. Are there any questions?

2

Case study

How can a popular ice-cream maker increase sales?

Background

Dino Conti Ice Cream Inc., based in Santa Barbara (USA), manufactures and distributes ice cream to consumers in California. It produces 15 flavours, which it distributes mainly to supermarkets and company-owned stores. Its most famous product is its classic chocolate ice cream, sold under the SupaKool label. Many people believe that Dino Conti's SupaKool chocolate ice cream is the best in the world.

Dino Conti has expanded rapidly in recent years, but now its growth is slowing down. A recent fall in profits has disappointed the management. The owner, Paolo Conti, wants the company to become more international.

🔊 **CD1.24** Listen to an excerpt from a board meeting. Make notes under these headings.

Reasons for falling profits

- Prices
- Products
- Equipment
- Environment
- Outlets

Chart 1: Dino Conti's main products (as a % of turnover)

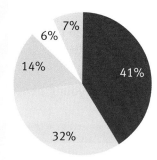

Classic SupaKool chocolate ice cream	41%
Six top-selling flavours	32%
Other flavours	14%
Iced yoghurt	6%
Novelty products*	7%

* iced fudge, chocolate bars, lollipops

The future

Paolo Conti has $3 million to invest in his company so that it continues to expand and become an international business. Here is an extract from a company profile that appeared in a business magazine recently.

Dino Conti can continue its remarkable growth, but only if it solves its present problems, develops new products, and finds new markets.

So how should Paolo Conti invest the $3 million? Chart 2 on page 21 lists the ways he could do that.

Chart 2: investment options

Option	Cost (estimated)	Benefit
1 Build a bigger factory	$2.4 million	More production capacity; lower unit costs
2 Export to China and Russia	$1.2 million	New markets – great sales potential
3 Buy out its major competitor	$2 million+	Reduce competition; increase production capacity
4 Develop a range of exotic fruit drinks	$2.5 million	Move into a new area
5 Upgrade its equipment and fleet of trucks	$1.2 million	Lower costs
6 Distribute to more outlets	$500,000	Increase sales and profits
7 Increase its advertising budget	$500,000	Increase sales / Improve company image
8 Make the company more 'green'	$800,000	Improve company image and sales
9 Improve the products' packaging	$400,000	Increase sales
10 Offer free ice cream to all consumers one day a year	$600,000+	Raise awareness of the company; good PR

Task

You are directors of Dino Conti Ice Cream. Meet to discuss your investment plan.

1 Work in pairs. Decide how to spend the $3 million. Prepare a presentation of your investment plan, with reasons for your choices.

2 Meet as one group and present your ideas.

3 As one group, agree on a final investment plan.

*Watch the Case study commentary on the **DVD-ROM.***

Writing

As a director of Dino Conti Ice Cream, write a proposal document to your CEO in which you:

- list the investment options you have chosen;
- give arguments for each option, as well as the cost and benefits.

Begin as shown on the right.

INVESTMENT PLAN

1 Objectives

To solve our current problems and enable Dino Conti to become a competitive international business, we propose an investment of $3 million.

2 Strategy and implementation

The Board of Directors has agreed the following investment plan.

→ *Writing file* page 127

'I'm very proud of my gold pocket watch. My grandfather, on his deathbed, sold me this watch.' **Woody Allen, American actor, writer, director and comedian**

STARTING UP   **A**   **What do you like about shopping? What don't you like? When did you last visit these retail outlets? What did you buy?**

- a (street) market
- a convenience store
- a supermarket
- a department store
- a specialist retailer
- a shopping centre/mall
- an online retailer

B   ◀)) CD1.25–1.27 **Listen to three people talking about their shopping habits and answer these questions.**

1   What do they like and dislike?

2   Which shopper are you most like?

3   How are shopping habits changing in your country?

VOCABULARY
Making sales

A Choose the correct word (a, b or c) to complete each sentence.

1 A _manufacturer_ is another name for a 'producer'.

a) supplier   b) distributor   (c) manufacturer)

2 Suppliers often sell large quantities of goods to ...., who do not usually sell directly to consumers.

a) wholesalers   b) retailers   c) manufacturers

3 We offer a .... to customers who buy in bulk.

a) refund   b) discount   c) delivery

4 We ask consumers who are not fully satisfied to .... goods within seven days.

a) discount   b) refund   c) return

5 In order to get a full ...., customers must send back goods in the original packaging.

a) discount   b) refund   c) return

6 Goods will be .... within 24 hours of your order.

a) dispatched   b) purchased   c) exchanged

7 Goods are kept in our .... until ready for delivery.

a) stock   b) storage   c) warehouse

8 Products and services offered at a large discount are generally a(n) ....

a) sale   b) bargain   c) offer

B Combine phrases from Box A with words from Box B to make word partnerships. Use the definitions (1–8) below to help you.

A

| after-sales ~~cooling-off~~ credit-card interest-free loyalty-card |
| method of   money-back   out of |

B

| credit   details   guarantee   payment   ~~period~~   scheme   service   stock |

1 the time when you can change your mind and cancel an order _cooling-off period_

2 the name, number and expiry date on your payment card

3 the way you pay for the goods you want

4 when you can pay some time after you buy, but at no extra cost

5 when the goods you require are not available

6 a promise to return your money if you are not happy

7 the help you get from a company when you start to use their product

8 method for customers to obtain a discount on future purchases from the same organisation

C Look back at the retail outlets in Starting up Exercise A. Where would you buy the following items? Why?

• a pair of shoes   • music   • fruit   • a bottle of perfume/cologne   • a holiday
• a watch / piece of jewellery   • furniture   • a book   • concert tickets

See the DVD-ROM for the i-Glossary.

D Which of the answers in Exercise B would you expect to be important in each situation/purchase in Exercise C? Discuss your ideas.

LISTENING

Selling on TV

Sue Leeson

A   🔊 CD1.28 **Sue Leeson is Director of Marketing at QVC, the global shopping channel. Listen to the first part of the interview and answer these questions.**

1   What are the six product groups that she mentions?

2   QVC sells to consumers in which countries?

3   Which two media are used to sell QVC's products?

B   🔊 CD1.29 **In the second part, Sue talks about the secret of a really good presentation and developing a sales pitch. Listen and complete this paragraph.**

Firstly, having a product that you can easily ....^{1} and a product that has a good ....^{2} behind it. Secondly, that the person who's actually giving the sales presentation can engage with their............^{3} in a credible fashion, can tell the story very clearly and can demonstrate the features and............^{4} of each product in a very............^{5} and easy-to-understand way.

C   🔊 CD1.29 **Listen again and complete these notes.**

You need to know:

* the product ....^{1}
* what the product can or can't............^{2}
* when the product is or isn't............^{3}.

D   🔊 CD1.30 **Listen to the third part and answer these questions.**

1   Why are beauty products easy to sell on TV?

2   Which type of product is difficult to sell, and why?

Watch the interview on the DVD-ROM.

E   🔊 CD1.31 **Listen to the final part. If customers want to buy a skincare product, what four things can they see on the QVC website?**

READING

Sales skills

A   **Look at these qualities needed to succeed in sales. Which do you think are the top four?**

• personality   • honesty   • appearance   • confidence   • knowing your product
• organisational skills   • ability to close a deal   • ability to deal with people

B   **Which of the qualities in Exercise A is the most important? Turn to page 136 to see how 200 sales professionals answered this question.**

C   **Work in pairs.**

Student A: Read the article on the opposite page and match each of these headings (a–h) to one of the paragraphs (1–8).

a) Motivation
b) Professionalism
c) TV
d) Personal qualities

e) Main finding of the survey   1
f) Why women make the best salespeople
g) What the survey asked
h) The woman who would make the best salesperson

Student B: Read the article on page 137 and match each of these headings (a–h) to one of the paragraphs (1–8).

a) Know your business
b) Appearance
c) Confidence
d) The sales mindset

e) Numbers, numbers, numbers
f) Know how far you'll negotiate
g) People dislike selling   1
h) Develop a sales process

Women on top in new sales industry survey

A new survey of the sales industry shows who sales professionals believe make the best salespeople and the qualities needed in order to succeed.

1 A new survey of over 200 sales professionals has found that two-thirds of women and over half of men believe that women make the best salespeople, underlining the growing reputation of women in the sales industry.

2 The survey was carried out for Pareto Law, a recruitment and training company. It questioned sales professionals on what they considered to be the most important qualities for a salesperson. It also asked who would be most likely to succeed.

3 Both men (53%) and women (66%) agreed that women do make better salespeople, with Hillary Clinton voted as the top female celebrity most likely to succeed in a career in sales.

4 When asked why women make the best salespeople, men believe the main reason is that women are better at actually closing a deal, while women stated they are better than men when it comes to dealing with people. Other female skills highlighted included being more organised and being able to handle more work, while male skills were identified as strong personalities and selling skills.

5 Jonathan Fitchew, Managing Director of Pareto Law, said: "Television programmes have increased people's interest in the sales industry, but have also highlighted the different approaches of men and women to the same sales issues."

6 When it comes to the individual qualities required to become a successful salesperson, men ranked honesty as most important (53%), while women placed most value on personality (47%). Both agreed that integrity was also key, coming third overall (41%). Good looks came at the bottom of the list, with only 3% of sales professionals ranking this as important.

7 This focus on professionalism, rather than the hard sell, supports the fact that over half of the sales professionals questioned believe that the reputation of sales has improved over the last 10 years, with 55% of men and 47% of women considering this to be the case.

8 Both men (87%) and women (86%) agreed that the top incentive for salespeople was money, with the average sales executive expecting to earn between £25–35k, including bonuses and commission, in their first year of work. Other incentives included verbal praise, overseas holidays and cars.

adapted from www.ukprwire.com

D **Work in pairs.**

Student A: Ask Student B these questions about their article.

1 What should you do if you are not inwardly confident?

2 What do you need to know well?

3 What do '30 seconds' and '15 seconds' refer to?

4 What should you do when you are rejected?

5 What should you focus on?

6 What do you need to know when negotiating?

7 What sales mindset should you have?

Student B: Ask Student A what these numbers refer to in their article.

a) two-thirds   b) half   c) 53   d) 66   e) 53   f) 47   g) third
h) 41   i) 3   j) 10   k) 55   l) 47   m) 87   n) 86   o) 25–35

LANGUAGE REVIEW

Modals 2: *must, need to, have to, should*

- We use *should* or *shouldn't* to give advice or make suggestions.
  *You **should** follow up all your leads.*
  *You **shouldn't** talk about yourself.*

- We use *have to* or *need to* to say that something is necessary or very important.
  *I think you **have to** pay a sales tax.*
  *I **need to** sell my car quickly.*

- We use *don't have to* or *don't need to* if something is not necessary.
  *You **don't have to** make a sale the first time you speak to a contact.*
  *If you buy now, you **don't need to** pay anything until next year.*

- *must* is very similar to *have to*.
  *You **must** sound and appear confident.*

  But *mustn't* is **not** the same as *don't have to*. We use *mustn't* to say that somebody is not allowed to do something.
  *You **mustn't** sell cigarettes to anyone under age. (= **Don't** sell cigarettes to anyone under age.)*

  ➡ *Grammar reference page 143*

A **Read these rules of a timeshare* vacation club. Then answer the questions below.**

- Timeshare members must have an income of $60,000 or over.
- You don't have to go to a timeshare sales presentation.
- You have to stay for a minimum of seven nights.
- You shouldn't play loud music after 10 p.m.
- You need to make your reservation 180 days in advance.
- You don't have to attend members' welcome nights.
- Timeshare members must be 25 or over.

* A timeshare is the right to use holiday accommodation for a specific amount of time each year.

1 Can you be a member if you earn $50,000? *No*

2 Is it necessary to sit through a timeshare sales presentation?

3 Is it necessary to stay for at least seven nights?

4 Can you play loud music after 10 p.m.?

5 Can you book 90 days in advance?

6 Is it necessary to go to members' welcome nights?

7 Can you be a timeshare member if you are 21?

B **Match each of these sentences (1–6) to a suitable ending (a–f).**

1 I can pay for the house now, a) so we don't need to work over the weekend.

2 We've reached our sales targets, b) so we must not offer any further discounts.

3 Our profit margin is low, c) so you must be confident.

4 My business is quite small, d) so you'll have to buy it on disk.

5 It isn't available as a download, e) so I have to be very careful with cashflow.

6 The job involves sales presentations, f) so I don't have to worry about a bank loan.

C **In pairs, write an advice sheet on how to be a good salesperson, including the qualities you need to succeed. You may use the reading texts on pages 25 and 137 to help you.**

example: *You must sound and appear confident.*

SKILLS

Negotiating: reaching agreement

A **Work in two groups, A and B.**

Group A: Look at the negotiating tips on page 132.
Group B: Look at the negotiating tips on page 136.

1 Each group agrees on the five most important negotiating tips on its list.

2 Form new groups with members from Groups A and B. Agree on a *single* list of the five most important tips from *both* lists.

B ◀) CD1.32 **You are going to hear a conversation between Martin, Sales Manager of Pulse, an electric-car company, and Chen, an official from the Urban Transport Department of a city in China. Listen and answer these questions.**

1 Why does Chen want to buy electric cars for the Transport Department?

2 Which of these do they discuss?

• quantity   • price   • discounts   • colours   • delivery   • warranty   • models

3 What will they discuss after lunch?

C ◀) CD1.32 **Listen to the negotiation again and complete these sentences.**

1 Chen: Yes, pollution is a big problem here. We're trying all sorts of ideas to reduce it … I see from your .... that a standard two-seater car will cost about €12,000.

2 Martin: If you order 10 vehicles, you'll be paying us about €100,000 , minus the 2% .... we offer a new customer.

3 Martin: We could possibly deliver by late August, all being well.

   Chen: Mmm, that might be OK, if you can .... by then.

4 Chen: Good, how about the .... ? We'd like a long period.

5 Chen: What about payment? Do you offer .... terms?

   Martin: I'm afraid not. It's company .... for a new customer. We need payment by bank transfer on receipt of the goods. Oh, and we ask for a .... of 20% of the value of the order.

D **Work in pairs to role-play this situation. Martin and Chen are continuing the negotiation. They discuss these points.**

• four-seater car

• colours

• after-sales-service

• radio/CD player and sat-nav system

Student A: Turn to page 138.   Student B: Turn to page 134.

Read your role cards. Try to agree on the points you negotiate.

USEFUL LANGUAGE

STATING AIMS

We're interested in buying 10 cars.

We'd like to start the scheme in June.

We must have delivery as soon as possible.

MAKING CONCESSIONS

We could possibly deliver by August.

That could be all right, as long as you pay more for a longer period.

We can do that, providing you make a down payment.

REJECTING SUGGESTIONS

I'm afraid not. It's company policy.

I'm sorry, we can't agree to that.

Unfortunately, we can't do that.

BARGAINING

If it works, we'll increase the order later on.

If you increased your order, we could offer you a much higher discount.

That might be OK if you can guarantee delivery by then.

GETTING AGREEMENT

That's very reasonable, don't you think?

That sounds a fair price to me.

Fine./OK./Great!

FINISHING THE NEGOTIATION

Right, we've got a deal.

Good, I think we've covered everything.

OK, how about dinner tonight?

A partnership agreement

How can a jet charter company stay ahead of the competition?

Background

EPJS (Executive and Private Jet Service) is a jet charter company. It arranges travel in private jets for top executives and VIPs (very important people). It provides a customised service, looking after all its customers' requirements, from booking tickets to transporting air travellers to their final destination.

It is currently negotiating a partnership agreement with the Megaluxe group of hotels. Based in Stuttgart, Germany, Megaluxe has five-star hotels across Europe, Asia and South America. EPJS has agreed to give Megaluxe 'preferred partner status'. This means that EPJS will always reserve rooms for its customers in a Megaluxe hotel, providing the customer has not expressed a preference for another hotel.

EPJS is a fast-growing company, but it is facing strong competition from other charter airlines. To beat the competition, it must offer customers a very attractive package: good-value prices, special assistance at airports, superb hotel accommodation and outstanding service.

EPJS and Megaluxe have met several times. They are now ready to negotiate some of the key terms of the contract.

🔊 **CD1.33** Listen to a conversation between a director of EPJS and a director of Megaluxe. They are discussing the agenda for the negotiation. Note down the agenda items.

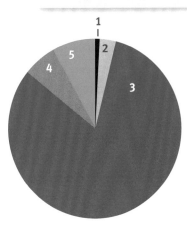

EPJS customer profile (% of total customers p.a.)

1 *Super-wealthy   1%
2 ** Wealthy   3%
3 Business executives   82%
4 VIPs   6%
5 *** Other   8%

Very high net worth (over $30 million)
***High net worth (over $1 million)**
****Clients chartering for special events, e.g. celebration trips, family reunions, sports-team travel, bands on tour, etc.**

SUITES ROOMS RESTAURANT SPA BARS POOL INDOOR TENNIS GOLF COURSE
BUSINESS CENTRE REST ROOMS CONCIERGE SERVICE MEETING ROOMS

Welcome to Megaluxe hotels

- Every modern convenience
- Splendid views of the city
- Elegance, luxury, relaxation

ROOM RATES

Format	Arrangement	Rate per night
Platinum Suite	Suite	$4,000 per night
Gold Standard	Double room	$1,000 per night
Executive Standard	Double room	$850 per night

Task

Work in two groups.

Group A: You are directors of Megaluxe. Turn to page 133.

Group B: You are directors of EPJS. Turn to page 138.

Read your role cards and prepare for the negotiation. Use the agenda items that you noted down during the telephone call. Try to agree on a partnership deal.

Watch the Case study commentary on the DVD-ROM.

Writing

As a director of EPJS or as a director of Megaluxe, write a letter to the person you negotiated with, summarising what you agreed.

27 November
Dear [name],
Below is a summary of the points we agreed at our recent meeting.

 Writing file page 128

1 Saying 'no' politely

A In groups, answer these questions.

1 What excuses do people make when they say 'no'?

2 Have you ever had to say 'no', but been embarrassed?

3 Have you ever said 'yes' to a request, but later wished you had said 'no'?

4 When is it rude to say 'no' in your country?

B ◀)) CD1.34 Listen to the first part of a short talk by a cross-cultural communications expert. Complete these five tips for saying 'no' politely.

1 Pay............

2 Offer............

3 Show............

4 Be............

5 Avoid............

C ◀)) CD1.35 Listen to the second part of the talk, which looks at saying 'no' in different countries. Decide whether these statements are true (T) or false (F). Correct the false ones.

1 In Japan, it is very important to focus on verbal communication.

2 In Japan, it will embarrass people if you turn down a request.

3 Indonesians do not like to embarrass people by saying 'no'.

4 Bahasa Indonesian has 12 ways of saying 'yes'.

5 In China, silence can mean there are problems.

6 In the Arab world, silence usually means 'no'.

7 Refusing a cup of coffee from an American host is considered rude.

D Match the invitations and requests (1–5) to the responses (a–e).

1 Would you like to go out for a meal later?

2 Would you like some more food?

3 Shall we meet up next Tuesday?

4 Please stay a little bit longer.

5 Can you check that the fire-exit notices are all in the right place, please?

a) I'm afraid you've come to the wrong person. You'll have to ask Ingrid in Health and Safety.

b) Thanks for the invitation, but I'm not feeling so well. Maybe some other time.

c) Nothing more for me, thanks. It was delicious.

d) I'm sorry. I'd love to, but I have other plans that evening.

e) I've had a wonderful time and I wish I could, but I really have to go.

E 🔊 CD1.36 **Listen and check your answers.**

Task

In pairs, role-play these situations. Read both roles (A and B). Take it in turns to play Role B, so you both get the opportunity to say 'no' politely.

	A	B
1	You are the host at a meal in a restaurant. Offer your client some champagne.	You do not drink alcohol. Say 'no' politely.
2	You have to complete a short report quickly. Ask a colleague to help you.	You are very busy, and this is not your job. Suggest your colleague asks Freya to help.
3	You are an investment director. Invite a client to an important hospitality event next month.	You cannot attend this event because you have already accepted another invitation. But you want to maintain a good relationship and you would like to attend another event in the future.
4	You are the host at a meal in your home for some business contacts. Offer your guest some lamb, rice and vegetables.	You hate lamb. Say 'no' politely. Say you are happy with just rice and vegetables.
5	You have just finished writing a very important report, which you need to submit in an hour. Ask your colleague to check it first.	You are very busy. You have to prepare for a meeting with your boss in an hour.
6	You are in a country where it is common to go out to eat late at night. Invite a business contact who has arrived from another country to go out for a meal at 10 p.m. tonight.	You are very tired and need to prepare for an important meeting tomorrow.

1 Careers

VOCABULARY

Choose the best word to complete each sentence.

1 Zoltan decided on his career *move* / *plan* when he was in his first year of university, and amazingly, he followed it until he retired.

2 Rupert hopes to make a *living* / *course* doing freelance consulting.

3 My company has a training programme that offers career *opportunities* / *breaks* to students who have just graduated from university.

4 Helena was very happy with the *bonus* / *progress* she got last month.

5 If you want to climb the career *plan* / *ladder*, you have to be prepared to work very hard.

6 Dominic was very pleased when he earned his first *job* / *commission*.

7 Begonia is ready to make a career *opportunity* / *move*, so she's applying for jobs with other companies.

8 Alicia did *a mistake* / *her best* when she completed her job application.

9 Some companies help their employees take a career *path* / *break* by giving them a few months off without pay.

10 Pietro was 55 years old when he took *early retirement* / *a pension*.

11 Mei-Mei didn't follow the usual career *ladder* / *path* for the CEO of a marketing firm. She started out working as a primary-school teacher.

12 Sharon never felt happy working *overtime* / *extra*.

13 Magnus earns *€60K per year* / *flexitime* in his new accounting job.

14 I wasn't surprised to hear that Dean got *the sack* / *a mistake*, but I feel very sorry for him.

MODALS

Complete each conversation with *can*, *could* and *would*. Use each word once in each conversation.

A: ....¹ I help you?

B: Yes. My name's Heinz Wagner. I'm here to see Martina López.

A: She'll be right out. ....² you like a cup of coffee or tea?

B: No, thanks. But ....³ you tell me where the men's room is, please?

***

A: My cousin ....⁴ speak French and German by the time she was five, and now she ....⁵ speak Russian and Greek as well.

B: Do you think she ....⁶ like to learn any more languages?

***

A: ....⁷ you like to ask any more questions about Fabian?

B: Yes. ....⁸ he drive? Does he have a licence?

A: I'm not sure. I ....⁹ phone him and ask him.

SKILLS

Match the halves of the expressions.

Part A

1 Can
2 Can I get him to
3 Can I leave
4 He seems to be
5 Could I speak
6 Could you
7 Could you ask
8 Could you tell

a) with someone right now.
b) her to call me back?
c) to Michael Sands, please?
d) you hold?
e) him that I called?
f) call you?
g) a message, please?
h) transfer me to the IT department, please?

Part B

1 Could you tell me
2 Can I take
3 I can transfer you
4 I'll
5 I'm afraid
6 I'm sorry, there's no
7 Is this the
8 Who's
9 Yes, this is

a) Larissa Schulton speaking.
b) a message?
c) answer.
d) there's no answer.
e) to her voicemail.
f) what it's about?
g) put you through.
h) marketing department?
i) calling, please?

2 Companies

VOCABULARY

Complete the text below with the words in the box.

> net profit   parent company   pharmaceutical   share price
> Spanish subsidiary   turnover   workforce

Espania-pharm

Espania-pharm today announced the opening of its new head office in Barcelona. The ....[1] company's efforts to boost its market share paid off in the first quarter, as its ....[2] was almost €15.6 million, leading to a ....[3] of €8 million. The company has also doubled the size of its ....[4] by hiring 50 new employees in the past four months. However, the company's ....[5] is unlikely to go up until investors feel confident that the company is strong.

Espania-pharm is the ....[6] of the global giant. The ....[7], based in Stockholm, reported profits of €950 million in the first quarter.

PRESENT SIMPLE AND PRESENT CONTINUOUS

Complete this text with either the present simple or the present continuous form of the verbs in brackets. Use contracted forms where appropriate.

I ....[1] (*be*) a trainee project manager and I ....[2] (*love*) my job. I ....[3] (*work*) for a well-known computer manufacturer, in the marketing department. Right now, we ....[4] (*develop*) an advertising campaign for our newest laptop computers. We ....[5] (*try*) to find the best artist for our print advertisements, so this week I ....[6] (*look*) at samples of artists' work every day.

I ....[7] (*feel*) proud to work for a big, well-known company. This week, I ....[8] (*start*) each day with a planning meeting that includes the CEO. He ....[9] (*be*) very well known around the world, and my friends all ....[10] (*think*) I'm lucky to work with someone famous.

SKILLS

Complete each gap in these presentation extracts with the correct word (a, b or c).

Good morning, ...[1] Mieko Murata, Director of Marketing, NHHC Telecommunications. Today, ...[2] to talk about our new projects. First, ...[3] some background information about the company. ....[4], I'll talk about our marketing activities.

............[5], I'll discuss some case studies. ....[6] some background information about the company and about what we've been doing in the past year.

***

If there are no more questions about background, I'll continue. ....[7] to our marketing activities – we've recently had a really big marketing event in Singapore.

***

Thanks ....[8] my talk. Are there any questions?

1 a) I'm	b) this is	c) it's
2 a) we're	b) it's	c) I'd like
3 a) I've given you	b) I'll give you	c) there's
4 a) Next	b) After	c) Finally
5 a) In the end	b) At last	c) Finally
6 a) Here's	b) Let's	c) There's
7 a) Changing	b) Moving on now	c) Then
8 a) for coming to	b) that you came to	c) for

3 Selling

VOCABULARY

Circle the odd word/phrase out in each group.

1 wholesaler / retailer / supplier / offer

2 return / discount / offer / bargain

3 return / exchange / purchase / refund

4 stock / sale / storage / warehouse

5 dispatch / deliver / distribute / manufacture

6 money-back guarantee / out of stock / loyalty-card scheme / interest-free credit

MODALS

Read these tennis-court rules, then tick the true sentence in each pair below.

Tennis-court rules	
No music	Respect our neighbours and play quietly
Payment not necessary	Park closes at 10 p.m.
Tennis shoes required	Age 12 and over only

1 a) You don't have to play music.   b) You mustn't play music.

2 a) You don't have to pay.   b) You must pay.

3 a) You must wear tennis shoes.   b) You don't have to wear shoes.

4 a) You don't have to play quietly.   b) You shouldn't make a lot of noise.

5 a) You should leave before 10 p.m.   b) You have to leave at 10 p.m.

6 a) You must be 12 or older to enter.   b) If you're 12 years old, you mustn't enter.

WRITING

Read these instructions and write a letter (60–90 words). Begin it with a salutation and end politely.

You had a meeting with Mr Ulrich last week. You want to move ahead with a distribution agreement with his company. You are sending him with this letter a draft contract for his approval. You want him to read through it and tell you if there are any changes or additions.

Cultures 1: Saying no politely

A Unscramble the polite refusals.

1 could / wish / I / I / , / really / but / have / I / go / to / .

2 the / invitation / for / Thanks /, / I'm / feeling / but / not / very / well / . / some / time / Maybe / other / .

3 more / me / Nothing / for / , / thanks / . / was / It / delicious / .

4 you've / I'm / afraid / come / the / to / wrong / person / . / Keith / You'll / to / have / ask / .

5 sorry / I'm / . / to / love / I'd / , / have / but / I / other / that / plans / day / .

B Match each polite refusal in Exercise A with one of these requests.

a) Would you like some more cake?

b) Shall we meet up for a game of golf on Saturday?

c) Please stay a little bit longer.

d) Would you like to go out for a curry with me and Mr Takahashi?

e) Can you arrange drinks and snacks for this afternoon's meeting?

Business skills

Objectives

Speaking

- Can answer simple questions and respond to simple statements in an interview.
- Can describe skills and abilities using simple language.

Writing

Can write simple sentences about personal skills.

Lesson deliverable

To prepare and participate in an interview describing skills and responsibilities.

Performance review

To review your own progress and performance against the lesson objectives at the end of the lesson.

A SPEAKING 1

What are the best ways to find a new job? How did you get your job? How would you look for a job?

B READING

Arjun Soni works as a project manager. He is thinking about changing his job. Complete his professional profile on a job search site which describes his skills and abilities. Complete it with the words in the box.

budgets   costs   ~~experience~~   opportunities   skills
team   understanding

Arjun Soni

Project Manager with 11+ years of experience[1] in leadership and problem-solving for government and business. Excellent _____[2] of company objectives and a team player.

Areas of expertise

Customer relations   Quality control   Client/Staff training

Project management   Risk management

Numeracy _____[3]

Mission: I'm looking for new career _____[4] to work in multi-national projects.

Experience

Dynamic Business Solutions, Delhi, India

Small company helping organisations to achieve objectives

I plan, manage and finalise projects, completing on time every time. I have helped many companies to reduce _____[5] and meet their objectives. I lead a _____[6] of eight people working with _____[7] from $5m to $20m.

Education

Institute of Technology, Bombay

Degree in Mathematics, First

C LISTENING

1 🔊 **BSA1.1.1** Jennifer, an employment agent, phones Arjun to discuss a job that might interest him. Listen to her voice mail message and answer the questions.

1 How did she hear about Arjun?

2 What does she want Arjun to do?

2 🔊 **BSA1.1.2** Arjun is meeting Jennifer. Listen and complete Jennifer's notes with the numbers you hear.

Arjun Soni – Danford Bank position

Skills	Experience and responsibilities
Project management?	_____[1] years in total – _____[2] years with Dynamic Business Solutions
Experience with large projects?	yes, _____[3]-year project – introduce telecommunications system; budget of $_____[4]
Team leading?	directly led a team of _____[5] people and indirectly a team of _____[6] people
Ability to work in international environment?	limited experience – only _____[7] project so far, but keen to get more experience

3 Read these extracts from the interview. Complete the gaps with what Arjun said about his experience and responsibilities. Use one or two words in each gap.

1 **J:** You're a project manager.

   A: Yes, that's .... I've worked .... project management for eleven years.

2 **J:** And you're working for Dynamic Business Solutions.

   A: Yes, I .... I've worked .... them for the last three years.

3 **J:** And what are some of your responsibilities there?

   A: ...., I .... manage a range of different projects.

4 **J:** And were you in charge of that project?

   A: Yes, I was. I had a small team .... four people.

5 **J:** And you've worked with companies abroad.

   A: Well, ... and ....

6 **J:** You worked with Dino Patel at METS.

   A: No, ..., it was Danford Management.

4 🔊 **BSA1.1.2 Listen again and check your answers.**

D SPEAKING 2

Work in pairs. Practise describing your responsibilities at work.

Student A: Turn to page vi.
Student B: Turn to page x.

Task

Pre-task: Research

1 **Turn to page vi and read the job posting and company information. Imagine you saw the job posting on the website of a recruitment agency and have decided to apply for the position. Take notes on the job and the company.**

2 **Write a personal profile for yourself with the skills you think you need for this job.**

Part 1: Preparation

1 **Work in pairs or small groups. Read the task.**

> **Context:** You are going to attend an interview with Total Staff, the recruitment agency, and a representative from the company, Gym Now. You need to prepare for the interview.
>
> **Task:** Attend an interview for the job.

2 **Allocate roles. Who will be the candidate? Who will be the interviewer/s?**

3 **Think about these points:**

Candidate:
• your current job and responsibilities
• the language you need to describe your skills, experience and responsibilities

Interviewers:
• questions you want to ask about the candidate's experience
• items on their professional profile that you want to know more about

4 **Make sure your interviewer has a hard copy of your professional profile, or access to it online.**

Part 2: Interviewing

1 **Hold your interviews. Think about these points:**

Candidate: your voice – how to sound professional and confident; the skills and abilities you want to stress

Interviewers: the skills required; the responsibilities the candidate will need to take on; beginning and ending the interview; how you will ask questions

2 **At the end, make notes on what you and your partner(s) did well during the interview and what you could each improve.**

E PEER REVIEW

Using your notes from Part 2 of the Task, complete these sentences to give feedback to your colleagues.

• You described these skills really well: ....

• You described these abilities really well: ....

• Your responses to questions were ....

• As the interviewer, your questions were: ....

• You could improve by ....

F SELF-ASSESSMENT

Write 50–80 words to assess your performance in the interview. Use the lesson objectives and the feedback from your colleagues as a guide.

Think about these points:

• your role in answering the questions or responding to statements

• your role as the interviewer

G PROFESSIONAL DEVELOPMENT AND PERFORMANCE GOALS

Think about the job you would like to do next and answer the questions.

1 What will your real professional profile look like?

2 What skills and abilities can you bring to a new job or role?

Presentations

Objectives

Speaking

- Can convey simple relevant information emphasising the most important point.

- Can express opinions using simple language.

Listening

Can deal with practical, everyday demands, exchanging straightforward practical information.

Lesson deliverable

To plan, prepare and give a presentation about a partnership agreement.

Performance review

To review your own progress and performance against the lesson objectives at the end of the lesson.

Ⓐ SPEAKING 1

1 Which of these are good workplace benefits? Choose your top three. Then compare in pairs.

extra holidays   free courses and training
free tickets to entertainment/sport events
free transport to and from work   gym membership
health insurance

2 Work in pairs. Look at three slides from a company presentation and agree on one sentence to describe what you think the presentation is about.

Ⓐ **Reasons for leaving Walker Investments**

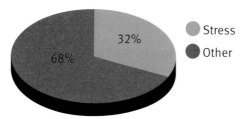

32% ● Stress
68% ● Other

Ⓑ **All other things being equal, would you prefer to work for a company with a free gym?**

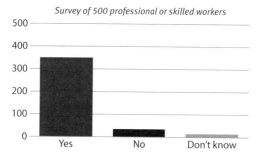

Survey of 500 professional or skilled workers

Ⓒ **When people exercise ...**

- 45–50% report fewer illnesses.

- 56–67% report having a good night's sleep.

- 54–62% said they're 'happy' to 'very happy' with their lives.

Ⓑ LISTENING 1

1 ◀)) BSA1.2.3 Priyanka Kaif, the Human Resources Manager at Walker Investments, is giving a presentation to team leaders. Listen to her introduction. What has the company decided to do?

2 ◀)) BSA1.2.3 Listen again. In what order does Priyanka mention these things?

a) the benefits of exercise ☐

b) what the company is going to do ☐

c) the value to the company of a free gym ☐

d) the company's attitude to its staff ☐

3 ◀)) BSA1.2.4 Listen to Priyanka presenting slide A. What is her most important point? What relevant information does she give on this point?

4 Match the phrases in italics (1–3) to their purpose (a–c).

1 *Slide A shows* the reasons people gave for leaving our company in 2015.

2 *As you can see from this slide*, 32 per cent said that stress was one of the reasons they decided to go.

3 *This means that* a large number of our workers probably suffer from stress on the job.

a) to summarise the visual

b) to reach a conclusion

c) to highlight the most important information from the visual

5 Work in pairs. Take turns to present slides B and C. Use the phrases in italics in Exercise B4.

C SPEAKING 2

1 **Look at four facts Priyanka presents about the partnership with a gym. Which word(s) does she use to emphasise positive points? Which word(s) does she use to explain more negative points?**

1 The gym is open from 6 a.m. to 10 p.m., so staff can use it before and after work or in the lunch hour.

2 The gym is a five-minute walk from our head office, so it's very convenient for most staff.

3 There are additional exercise classes available, but staff have to pay for those.

4 Staff can use the free lockers to store clothes, but they must leave a £10 deposit.

2 **Work in pairs. Practise presenting information about another partnership deal.**

Student A: Turn to page vii.
Student B: Turn to page x.

D LISTENING 2

🔊 **BSA1.2.5 Listen to the end of Priyanka's presentation. Summarise the benefits of a partnership with Fit Now gym.**

Benefits of a partnership with Fit Now gym

- ....
- ....
- ....

Conclusion

- For the company: ....
- For management: ....
- For HR: ....

Task

Pre-task: Research

What are the benefits of providing good quality food to staff in the workplace? What could companies do to improve the standard of food they offer their staff? Think and make notes.

Part 1: Preparation

Context: You work for a large company. You have agreed a new partnership with a catering company in order to improve food and diet choices in the company.

1 **Work in two groups, A and B. Turn to page vii to read about your partner companies.**

2 **Prepare a five-minute presentation to senior management about the new partnership. Think about these points:**

Structure:
- introducing the presentation: Mention the company's attitude to its staff, the benefits of healthy eating, the value of a healthy staff restaurant, what the company is going to do.
- main part of the presentation: Organise your evidence. Prepare slides to emphasise your points. Give the facts about the new partnership.
- ending: What main points do you need to repeat?

Techniques and language:
- use phrases to summarise a slide, highlight the most important information and reach a conclusion.
- explain the key facts about the partnership using so … , but …
- use phrases for summarising and concluding (*So, as you can see,* … ; *For these reasons,* …).

Part 2: Presentation

Give your presentation.

Presenters: use the structure in Part 1 to give your presentation.

Audience: make notes while you listen. What are the benefits of the new partnership? Write one question you can ask the presenter.

E PEER REVIEW

Think about another presentation. Give feedback.

1 What important points did the presentation cover?

2 Which parts of the presentation went well?

3 What good techniques/language did the presenter use?

4 What could the presenter improve?

F SELF-ASSESSMENT

Look back at the lesson objectives and complete the sentences.

1 As the presenter, I performed well because …

2 As the presenter, one thing I did less well was …

3 As the audience, I understood .... per cent of the information.

4 As the audience, I asked / didn't ask a good question.

G PROFESSIONAL DEVELOPMENT AND PERFORMANCE GOALS

What new projects has your company introduced? Could you present these ideas in a positive way? Write three sentences about how you could use the skills in this lesson.

'All the great ideas are controversial, or have been at one time.'
George Seldes (1890–1995), US investigative journalist

STARTING UP

A **Which of these statements do you agree with? Which do you disagree with? Why?**

1 There are no *new* ideas.

2 Most of the best ideas are discovered by accident.

3 Research and development is the key to great business ideas.

4 There is nothing wrong with copying and improving the ideas of others.

5 The best way to kill an idea is to take it to a meeting.

B **Discuss these questions.**

1 What do you think are some of the best ideas in the last 20 years?

2 What is the best idea you have ever had?

3 Which creative person do you most admire? Why?

4 What should companies do to encourage new ideas?

VOCABULARY
Verb and noun combinations

A **Match the word partnerships (1–6) to their definitions (a–f).**

1 to take advantage of an opportunity

2 to raise somebody's status

3 to enter a market

4 to extend a product range

5 to meet a need

6 to make a breakthrough

a) to offer a larger variety of goods

b) to do or provide something that is necessary

c) to do something when you get the chance to do it

d) to make an important discovery or change

e) to start selling goods or services in a new area

f) to make somebody look or feel more important

B Read this extract from a talk by the head of a research and development department. Then complete the gaps (1–6) with the correct form of a word partnership from Exercise A.

Great ideas are generated in different ways. Sometimes an idea may simply be when a company *takes advantage of an opportunity*[1] to ....[2], to offer more choice to existing customers. Or a great idea could allow a company to ....[3] which was closed to it before.

Companies which are prepared to spend a lot on R&D may ....[4] by having an original idea for a product which others later copy, for example Sony and the Walkman.

On the other hand, some products are developed in response to customer research. They come from customer ideas. These products are made to ....[5], to satisfy consumer demand. Or the product does something similar to another product, but faster, so it saves time. Some people will buy new products because the product ....[6] – gives them a new, more upmarket image.

C ◀)) CD1.37 Listen and check your answers to Exercise B.

D ◀)) CD1.38 Listen carefully to the last part of the talk and complete the gaps to form word partnerships with the words in *italics*.

Other people will buy any 'green' product which ....[1] *waste* or ....[2] *the environment*, even if it is more expensive. If an idea is really good and the product ....[3] *a gap* in the market, it may even ....[4] *an award* for innovation.

E Work in pairs. Exercise B refers to the Sony Walkman. Can you think of any other examples of products which:

1 were completely original and later copied?

2 are green?

3 won an award?

4 were developed from customer ideas?

Compare your ideas in small groups.

*See the **DVD-ROM** for the i-Glossary.*

LISTENING

Great business ideas

Dr Kate Pitts

A Dr Kate Pitts is a researcher at the e-Research Centre, University of Oxford. She was asked the question: *In your opinion, what were the best business ideas of the last 15 years?* Predict what she will say. Think of products and services.

B ◀)) CD1.39 Listen to the first part of the interview. What products and services does Kate mention? Why does she think they were excellent ideas?

C ◀)) CD1.40 Listen to the second part and answer these questions.

1 What types of company spend a lot of time and money on research and development?

2 Which company spends nearly 25% of the cost of sale on research and development?

*Watch the interview on the **DVD-ROM.***

D 🔊 CD1.40 **Listen to the second part again and complete the gaps in the audio script.**

I strongly believe that most companies can benefit from using ....[1] and ....[2] within their own company to actually develop new ....[3] and services. My definition of ....[4] is to look at what everybody else sees, and see something ....[5].

So that might mean looking at what you already do, and looking at where you can do it slightly differently to ....[6] your product range, or ....[7] your products into new markets. This can save ....[8] and money.

E **Discuss these questions.**

1 What will be the best business idea in the next 15 years?

2 What would you like someone to invent?

READING

Three great ideas

A **What makes a business idea a really *great* idea? Brainstorm as many points as you can.**

example: *It results in an increase in sales and profit.*

B **Work in groups of three. Make quick notes in answer to the questions below about your article.**

Student A: Read Article 1 on the opposite page.
Student B: Read Article 2 on the opposite page.
Student C: Read Article 3 on the opposite page.

Questions	Who needs translators?	Safer cycling	Going for gold
1 What is the great/unusual idea?			
2 What problem does this idea solve?			
3 Which markets are mentioned in relation to this idea?			
4 In terms of time, at what stage of development is the idea?			

C **Ask your partners the four questions in Exercise B and make notes on what they say.**

D **Discuss these questions in pairs.**

1 Which of the ideas do you find the most interesting? Why?

2 Which idea do you think will be the most profitable?

3 Which idea will reach the most markets?

4 Can you think of any problems any of the ideas might have?

adapted from www.timesonline.co.uk

+ Article 1

WHO NEEDS TRANSLATORS?

Google is developing software for the first phone capable of translating foreign languages almost instantly. By building on existing technologies in voice recognition and automatic translation, Google hopes to have a basic system ready within a couple of years. If it works, it could eventually transform communication among speakers of the world's 6,000-plus languages.

The company has already created an automatic system for translating text on computers, which is being honed by scanning millions of multilingual websites and documents. So far, it covers 52 languages. Google also has a voice-recognition system that enables phone users to conduct web searches by speaking commands into their phones rather than typing them in.

Now it is working on combining the two technologies to produce software capable of understanding a caller's voice and translating it into a synthetic equivalent in a foreign language. Like a professional human interpreter, the phone would analyse "packages" of speech, listening to the speaker until it understands the full meaning of words and phrases, before attempting translation.

adapted from www.thisislondon.co.uk

+ Article 2

SAFER CYCLING

Swedish designers have created a cycling "collar" that is worn around the neck with an airbag hidden inside. When sensors in the device determine a crash has happened, an airbag instantly inflates around the cyclist's head to form a helmet.

The invention was presented today in Stockholm. It will go on sale in Sweden early next year for about £50. The designers have spent six years developing it. Terese Alstin, one of the inventors, said, "The protection should include keeping the sense of freedom and not ruining your hairstyle."

The device has been improved by recreating hundreds of accidents using crash-test dummies and real riders. "We have developed a unique, patented, mathematical method to distinguish these movement patterns," say the inventors. A small helium-gas cylinder inflates the airbag in 0.1 seconds and is designed to let cyclists see at all times.

The airbag stays inflated for several seconds. It is powered by a rechargable battery. Co-inventor Anna Haupt said, "The shell of the collar is removable and available in many different styles and fabrics, and will be launched in new fashion collections."

adapted from www.guardian.co.uk

+ Article 3

Going for gold

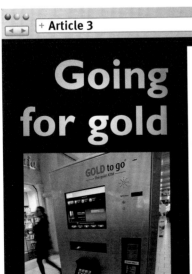

Apart from being gold-plated – and the fact that they are bulletproof – they seem much like any other vending machine. But instead of chocolate bars, a network of "gold-to-go" machines dispenses 24-carat bullion in a smart presentation box.

Originally designed as a marketing device for an online gold-trading business, the machines have become such a success that their inventor plans to build a global network, installing them everywhere from fitness centres to cruise ships.

Thomas Geissler, the German businessman behind the machines, said their unexpected success was the result of a recent interest in gold. "Our customers are those who are catching on to the idea that gold is a safe investment at a time of financial instability," he said.

Since the first machine was installed in May, in the lobby of Abu Dhabi's Emirates Palace hotel, 20 gold-to-go machines have appeared across Europe. Germany already has eight. Next month, the first machines will open in the United States – in Las Vegas and Florida.

The company claims its gold is cheaper than that available from the banks, largely because its overheads are lower, and that unlike at a bank, the machine gold is available immediately.

Past simple and past continuous

Study these examples.

a) *Yesterday afternoon, the CEO **was meeting** the research team in Dublin.*
(past continuous)

b) *We were **having** a successful negotiation when suddenly they **made** new demands.*
(past continuous)   (past simple)

c) *The advertising agency **started** in 1982, and Wieden **came up with** the 'Just Do It' slogan for Nike in 1988.*   (past simple)   (past simple)

Now read through these rules.

- We use the **past continuous** to talk about something that was going on around a particular time in the past, as in example a).

- We often use the **past continuous** to describe an action which was already in progress when something else happened, as in example b).

- We use the **past simple** to talk about actions or events that we see as completed, as in example c).

➡ *Grammar reference page 144*

Laszlo Biro

A ### Read the Laszlo Biro story and choose the correct form of the verbs.

People *wrote / were writing*[1] with quills, pens and pencils long before Laszlo Biro *invented / was inventing*[2] his biro in 1938. While he *worked / was working*[3] as a journalist in Hungary, he *noticed / was noticing*[4] that the ink used in newspaper printing dried quickly. But this ink would not flow into the tip of a fountain pen. In 1938, he *developed / was developing*[5] a new tip using a ball that was free to turn in its socket. He *died / was dying*[6] in Buenos Aires in 1985.

B ### In pairs, take it in turns to tell your partner that you saw them doing these things at work. Your partner has to think of a good reason why they were doing it.

EXAMPLE:

Student A: When I saw you, you were putting a pack of paper in your bag.
Student B: Oh, my boss asked me to print out a long report at home tonight.

When I saw you, you were:

- looking at Facebook during office hours.
- studying Japanese instead of working.
- talking with friends in the staff restaurant.
- playing games on your mobile phone.
- reading a book.
- collecting money from your colleagues.

Successful meetings

A ### Which of these statements do you agree with? Why?

1 The best number for a meeting is six people or fewer.

2 Never have food or drink during a meeting.

3 Always start and finish a meeting on time.

4 You should sit round a table when you have a meeting.

5 A meeting must always have a leader.

6 At a formal meeting, each person should speak in turn.

B 🔊 CD1.41 **DC Dynamics is an electronics company based in Boston, USA. The marketing department held a meeting to discuss their new smartphone. Listen to the meeting, then answer these questions.**

1 What were the main aims of the meeting?

2 Which month did they choose for the launch?

C 🔊 CD1.41 **Listen again and tick the expressions which the chairperson uses.**

1 OK, everyone, let's begin, shall we? ☐

2 Our main purpose is to decide the date of the launch. ☐

3 Mei, what do you think? ☐

4 Cheng, can you give us your opinion about this? ☐

5 Any thoughts on that? ☐

6 Let's get back to the point. ☐

7 Now, I'd like to move on to sales outlets. ☐

D 🔊 CD1.41 **Listen to the meeting again and complete these extracts.**

Mei: Personally, I'm _in favour_ [1] of June. Let's get into the market early and surprise our .... [2].

Wan: Yeah, June's too early. I think September's the best time. We can promote the smartphone strongly then, with a multimedia .... [3].

Lincoln: What about the recommended retail price for the phone? Any thoughts on that?

Mei: .... [4] a minute. I thought we were talking about the .... [5] date, not the price.

Lincoln: OK, Mei, maybe we are moving a little too fast. Let's get back to the .... [6].

Lincoln: Good. We need to be sharp on pricing. Now, what sales outlets do you think we should .... [7], Wan?

Wan: No problem there. We could start with the specialist mobile-phone stores and big .... [8] stores. After that, we could look at other distribution .... [9].

E **Work in groups of four. GLP of Buenos Aires has developed a new wallet, code-named 'The Hipster'. It will be launched in the US. The marketing department holds a meeting to discuss a strategy for selling it.**

Student A: Turn to page 134.   Student C: Turn to page 132.
Student B: Turn to page 138.   Student D: Turn to page 136.

Read your role card, then hold the meeting.

USEFUL LANGUAGE

CHAIRPERSON/LEAD

Beginning the meeting
Can we start, please?
Right, let's begin.

Stating the aim
The main aim/purpose of this meeting is to ...

Asking for comments
What do you think?
How do you feel about this?

Changing the subject
Let's move on now to ...
The next thing to discuss is ...

Clarifying
What do you mean by ...?
Sorry, I don't quite understand.

Summarising
OK, let's summarise.
Right, let's recap.

PARTICIPANTS

Giving opinions
I think we should ...
I'm in favour of ...

Making suggestions
Perhaps we should ...
We could ...

Agreeing
I think you're right.
I (totally) agree.

Disagreeing
I don't know about that.
(I'm afraid) I don't agree.

Interrupting
Hold on (a moment).
Can I just say something?

The new attraction

An international competition will encourage great ideas for a new visitor attraction

Background

Dilip Singh is a very rich man. He gives money generously to charities all over the world and provides finance for projects which will help local communities.

He has recently organised an international competition for people wanting to create a new attraction in their country. The winner(s) will receive $20 million to finance and develop their project.

🔊 **CD1.42** Listen to a conversation between Dilip and his personal assistant, Jane Ferguson. Note down the three key points that Dilip makes about the new attraction.

Here are three attractions that have impressed Dilip because they are unusual and exciting.
He has put them on the website as examples to stimulate the imaginations of competitors.

Which one would you like to visit? Why?

Have you visited any attraction which greatly impressed you? If so, talk about it with your colleagues.

Unusual attractions

1 Shakespeare's Globe Theatre – London, England

Opened in 1997, this modern building is a reconstruction of the original Globe Theatre, which was built in 1599. It was an open-air playhouse where Shakespeare's plays were performed. An exhibition and tour show what life was really like in Shakespeare's time. The Globe Theatre is a popular London attraction. *MORE*

2 The Vulcan Tourism and Trek Station – Alberta, Canada

The town of Vulcan is in Alberta, Canada, and its name has helped it to become a tourist attraction. It has built a tourist station based on the theme of the famous *Star Trek* television and feature-film series. It shows many objects from the series, and there is a replica nearby of the starship Enterprise from *Star Trek V*. *MORE*

3 The Sunken Ship Museum – Yangjiang, South China

Opened in 2010, the museum is located underwater. The main exhibit is an 800-year-old ship which is 24 metres below the surface of the sea. Visitors can see the ship from underwater corridors. In addition, they can view the precious objects which have been taken from the ship. *MORE*

Task

Work in small groups.

1 **Brainstorm ideas for a new attraction in your area/country.**

2 **Choose the best idea. Then discuss your concept, using these questions as a guide. Choose someone to lead your discussion.**

1 What are the strong points of your great idea?

2 What kind of experience will your attraction offer visitors?

3 How will it make money for the local community?

4 How can you attract tourists?

5 What are your plans for marketing and promoting the attraction?

6 What corporate sponsorships will you try to obtain?

3 **Describe your ideas to the other groups. Answer their questions.**

4 **Meet as one group. Choose someone to lead the meeting. Discuss all the projects and decide which one should be presented to Dilip Singh's committee. If you cannot agree, take a vote.**

Watch the Case study commentary on the **DVD-ROM.**

Writing

You are a member of the committee which helps Dilip to judge the projects. He has asked you to write a short report on the project you think should win, with your reasons for recommending it.

Outline the key features of the project and say why it would be a commercial success.

NEW ATTRACTION – RECOMMENDATION FOR WINNING ENTRY

Introduction

This report outlines the key features of the new attraction that we feel should win the competition. It gives reasons why the project was selected and explains why the new attraction should be a commercial success.

➡ *Writing file page 129*

43

'*Rest is a good thing, but boredom is its brother.*'
Voltaire (1694–1778), French philosopher

STARTING UP

A Add the verbs from the box to the phrases below to create some common stressful situations.

being   finding   ~~going~~   having   making   moving   shopping   travelling   taking   waiting

1 .*going*. to the dentist
2 .... in a long queue
3 .... stuck in a traffic jam
4 .... a parking space
5 .... with your partner/family
6 .... house
7 .... an interview
8 .... a speech
9 .... by air
10 .... an exam or test

Which of the above situations is the most stressful for you? Can you add any others to the list?

B **What do you do to relax? Which of these activities are the most effective for you, and why? In what other ways do you relax?**

• playing a sport • reading • eating/drinking • having a bath • walking
• gardening • massage • shopping • listening to music • watching TV
• meditating • browsing online • blogging • using Facebook/YouTube

C **Rank these situations from 1 (most stressful) to 10 (least stressful). Then discuss your choices.**

- making a presentation to senior executives
- leading a formal meeting
- telephoning in English
- writing a report with a tight deadline
- negotiating a very valuable contract

- meeting important visitors from abroad for the first time
- asking your boss for a pay rise
- dealing with a customer who has a major complaint
- covering for a colleague who is away
- taking part in a conference call

VOCABULARY

Stress in the workplace

A **Match the words (1–8) to their definitions (a–h).**

1 lifestyle
2 workaholic
3 workload
4 deadline
5 flexitime
6 work–life balance
7 quality of life
8 working environment

a) a system where employees choose the time they start and finish work each day

b) a time or date by which you have to do something

c) how personally satisfied you are with the way you live and work

d) someone who cannot stop working and has no time for anything else

e) the ability to give a good amount of time to your work and to outside interests, e.g. family

f) the amount of work a person is expected to do

g) the people, things and atmosphere around you at work

h) the way people choose to organise their lives

B **Complete each sentence with an appropriate word or phrase from Exercise A.**

1 I worked until 11 o'clock at night to meet the .... for presenting the report.

2 I work six days a week and never have a holiday. My girlfriend says I'm a ....

3 Karl has a heavy .... at the moment because several colleagues are off sick.

4 She gave up a highly paid job to join a meditation group in India. She's completely changed her ....

5 A .... system can help to reduce stress levels of employees by giving them more control over their working hours.

6 If you have children, working from home may help improve your ....

7 Many people argue that technology has greatly improved our .... and the way we feel about work. Others disagree, arguing it actually increases stress.

8 A clean, quiet, comfortable and friendly .... can actively reduce levels of stress.

C **Make sentences using some of the vocabulary items from Exercise A to describe your own situation.**

D **Discuss where to put the jobs in the box in the stress league on the next page. Rating is from 10 to 0: the higher the rating, the greater the pressure. Then turn to page 132 and check your answers.**

Advertising executive Architect Banker Diplomat
Hairdresser Firefighter Sales assistant

Your place in the stress league

Miner	8.3	Film producer	6.5	Psychologist	5.2	Optician	4.0
Police officer	7.7	....	6.3	....	4.8	Postman	4.0
Construction worker	7.5	Musician	6.3	Farmer	4.8	....	3.7
Journalist	7.5	Teacher	6.2	Vet	4.5	Minister/Vicar	3.5
Airline pilot	7.5	Social worker	6.0	Accountant	4.3	Nursery nurse	3.3
....	7.3	....	5.7	....	4.3	Librarian	2.0
Actor	7.2	Stockbroker	5.5	Lawyer/Solicitor	4.3	
Doctor	6.8	Bus driver	5.4	....	4.0	

Source: University of Manchester Institute of Science and Technology (UK)

E Choose three jobs from the stress league in Exercise D. What do you think makes these particular jobs stressful? Compare your ideas.

F Is your own job (or one you intend to do) included in the stress league? Do you think it is in the right place? What about the other jobs in the league? If your job is not included, where would you place it?

G Discuss these questions.

1 Do you like working under pressure? Why? / Why not?

2 What deadlines do you have to meet in your daily life? Which are the most difficult to meet?

3 Why do people become workaholics?

4 How important is the working environment in reducing stress?

*See the **DVD-ROM** for the i-Glossary.*

LISTENING
Dealing with stress

Jessica Colling

A What are the main causes of stress at work?

B ◀)) CD1.43 Jessica Colling is Director of Marketing at Vielife, a consultancy that advises businesses on health at work. Listen to the first part of the interview and answer these questions.

1 What three examples are given of things that make people feel under pressure at work?

2 What is *resilience to stress*?

C ◀)) CD1.44 Listen to the second part. What can happen if you have to manage stress for a long time without a break?

D ◀)) CD1.44 Listen again and complete this extract.

It's difficult to say really what's a ....[1] level of stress for somebody to feel at work. The problem with that is that what one person finds really ....[2] and it excites them to be able to do their job well, somebody else might find really, really ....[3]. What we do see is that actually a high level of continued ....[4] can actually sometimes spill over into feelings of stress.

E ◀)) CD1.45 Listen to the third part. What two examples are given of companies being flexible in how they expect staff to work?

*Watch the interview on the **DVD-ROM**.*

F ◀)) CD1.46 Listen to the final part. What two reasons are given for why women report higher levels of stress than men?

G Discuss these questions.

1 What is a good work–life balance for you? Is it easier for men than women to be a manager?

2 Is it important to have a certain level of stress in the workplace?

A In pairs, rank these countries according to those where you think business leaders feel the most stress (1 = most stress, 9 = least stress).

- Australia
- China
- Denmark
- Finland
- Greece
- Mexico
- Sweden
- Turkey
- Vietnam

B Read the first two paragraphs of this article. Then check your answers to Exercise A.

Over half of business owners feeling increasingly stressed

More than half the leaders of privately held businesses globally feel their stress levels have increased over the last year. The research from 5 the Grant Thornton International Business Report (IBR) 2010 covers the opinions of over 7,400 business owners across 36 economies. Mainland China tops the league for 10 the most stressed leaders, with 76% of business owners saying their stress levels have increased over the last year.

Other economies that were high in 15 the stress league table were Mexico (74%), Turkey (72%), Vietnam (72%) and Greece (68%). At the opposite end of the scale, business owners in Sweden (23%), Denmark (25%), Finland 20 (33%) and Australia (35%) have the lowest stress levels in the world.

There appears to be a link between stress levels and GDP. Business owners in mainland China, Vietnam, 25 Mexico, India and Turkey are all high on the stress league table and are working in environments where high growth is expected. But it's not just in countries expecting high growth that 30 stress levels are high – at the opposite end of the growth scale, Ireland, Spain and Greece are all high on the league table. Said Alex MacBeath, Global Leader – Markets at Grant Thornton 35 International, "We have businesses at both ends of the GDP growth scale experiencing high stress for very different reasons. In mainland China, the pressure is on to keep up with the 40 speed of expansion, while in Ireland, for example, the economy is shrinking, and business owners are worried about how they will keep their business alive."

45 Business owners were asked about the major causes of workplace stress.

Not surprisingly, the most common cause during 2009 was the economic climate, with 38% of respondents 50 globally saying this was one of their major causes of stress. This was followed by pressure on cashflow (26%), competitor activities (21%) and heavy workload (19%). Alex 55 MacBeath comments, "The causes of workplace stress can be put into three distinct groups – economic, business and personal. An employee may place more importance on personal elements 60 such as their work–life balance. The business owner has additional pressures to consider."

The survey also found a link between stress levels and the number 65 of days taken off by an individual in a year. Countries at the top of the stress league are those where business owners, on average, take fewer holidays each year.

adapted from http://www.grantthorntonibos.com

C Read the whole article and answer these questions.

1 What is the difference between these groups of countries in terms of reasons for high-level stress?

   a) China, Vietnam, Mexico, India and Turkey

   b) Ireland, Spain and Greece

2 According to Alex MacBeath, how do business leaders experience stress differently in China and Ireland?

3 What are the four major causes of workplace stress?

4 According to Alex MacBeath, what three types of pressure are there?

D Look at this list of countries.

Vietnam   Sweden   Denmark   Mexico   China   Finland

In which countries do business owners take:

1 fewer holidays?

2 more holidays?

(You will need information from paragraphs 1, 2 and 5.)

E In pairs, discuss these questions.

1 What are the additional pressures that business owners might have?

2 Should companies do more to reduce stress at work? What could they do?

3 How many days' holiday per year do you think people should get?

Past simple and present perfect

Answer the questions in brackets about the sentences in *italics*.

1 She **has worked** in Paris for five years. (Does she work in Paris now?)

2 She **worked** in Hong Kong for three years. (Does she work in Hong Kong now?)

Which sentence above (1 or 2) uses the past simple? Which uses the present perfect?

We use the past simple to:

- talk about completed actions that happened in the past.
  *Larry Page and Sergey Brin **created** Google in January 1996.*

- refer to a definite moment or period in the past.
  *I **spoke** to her on Tuesday.*

The present perfect connects the past and the present. We use the present perfect to:

- talk about past actions that affect us now.
  *The boss **has** just **given** her a pay rise, and she's very pleased.*

- talk about life experiences.
  *I've **worked** with many companies where stress was a problem.*

- announce recent news.
  *Coca-Cola **has** just **confirmed** it has dropped Wayne Rooney.*

→ *Grammar reference* page 145

A **Cross out the incorrect sentence in each pair.**

1 a) Stress levels have increased in recent years.

   b) ~~Stress levels increased in recent years.~~

2 a) The finance sector changed dramatically over the past five years.

   b) The finance sector has changed dramatically over the past five years.

3 a) The risk factors for stress have risen significantly since 2009.

   b) The risk factors for stress rose significantly since 2009.

4 a) I resigned three months ago.

   b) I have resigned three months ago.

5 a) Have you ever been to a stress counsellor before?

   b) Did you ever go to a stress counsellor before?

B **Write the time expressions from the box in the correct column of this chart.**

Past simple	Present perfect
two years ago	so far

> ~~so far~~ ~~two years ago~~ ever in 2009 yet just yesterday for the past two weeks already never last Friday during the 1990s in the last few days since 2005 when I was at university

Now talk about your life using the time expressions.

C **The present perfect is often followed by more detailed information in the past simple. Work in pairs. Ask and answer questions about these subjects.**

- attend a conference
- be late for an important meeting
- make a telephone call in English
- travel abroad on business
- make a presentation
- go on a training course

example:

A: Have you ever travelled abroad on business?   B: Yes, I have.

A: Where did you go?   B: Frankfurt. I went there three years ago, on a sales trip.

SKILLS

Participating in discussions

A You are going to hear three members of the human resources department of a transportation company discussing ways of improving the staff's health and fitness. What ways do you think they will mention?

B ◀)) CD1.47 Listen to the conversation and check your answers.

C ◀)) CD1.47 The speakers use several expressions to make suggestions. Listen to the conversation again and complete the gaps in these sentences.

1 Well, I think............ .... carry out a survey, find out why the staff are so stressed ...

2 I have another idea. .... we encourage staff to keep fit? .... paying for their subscription to a gym?

3 We .... more staff for them, give them an assistant.

4 Well, it might be a .... to set up a counselling service ...

5 .... meet tomorrow, same time, and try and come up with a plan ...

D ◀)) CD1.48 At the next meeting, the team discusses plans for staff to attend a local sports centre. Listen and tick the expressions they use in their conversation. Then write 'A' if the expression shows agreement or 'D' if it shows disagreement.

1 Mm, I don't know.

2 It would be popular, but it could be expensive.

3 I think I agree with you.

4 OK, but we can solve it. The sports centre has great facilities ...

5 Exactly. It would really help staff to be more healthy...

6 I'm not in agreement, Danielle. It isn't a great idea.

7 I still think it's a good idea. It's well worth trying.

E Work in pairs. You work in the human resources department of a large company. Discuss how you would deal with these problems. Use expressions from the Useful language box below to help you.

1 More and more staff are taking medicine, e.g. anti-depressants, because they feel highly stressed at work. They are often sick, or pretend they are sick, and take days off work.

2 Many employees feel uncertain about their jobs and careers in the company. They worry about the future. They are constantly anxious and don't sleep well.

3 Some staff are stressed because they feel they have no control over their work and they don't participate in decisions. They say they feel 'worthless' and are not valued by management.

USEFUL LANGUAGE

MAKING SUGGESTIONS	GIVING OPINIONS	AGREEING	DISAGREEING
I think we should carry out a survey.	We've got to do something about it.	I suppose we could do that.	Mmm, I don't know.
Why don't we encourage staff to keep fit?	I think we should definitely pay staff's subscriptions.	I think I agree with you.	I can't agree with you there.
How about paying for their subscription to a gym?	It would be popular, but it could be expensive.	Yeah, you're right.	I'm not sure it's a good idea.
It might be a good idea to set up a counselling service.	It'd cost a lot, and attendance would be difficult to monitor.	Exactly.	I still think it's a good idea.
		Good. / Excellent idea. / Great.	I'm afraid that's out of the question because ...
		I completely agree.	

DAVIES–MILLER ADVERTISING

Too much stress is damaging work at a large advertising agency

Background

Davies–Miller is a large advertising agency on Madison Avenue in New York. It has expanded rapidly in recent years and has a number of famous companies as its clients.

There is very strong competition in the US advertising industry. Agencies compete to win new contracts or take clients away from their rivals. Advertising staff are well paid, but they work long hours. They worry about job security and become anxious if their company loses an important client.

Recently, Davies–Miller lost two of its major accounts. This had a significant effect on the employees. The agency decided to carry out a survey of the staff's opinions about their working conditions. It showed that 65% of staff felt 'highly stressed' in their jobs.

Discuss how the high levels of stress could affect the performance of the agency.

Listen to / read on page 51 about four incidents at Davies–Miller which involved stress. In each case, note down briefly the key points of each incident.

1

James,
Account Executive

 CD1.49 Jessica Parker, a junior account executive, calls Sheila Murray in the human resources department from Rio de Janeiro, Brazil, about her boss, James. They are currently negotiating an important contract with a client there.

2

Birgitte,
Schedule Coordinator

Summary of an interview with Birgitte by a member of staff (HR)

Birgitte regulates the flow of work, coordinates scheduling and prepares cost estimates. According to her, she is stressed because she is often interrupted at work by visits from other members of staff. She believes there is too much gossiping in the office, which stops her from doing her work.

She says that her supervisor favours certain members of staff and does not want to send her on training courses.

She lives a long way from work. Because of this, she gets back home very late and has no time to relax.

3

Juliana, *Art Director*

Extract from an e-mail sent to Head of HR

I've never been under such pressure in my work since I joined the agency. I have no time to listen to the problems of my colleagues. I spend all my time trying to meet impossible deadlines to produce designs for the Account Executives. We're competing for too many contracts, that's the problem. I just don't understand the policy of the agency. It won't help to hire more staff. Most of the creative ideas in the agency come from me. Sometimes I wonder if they want me to leave and bring in someone younger. I'm worried because the situation's beginning to affect my health. I can't seem to relax when I get back home.

4

Jolanta, *Assistant to Art Director*

Part of an informal conversation between Jolanta and a member of the HR department

"I'll be looking for another job soon. I feel really stressed out. Juliana never tells me anything. She never asks for my opinion. It's incredible. I've got a Master's in advertising, but it doesn't seem to impress her. She only gives me boring jobs and shouts at me if I make a mistake. I think she'll have a nervous breakdown soon. She never praises anything I do – it really upsets me. I was hoping to have a career here. No chance of that."

Task

1 **You are members of the HR department. Work in small groups and discuss these questions.**

1 What are the main reasons why the staff mentioned above are highly stressed or demotivated?

2 What action(s) should the HR department take in each case?

2 **Compare the results of your discussion with other groups.**

3 **Meet as one group. Make suggestions for practical ways of reducing the stress levels of staff in the agency.**

*Watch the Case study commentary on the **DVD-ROM**.*

Writing

As Head of Human Resources, write the recommendations section of a report to Davies–Miller's CEO. Outline your practical suggestions for reducing stress in the company, both in the short and long term.

Recommendations
The management team met on July 5 to discuss ways of dealing with stress in the company. The following recommendations were made:

 Writing file page 129

6 | Entertaining

'Food is our common ground, a universal experience.'
James Beard (1903–1985), American chef and food writer

STARTING UP

A Imagine you have to entertain a group of foreign businesspeople. Which of these activities would you choose? What would you add?

• historic site(s) • an opera / a concert • motor racing • tennis
• a bar / a nightclub • wine tasting • a game of golf • a restaurant
• the theatre • horse racing • a football match • an art gallery

B Many companies are spending less on corporate entertaining. Do you think this is a good idea? Why? / Why not?

VOCABULARY

Eating and drinking

A Work with a partner. Which adjectives in the box form partnerships with the words below (1–6)?

convenient cosy efficient exciting local/regional reasonable

1 atmosphere   3 location   5 service
2 food   4 prices   6 entertainment

You plan to take a foreign visitor out for dinner. How important are the above factors for you when entertaining guests? Discuss your ideas in pairs.

B Match the words in the box to the correct food categories below (1–4).

> ~~beef~~ broccoli cabbage chicken crab cucumber duck lamb
> lobster mushroom onion pork prawns/shrimp salmon
> spinach tuna turkey veal venison

1 meat *beef*

2 poultry

3 fish/seafood

4 vegetables/salad

C Combine the words in the box with the headings below (1–3) to create word partnerships related to drinks.

> alcohol-free bottled draught ~~dry~~ house medium mineral red
> rosé sparkling still sweet tap vintage white

1 wine *dry wine, ...*

2 beer

3 water

D Think of a typical or unusual dish from your country. How would you describe it to a foreign visitor? Use these phrases to help you.

It's a meat/fish/rice/vegetarian dish.

It's a kind of seafood/vegetable/dessert, etc.

It's quite spicy/rich/hot/sweet/salty/bitter/sour.

It's called .... and tastes a bit like chicken/cabbage, etc.

It comes with / We usually eat it with ...

People often have a glass of .... with it.

It's got an unusual taste.

It's served with rice / pasta / a salad / a side dish, etc.

It's quite healthy/fattening/unusual, etc.

E Put these stages into a logical order for entertaining in a restaurant.

a) Look at the menu. ☐

b) Ask for the bill (*BrE*) / check (*AmE*). ☐

c) Book a table (*BrE*). / Make a reservation (*AmE*). ☐1☐

d) Leave a tip. ☐

e) Have the main course. ☐

f) Have a dessert. ☐

g) Order a starter (*BrE*) / appetizer (*AmE*). ☐

h) Have an aperitif. ☐

F 🔊 CD1.50 Listen to the dialogues and check your answer to Exercise E.

G Imagine a small group of foreign visitors is coming to your city.

1 Decide where you would take them for dinner. Choose a menu and a location to give them a 'taste' of your city/region/country.

2 Explain your choices to a partner.

3 Join up with another pair and compare your ideas.

*See the **DVD-ROM** for the i-Glossary.*

Corporate events

Dr Chris Bruton

A 🔊 CD1.51 **Dr Chris Bruton is Chief Executive of the Cavendish Consultancy, a corporate entertainment company. Listen to the first part of the interview and answer these questions.**

1 Which sports are popular?

2 Which sport is not popular? Why?

3 What was the most popular musical at the time of the interview?

B 🔊 CD1.52 **Listen to the second part. What is surprising about how the financial sector has reacted to the latest recession?**

C 🔊 CD1.53 **Listen to the third part. What makes a corporate event successful? Complete these notes.**

> 1 Identify your ....
>
> 2 Planning: having ...., e.g. umbrellas
>
> 3 Catering: high standard of .... and ....
>
> 4 Staff: ...., ... and briefing
>
> 5 Always .... up afterwards

Watch the interview on the DVD-ROM.

D 🔊 CD1.54 **Listen to the final part and answer these questions.**

1 Which two events were offered together on the same day?

2 How did people travel from London to the first event?

3 How did people travel from London to the second event?

E **In groups, discuss these questions.**

1 What event would you most like to be invited to? Why?

2 How does entertaining affect a company's image?

3 When can corporate entertainment become bribery?

Corporate entertainment

A **Discuss these questions.**

1 How important is corporate entertaining in your a) country? b) company/organisation?

2 What corporate-hospitality event would you like to be invited to?

B **The corporate-hospitality club asked three entertainment experts some questions. In pairs, read the article on the opposite page and put four of these questions in the appropriate places.**

a) What is the most effective way of measuring corporate hospitality?

b) What are the key elements required to produce successful corporate hospitality?

c) If you had an unlimited budget, what would be included in your dream corporate-hospitality package?

d) What is the best corporate-hospitality programme you have witnessed that wasn't your own?

e) What are the biggest challenges in creating corporate hospitality?

f) How have corporate-hospitality offerings changed in the past decade?

1 Question ......

Kate Kassar (Director, Beyond Events)
Listen to the client's aspirations and needs. Success then depends on the creation of a dynamic event, which matches and reflects the company culture and the tastes of guests.

5 **Andrew Hodgkins (Premier Service Director, Keith Prowse)**
What makes corporate hospitality so successful is being able to offer tickets or packages for events that are sold out or extremely popular.

10 **Alex Hewitt (Managing Director, AOK Events)**
Invite your guests to something they genuinely want to attend and ensure you get the right clients attending. Make sure the event is memorable. This way the event lives forever and makes your marketing budget go further.

2 Question ......

15 **Kate**
Creating an event with universal appeal to a potentially highly diverse audience. Finding the balance between limitless client aspirations and the boundaries of logistics and cost.

Andrew
20 The biggest challenge is to make corporate hospitality accessible to everyone – no matter what their budget is.

Alex
Getting the pricing right and making it easy for people to attend. Few of us want to be entertained on a Sunday night at a venue
25 with poor transport links.

3 Question ......

Kate
Six Nations rugby hospitality in a brewery next to Murrayfield Stadium. It captured the spirit of the rugby audience. Whereas other facilities offered the usual fine dining, this one boasted
30 draught beer, wooden benches, wintery food, rugby celebrities mingling and a party spirit, all on a lower budget.

Andrew
The packages at the Emirates, Arsenal's home ground, are spectacular, and we wish we could have been involved in the
35 Ryder Cup Europe packages.

Alex
A few years ago, my sister invited me to a private sponsor's concert in a tiny London venue in the middle of the Wimbledon fortnight, which featured John McEnroe and Pat Cash on guitar,
40 Nick Mason on drums and Chrissie Hynde on vocals. Fantastic food and an unlimited bar made it the perfect event.

4 Question ......

Kate
A one-off interactive experience that money can't buy. An event that gives its audience a real feel of the host brand,
45 combining the adrenaline of sport with the feel-good factor of entertainment and the glamour of the Monaco F1 Grand Prix.

Andrew
If we had an unlimited budget, we'd love to offer sporting packages with a twist. For example, offering high-profile former
50 sportsmen and women to give clients a coaching session in their chosen sport before the event.

Alex
Morning golf at Wentworth with Tiger Woods and Sean Connery, followed by a helicopter ride to Le Manoir, where
55 Raymond Blanc would oversee a spectacular lunch.

adapted from www.eventmagazine.co.uk

C Work in pairs. Overall, who do you think gave the most interesting answers, and why?

D In pairs, answer this question.

If you had an unlimited budget, what would be included in your dream corporate-hospitality package?

Multiword verbs

A multiword verb is a verb and one or two particles (prepositions or adverbs).

- It is sometimes possible to guess the meaning from the context.
  August is too early for our conference. Let's **put** *it* **off** *until October.*
  (= to delay, to arrange to do something at a later date)

- However, sometimes the meaning is difficult or impossible to guess.
  I **turned down** *their offer.* (= to refuse)

➡ *Grammar reference* page 146

A **Match the multiword verbs in bold (1–8) with their definitions (a–h).**

1 Who's going to **look after** our guests tonight?
2 We have two hours to **look around** the city.
3 We're really **looking forward** to the Tokyo trip.
4 Let's **take** the clients **out** to a Chinese restaurant.
5 Seventy staff **took part** in our fundraising events.
6 The CEO would like to **take up** your kind offer.
7 We were delighted that so many sponsors **turned up** at the event.
8 As we had another engagement, we had to **turn down** their invitation.

a) see the sights
b) arrive/appear/come
c) get involved in
d) give attention to / protect / take care of
e) accept (an offer)
f) await with pleasure
g) entertain
h) refuse/decline

B **Choose the correct options to complete this e-mail extract.**

Just a quick e-mail to say thank you for organising the Monaco Grand Prix hospitality event. Everyone who took *care of / part in / up* [1] the event thoroughly enjoyed looking *around / forward to / after* [2] the city and the Grand Prix itself. Our clients were looked *around / forward to / after* [3] very well by your events team. I am afraid I am going to have to *take care of / turn down / turn up* [4] your kind offer of free tickets for the film premiere as I have another engagement that night. However, we would like to *take up / turn up / turn down* [5] your offer of organising our corporate events next year. We are all really looking *forward to / around / after* [6] discussi**ng your proposals.**

C **In pairs, take turns to ask and answer these questions.**

1 What are you looking forward to most this month?
2 Have you ever turned down an important invitation?
3 What is the best team event you have taken part in?
4 Which famous person would you most like to look after for a day?

Socialising: greetings and small talk

A **What do you say to a business contact when you:**

1 introduce yourself?   2 introduce another person?   3 are introduced to another person?

What topics can/do you talk about?

B 🔊 CD1.55–1.59 **Listen to five conversations at a conference. Match the speakers in each one, then decide whether they know each other or not.**

Speaker 1		Speaker 2	Do they know each other?
1	Liz	a) Linda Eriksson	
2	James	b) Jürgen	
3	Julia	c) Lisa	
4	John	d) Jane	Yes
5	Carla	e) Sam Clarke	

C 🔊 CD1.56, 1.58 **Try to complete the gaps in Conversations 2 and 4. Then listen again and check your answers.**

Conversation 2

A: James, ...*have*... you ....^{1} Sam Clarke?

B: No. Hello, Sam. .... to meet ....^{2}. I think we both ....^{3} Mike Upton. We............^{4} together in Turkey.

C: Oh, yes ... Mike. He's in China now.

B: Really? I didn't know that. .... him my............^{5} next time you see him.

C: Yes, I will.

Conversation 4

A: Hi, I'm John.

B: Hello, John. ....^{6} to meet you. I'm Lisa, from the Amsterdam office.

A: Oh, Amsterdam. I've never been, but I............^{7} it's a............^{8} city, very lively.

B: Yes, it is. It's great. You should come. The conference is going to be there next year.

A: I'd............^{9} to. I'll look............^{10} to it.

D **Read these expressions (1–10). Decide whether each one is said by the host (H) or the guest (G).**

1 Can I get you a drink?   *H*

2 Yes, it's just down there on the left.

3 It all looks good. What do you recommend?

4 Would you like me to show you round?

5 Help yourself to some food.

6 Yes, please. I'll have a white wine.

7 Can I give you a lift to the airport?

8 Yes, I'd love to see some of the sights.

9 Could you tell me where the toilet is, please?

10 Thanks, but my taxi's coming.

E **Put the sentences from Exercise D in logical pairs.**

examples: 1 + 6   *Can I get you a drink?   Yes, please. I'll have a white wine.*

F **Work in pairs. Role-play the conversation.**

Student A: Turn to page 134.   Student B: Turn to page 139.

USEFUL LANGUAGE

INTRODUCING PEOPLE
Jurgen, this is Lisa.
Anita, do you know Ian?
Have you met Mauro?

ACCEPTING
Yes, I'd love to.
Thank you. That would be very nice.

RESPONDING
Pleased/Nice to meet you.
Good to see you again.

MAKING SMALL TALK
How's business?
We're having a great year.
Have you heard about ...?
How are things?

REQUESTS
Could I use your printer, please?
Do you mind if I take a map?

CLARIFYING
Sorry, I didn't catch your name.
I'm afraid I missed the name of your company.

OFFERS
Would you like to have dinner with us tomorrow night?
How about coming to the Cabaret Club with us?

REFUSING POLITELY
I'm really sorry, but I'm meeting a client then.
Thank you very much for asking, but I'm afraid I can't make it tomorrow.

THANKING
Thank you for the meal. It was really good.
Thank you for a lovely evening. I had a great time.

ORGANISING A CONFERENCE

A multinational is choosing the best location for its next sales conference

Background

Global Food and Drink Corporation (GFDC), a multinational company based in Dubai, is holding an international conference later this year. The Chief Executive, senior managers from the head office and about 100 managers from its overseas subsidiaries and sales offices will attend. The aims of the conference, in order of priority, are to:

- discuss how the company can improve its products and services;

- thank managers for their hard work;

- give managers the opportunity to get to know each other better.

The conference will take place in July. Participants arrive on Thursday evening, have a free day on Friday and leave on Monday morning. The budget is $4,000 per participant.

> 🔊 **CD1.60** Listen to two colleagues in the marketing department discussing the planning of the conference. Make notes about the key features the conference location must have.

Hotels

Seagreen Hotel, Miami, Florida (US)

- Location: seafront, close to beach
- Access: half an hour from airport, no shuttle service
- Conference facilities: one conference room (capacity 200), two meeting rooms, a large lounge (capacity 60 people) – could be used for workshops if necessary
- Bedrooms: small, all with sea views, well-designed with modern furniture/facilities
- Leisure: Olympic-size swimming pool, gift shop, art gallery, small fitness centre (not much equipment)
- Price: $2,200 per participant, including meals and all entertainment
- Restaurant: spacious (capacity 250), mainly Spanish and Mexican dishes, famous Hispanic chef.
- Entertainment: local musicians and singers, lively and noisy at night
- Guest reviews: excellent service, business centre – limited hours

Bamboo Conference Centre, Macau (south-east China)

- Location: city centre
- Access: 40 minutes from the airport, shuttle service, taxis, buses
- Conference facilities: conference room (capacity 300), eight meeting rooms (extra reservation charge $100 per room per hour)
- Bedrooms: spacious, luxurious, satellite television, free mini bar
- Leisure: casinos, night clubs, shopping mall (five minutes from hotel)
- Price: $3,100 per participant, including meals and two guided tours
- Restaurant: private dining hall (capacity 150), chef James Lee offers Cantonese cuisine, many unique dishes
- Entertainment: wide range available in the area
- Guest reviews: beautifully furnished rooms, reception desk slow to respond to service calls

The marketing team sent out a questionnaire to find out what type of venue the participants preferred. They have selected four to choose from (see below). All prices include the cost of flights.

Preferred location

Seaside 31%   City 28%   No preference 6%   Rural area 35%

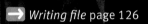

Task

You are members of GFDC's marketing department.

1   Work in small groups. Discuss the advantages and disadvantages of each hotel as the venue for the conference.

2   Rank the hotels 1–4 (1 = the most suitable hotel for the conference, 4 = the least suitable).

3   Meet as one group and listen to each other's ideas. Make your final choice. Take a vote if necessary.

*Watch the Case study commentary on the **DVD-ROM**.*

Writing

As Chief Executive of GFDC, write an e-mail inviting the overseas sales managers to attend this year's conference. Inform them of the dates, the purpose of the conference and the details of the location.

I am writing to invite you to attend this year's conference. It will be held ...

➡ *Writing file page 126*

3

Hotel Porte Ouverte, Monte Carlo (Monaco)

- Location: on a hill overlooking city, 10 minutes to the Palace and beach
- Access: at least 45 minutes from Nice airport, longer if traffic jams, no shuttle service
- Conference facilities: conference room (capacity 500), many meeting rooms, with up-to-date equipment
- Bedrooms: award-winning designs, well equipped, some have balconies/sea views
- Leisure: outdoor swimming pool, spa and fitness centre, free trips to old town of Nice
- Price: $4,000 per participant
- Restaurant: capacity for 250 diners, international cuisine
- Entertainment: pianist plays every night in the hotel lounge
- Guest reviews: service OK, but not outstanding; bars very busy at night, expensive drinks

4

Hotel Steffanberg, rural area (Sweden)

- Location: a modernised castle, 200 kilometres from Stockholm Airport
- Access: regular hotel bus service from the airport to the castle (three-hour journey)
- Conference facilities: conference room (150 capacity), five meeting rooms, all rooms large and bright
- Bedrooms: bright and comfortable, antique furniture, well equipped, no mini bar
- Leisure: nine-hole golf course near the castle, extra charge for pool and sauna, excellent spa
- Price: $3,600 per person
- Restaurant: dining hall for 200 people, two other smaller dining rooms, Swedish dishes, other dishes if requested
- Entertainment: evening entertainment by young Swedish musicians, classical music at lunch
- Guest reviews: beautiful views of castle grounds; owners friendly/helpful, but staff need more training on customer service

2 Doing business internationally

A **A meeting in Morocco**

What do you know about Morocco? In pairs, do this quiz. Decide whether each statement is true (T) or false (F). If the statement is false, correct it. Check your answers on page 134.

1	Morocco, a country in North Africa, has a border with Egypt ....
2	Religion plays a big role in Morocco's day-to-day life and business culture. ....
3	Moroccans always use Arabic when they do business internationally.
4	It is good to ask Moroccans about their family and work. ....
5	Friday is a good day to do business. ....
6	Networking is very important in Moroccan business culture. ....
7	Moroccans value greatly the reputation of their business. ....
8	In Moroccan business, who you know is more important than what you know. ....
0	Meetings often go on longer than scheduled. Moroccans do not like time pressure when doing business. ....
10	Moroccans are usually looking to build long-term business relationships. ....

Task 1

1 ◀) CD1.61 **Andrew Morgan is not very familiar with Moroccan business culture. He is meeting an Arab businessman, Karim Mansour in Rabat, who has been recommended by a colleague at head office. Listen and answer these questions.**

1 Why is Andrew Morgan visiting Morocco?
2 How does Morgan's company plan to distribute its products in Morocco?
3 What contacts does Morgan want to get during the visit?

2 ◀) CD1.61 **Listen again and note down the cultural errors Andrew Morgan makes. If necessary, refer to the audio script of the conversation on page 159. Compare your answers with those on page 135.**

B A posting to Mexico

Joanna Simmons works for a large food company based in Dallas, Texas. She has been posted to the company's subsidiary in Monterrey, Mexico. Unfortunately, she is having difficulties adjusting to the local business culture. Joanna sends some e-mails to her friend, Samantha, who works at head office. Work in groups of three. Each of you reads one e-mail. Summarise it briefly to the others in your group. Then do Task 2 below.

1

11 March

Hi Samantha!

You wanted to know how I'm getting on here. Not too well, I'm afraid. I'm having problems adapting to the business culture.

My knowledge of Spanish is not as good as I thought. I sometimes get invited to dinner at colleagues' homes. My hosts ask me a lot of questions about serious topics back home, but it's really difficult for me to have a conversation in Spanish with them. So I'm taking Spanish classes at the weekend to improve my language skills.

Actually, I've been trying to make things easier for myself by asking questions about Mexican culture. That way, my hosts do most of the talking!

2

4 May

You know, the Mexican way of doing business is so different. I have to go to business breakfasts every week, usually from 8 to 11. I'm not used to that. And business lunches are very important here. They go on for hours, and business is discussed only at the end of the meal. Also, no one seems very interested in my marketing ideas. I feel my Mexican colleagues are watching me and trying to decide if they like me.

3

13 June

I've noticed a few things about the business culture here. Mexicans don't seem to like much eye contact. Maybe they think it isn't polite. And they've got strange ideas about personal space. They stand very close to you and they often touch your shoulder or arm. But if I step back to get a bit more space, they're not happy.

Task 2

In small groups, discuss these questions.

1 What features of Mexico's business culture is Joanna having difficulties dealing with?
2 Has she done anything to overcome her difficulties? If so, what has she done?
3 What advice would you give her to help her adapt to the local business culture?
4 Is she the right person for a posting to Mexico? Why? / Why not?
5 Do you think you would have any problems working in a situation like this? If so, why?

C Doing business in South Korea

In a radio programme called *Business Today*, four people talked about their experiences of doing business in South Korea.

Task 3

1 🔊 CD1.62 – 1.65 Listen and make notes about the key points in each extract. Listen again if necessary.

2 Write a list of dos and don'ts for someone visiting Korea.

examples:

Do
Get information about people you are going to do business with.
Don't
Forget that the oldest person is often the most senior in a group of Korean executives.

D Work in groups. Consider the business cultures of the three countries featured in this section: Morocco, Mexico and South Korea.

1 If you could have a one-year posting to one of these countries, what would be your order of preference? Discuss your ranking with other members of your group and give reasons.

2 Choose one of the three countries. How does the business culture in your own country differ from the country you have chosen? In what ways is it similar?

3 Choose a country that interests you. Do some research into its business culture, then present what you've learned to your colleagues.

4 Great ideas

VOCABULARY

Complete the text below with the words in the box.

| enter extend fill made meet protect reduce take |

Company news

The Research and Development team have recently ....[1] a breakthrough that will allow us to significantly reduce the size of our 5,000-watt generator. We plan to ....[2] advantage of this opportunity to ....[3] a gap in the market by introducing a product that is not only powerful, but also very compact. This will ....[4] the needs of customers who need to limit the size and weight of their equipment because of the restrictions of their working environment. On the production side, making a smaller product will help us ....[5] waste and energy use in the manufacturing process. This will demonstrate that we are keeping our commitment to ....[6] the environment. We aren't planning to stop making our larger generators; we will ....[7] our generator product range to include the new 'micro-generator' line. We're hoping to ....[8] the highly competitive North American market with the new product next year.

PAST SIMPLE
AND PAST
CONTINUOUS

Complete this text with either the past simple or the past continuous form of the verbs in brackets.

While Trevor Baylis ....[1] (*listen*) to a radio programme about villages in rural Africa, he ....[2] (*have*) a great idea. According to the programme, most villages ....[3] (*not have*) electricity, so communication with the outside world ....[4] (*be*) a problem. While people in cities ....[5] (*receive*) the latest health information, people in the countryside ....[6] (*not get*) enough information and education. Baylis ....[7] (*go*) to his workshop and ....[8] (*begin*) experimenting. He soon ....[9] (*make*) a working radio with no batteries – wind-up radio. While he ....[10] (*try*), without luck, to sell his idea to companies, he ....[11] (*have*) a lucky break. His radio ....[12] (*appear*) on a BBC TV programme, and someone who had money to invest in the project ....[13] (*watch*). As a result, the Freeplay radio ....[14] (*become*) a huge success.

Put this conversation into the correct order.

a) Ben: I think we should hire Jenny Wong.   ☐

b) Lisa: I totally agree with Ben. Jenny's the strongest candidate.   ☐

c) Lisa: Yes, OK. I think everyone's here.   ☐

d) Lisa: I mean that she has a lot of experience.   ☐

e) Anna: Yes, she's experienced. But I think we should consider Klaus Lehman, too.   ☐

f) Tom: Can we start, please?   ☐

g) Tom: The main aim of the meeting is to decide who to hire as the new office assistant. Ben, what do you think?   ☐

h) Anna: Sorry, I don't quite understand. What do you mean by 'strongest'?   ☐

5 Stress

Complete the sentences below with the words in the box.

> deadline   flexitime   lifestyle   quality of life   work–life balance
> workaholic   working environment   workload

1   A firefighter's .... can be extremely dangerous. Lars had special training to deal with emergency situations.

2   Ahmed loves the .... associated with his job as an international airline pilot. He travels the world and he's paid very well.

3   Construction workers sometimes have to work hard to meet a .... Building work must be done to a strict schedule.

4   Lois, an accountant, likes to start work very early in the morning, so working .... allows her to start at 7.30 and finish at 4.30.

5   Su-Lee's .... as an actor is very good. She is well paid and she loves what she does.

6   Pietro is a nursery nurse. His young children attend the nursery, so he can see them during the day. This gives him a good ....

7   Steve's .... as a social worker can be a real challenge for him. Sometimes he has to visit 10 or 12 families in one day.

8   To succeed as an advertising executive, Joanna has to be a .... She works 12-hour days, six days a week.

Match the halves of these expressions.

1 How about	a) a good idea.
2 I can't agree	b) further thought.
3 I still think it's	c) encourage staff to work flexitime?
4 I think	d) buy new laptops for them.
5 I think I	e) about it.
6 I think this needs	f) paying for the cost of car parking?
7 It might be a good idea	g) we should do more research.
8 We could	h) with you there.
9 We've got to do something	i) agree with you.
10 Why don't we	j) to set up a childcare service.

WRITING

Read these notes, then write an e-mail (70–100 words) to your boss, Mike.

Points for update e-mail to Mike:

- Had a project meeting this morning.
- Project going well – on time because everyone working hard.
- Everyone loves work, but feeling very stressed.
- We work late, but must start next day at 8.30.
- Consider flexitime system – reduce stress and overwork?

6 Entertaining

VOCABULARY

Choose the best options to complete this text.

For business dinners, I usually go to Peking House, a Chinese restaurant. It has a *regional / convenient*[1] location about five minutes from the office, and the atmosphere is *cosy / reasonable*[2], so we can talk quietly and comfortably. It's also very important for a business meal to have *local / efficient*[3] service, and the staff at Peking House are the best. Chinese food is good because they have something for everyone. Peking House is famous for its seafood, especially the dishes with *prawns / veal*[4]. They also serve a wonderful *lamb / cabbage*[5] soup that's very popular with vegetarians. It isn't the cheapest Chinese restaurant in the area, but the prices are very *exciting / reasonable*[6], especially when you consider that the service and atmosphere are both excellent. Chinese restaurants don't always have a wide selection of drinks, but Peking House has a wonderful choice of good *wines / poultry*[7] and beers, including several *mineral / non-alcoholic*[8] ones for people who don't like alcohol.

MULTIWORD VERBS

Complete the text below with the words in the box.

after	around	down	out	part	to	up	up

1 Leyan and Rupert took............ in a charity marathon.

2 Beatta turned............ the invitation to go out for a meal after work because she was very tired.

3 We always take visitors............ for an expensive meal.

4 I'd like to take............ your kind offer to organise the after-work entertainment for next week's meeting.

5 Did you have a chance to look............ Barcelona when you were there?

6 How many people turned............ for your presentation?

7 Marcus is really looking forward............ his visit to Moscow.

8 Alberto's going to look............ the team from the Beijing office.

SKILLS

Match each statement (1–8) to a response (a–h).

1 Would you like to have lunch with us?

2 Piet, this is Alfonso.

3 How's business?

4 Sorry, I didn't catch your name.

5 Sorry, did you say you're from Poland?

6 Ingrid, do you know Dugald?

7 Could I use your pen, please?

8 Have you heard Liam's news?

a) We're having a great year.

b) Yes, that's right. Warsaw.

c) Sure. No problem.

d) Thank you. That would be very nice.

e) No, I haven't. What is it?

f) Yes, we met last year. Good to see you again.

g) It's John. John Hicks.

h) Pleased to meet you.

Cultures 2: Doing business internationally

Complete the tips below on doing business internationally with the words in the box.

> business breakfasts and business lunches   business card
> business culture   eye contact   food   local language   personal space
> red tape   the oldest person   trust and respect

Seniority

- Pay attention to who's who. In a group of Korean executives, ...[1] is often the most senior. In Mexico, you may need to take the time to socialise with other businesspeople so you can earn their ....[2].

Communication

- In most cases, your............[3] should be translated into the local language where you're doing business. This helps people understand who they're dealing with.

- If you need to socialise in the ....[4], work as hard as you can to improve your ability to speak it.

Business culture

- In Mexico, you can expect long............[5], but you might not talk about business
until the very end of the meal.

- Wherever you go, try to learn as much as you can about the ....[6] before your visit. The more you know, the easier it is to do business. For example, in some countries, there can be a lot of............[7]. You'll need a lot of official documents before you can go ahead with a project. You need to be patient.

Politeness and personal space

- Accept............[8] when someone offers it. It's better to accept it and leave some of it on your plate, rather than say 'no' to the offer.

- In some cultures, looking directly into someone's eyes shows honesty. But in other cultures, too much ....[9] may be impolite.

- Different cultures also have very different ideas about............[10]. In Mexico, people may stand very close to you and they often touch your shoulder or arm.

Small talk

Objectives

Speaking

- Can use simple, everyday polite forms of greeting and address.

- Can participate in short conversations in routine contexts on topics of interest.

Listening

Can follow short, simple social exchanges.

Lesson deliverable

To participate in an activity to practise small talk in a business context.

Performance review

To review your own progress and performance against the lesson objectives at the end of the lesson.

A SPEAKING 1

1 Complete these statements. Then discuss in pairs.

1 When I meet someone for the first time, I usually …

2 I enjoy/don't enjoy small talk because …

2 In pairs or groups, discuss these points.

1 what you say when you meet someone for the first time

2 how you introduce someone to another person

3 what topics you talk about with someone you have just met

4 what you say to someone you have met somewhere before

5 what you say if you don't understand what someone says

3 Discuss these questions.

1 Are these important when you meet someone? Why/Why not?

- handshake

- eye contact

- how close you stand to someone

- hand movements/gestures

2 Do all cultures use the same body language? Why is this important when meeting people from different countries?

B READING

Read these tips for small talk. Then match the tips (1–7) to the examples (a–g).

1 Greet appropriately (e.g. Hello/Pleased to meet you, shake hands/bow).

2 Remember names – try to use the person's name in conversation.

3 Ask and answer questions – is there any helpful extra information you can give?

4 Listen carefully and show interest in what the other person says.

5 Find common interests to talk about.

6 Avoid 'difficult' topics (e.g. religion, politics, salary, personal relationships).

7 End the conversation politely.

a) 'Mm, I see what you mean.'/'Really? I didn't know that.'/'Absolutely!'

b) 'I enjoy playing golf. What about you? Do you do any sport?'/ 'Yes, I like to travel, too.'

c) 'Please excuse me, I have to go now. It was good to talk to you. See you later, I hope.'

d) 'Good morning, Mr Kimura, pleased to meet you.'

e) 'I work for XYZ. It's a multinational based in India, but I work in the London office.'

f) 'What do you think about our new government?' 'What's your salary?'

g) 'Simon, pleased to meet you.'/'That's right, John.'/ 'I agree, Maria.'

C LISTENING

1 🔊 BSA2.1.6 Listen to a conversation and answer the questions.

1 Have Susan and Mike met before?

2 Have they spoken to each other on the phone before?

3 Do Susan and Massimo know each other?

4 What are Susan, Mike and Massimo going to do this evening?

2 🔊 BSA2.1.7 Listen to a second conversation and answer the questions.

1 Where do you think they are?

2 Which of these topics do they talk about?

- living in another country

- studying at university

- working in another country

- family

- languages they speak

- salary

- listening to a presentation

3 🔊 **BSA2.1.8 Listen to a third conversation and answer the questions.**

1 Why is Massimo late?
2 Who is flying back to Italy tonight?
3 What is Massimo going to do tomorrow?
4 Has Susan been to Italy before?
5 What food does Mike recommend?

	A	B
1	A: met before?	B: no; been to Italy?
2	A: no; speak before?	B: yes; work abroad before?
3	A: yes; work in Germany?	B: yes; where/work?
4	A: USA; like working there?	B: no; enjoy working there?
5	A: yes; (Add a question of your own.)	B: (Reply and add a question of your own.)
6	A: (Reply.)	

D SPEAKING 2

Work in pairs. Practise asking and answering the questions.

Task

Pre-task: Discussion

Companies often meet clients over lunch or dinner. Do you think this is a good idea? What are the advantages and disadvantages?

Part 1: Preparation

Context: A company which manufactures electronic components is planning a dinner to welcome some international customers who are visiting for the first time. You have spoken to some of the employees/customers previously on the phone.

Work in two groups, A and B, and prepare.

Group A
Your company is arranging the dinner. Discuss how to welcome the visitors and the language you are going to need (greetings, introductions, clarification, etc.). Decide which topics you can talk about with your clients and suggest how to deal with any unsuitable topics that occur in conversation. Also think about offering drinks and what food/drink to recommend. Think of something else you can offer to do for your guests.

Group B
You are the clients visiting the supplier. Talk together about the language you are going to use (greetings, introductions, clarification, etc.). Decide what topics you can talk about with your supplier and include one unsuitable topic to talk about with the people you are meeting. Also be prepared to accept or refuse offers.

Part 2: Role-play

The two groups meet at the restaurant. Role-play a conversation over dinner with people from the other group and talk to as many of them as you can. Make sure you introduce yourself and a partner, discuss at least three topics and offer/accept food/drink/invitations/etc. to keep the conversation going. Don't forget to use suitable body language.

Part 3: Reporting back

Return to your original group (A or B). Tell each other about the people you met in the other group and discuss how you dealt with unsuitable topics. Were you able to offer/refuse/accept successfully?

💿 **EXTRA PRACTICE: DVD CLIP AND WORKSHEET 4**

E PEER REVIEW

Look back at the lesson objectives and think about the dinner meeting. Then answer these questions.

1 Which conversation(s) went well?
2 What did your partner(s) do that was good?
3 What can you and your partner(s) do better next time?

F SELF-ASSESSMENT

Write 80–100 words to assess your performance.

Think about these points:

• what you did well
• feedback from your partners
• what you can do better

G PROFESSIONAL DEVELOPMENT AND PERFORMANCE GOALS

Think of ways to practise and improve your skills. Write two or three sentences about ways you can improve your small talk skills. What can you do to prepare when you plan to meet someone for the first time?

Meetings

Objectives

Speaking

Can make and respond to suggestions.

Listening

Can understand enough to respond to direct requests expressed slowly and clearly.

Lesson deliverable

To participate in two meetings and produce a business memo.

Performance review

To review your own progress and performance against the lesson objectives at the end of the lesson.

A SPEAKING

Work in pairs. Make a list of ideas about these questions. Then compare your ideas with the rest of the class.

1 What happens at the beginning, middle and end of meetings? Think of the role of the leader and of the participants.

2 What kind of preparation is useful for a meeting?

3 What does a good meeting leader do?

4 What do good meeting participants do?

B LISTENING

1 ◀》 BSA2.2.9 **The Human Resources Manager of a small international company has called her team to a meeting. Listen to the meeting and say if these statements are true (T) or false (F). Then compare your answers with a partner and correct the false statements.**

1 The HR Manager went to a recruitment seminar.

2 She is worried that the employees are not working hard enough.

3 The Korean engineers and their wives organised a Korean culture evening.

4 Now there are a lot of clubs and events.

5 The HR Manager asks her team to create some clubs.

6 They are going to meet again on Tuesday.

2 ◀》 BSA2.2.9 **Listen again and tick the expressions you hear.**

1 Well, I think it's a great idea.

2 What do you think?

3 I don't think …

4 I see what you mean.

5 I can see your point …

6 I totally disagree there.

7 Maybe we will …

8 Exactly!

Task

Pre-task: Preparation

Context: You are members of your company's social committee. The senior management team believes that more company clubs and events will improve staff morale. You are going to hold a meeting to brainstorm ideas.

Work in groups of three or four. Turn to page viii and choose a role card. Read your role card and look at the useful language box. Then choose a meeting leader.

Part 1: The meeting

1 Hold your meeting. By the end of the meeting, you must agree on a list of three or four possibilities. (Meeting leader: give your opinion, but make sure everyone contributes.)

Turn to pages 41 and 49 for useful meetings and discussions language.

2 Join up with another team and have another meeting, with a different meeting leader. You must decide on a final list of four or five possibilities.

Part 2: Follow up

You need to tell the rest of the company about your ideas. Follow these steps.

1 In pairs, write an e-mail to the employees in your company explaining the idea of starting up regular social events and company clubs.

2 Invite them to attend a meeting next week to discuss the idea.

3 Encourage them to think of suggestions for events and clubs, and to submit their ideas to you by e-mail before the meeting.

◎ EXTRA PRACTICE: DVD CLIP AND WORKSHEET 5

C PEER REVIEW

Give your opinion on the meetings. Think about these questions:

1 What did your colleagues do well?

2 Which parts of the meetings went well? Why?

3 Were some people easier to understand? Why?

D SELF-ASSESSMENT

Think about your performance in B and the Task. Look back at the lesson objectives and consider what you have learnt about running an effective meeting. Write 150 words about how well you achieved the objectives. What could you improve? How will you do this?

E PROFESSIONAL DEVELOPMENT AND PERFORMANCE GOALS

Think about how you will use and develop the meeting skills you have learned in your place of work/study. Write a SMART action plan for developing these skills.

A8

'Three components make an entrepreneur: the person, the idea and the resources to make it happen.' *Anita Roddick (1942–2007), British founder of The Body Shop*

STARTING UP

A **Discuss these questions.**

1 Would you like to start your own business? Why? / Why not?

2 What conditions are important for people starting new businesses? Choose the three
most important from this list. Can you think of any others?

- low taxes   • good transport links   • skilled staff   • training courses
- low interest rates   • high unemployment   • cheap rents
- a strong currency   • a healthy economy   • government grants
- a stable political situation   • easy access to credit

B **Many economies contain a mix of public- and private-sector businesses.
Think of companies you know in the areas below. Which are public-sector
companies, and which are private-sector ones?**

- post office   • railways   • television   • water   • energy   • telecoms
- cars   • banks   • newspapers   • airlines   • roads   • mining

C **Many companies in the UK have been privatised. What are the trends in
your country? Talk about the business sectors in Exercise B.**

VOCABULARY
Economic terms

A **Match the economic terms (1–10) to their definitions (a–j).**

1 interest rate
2 exchange rate
3 inflation rate
4 labour force
5 tax incentives
6 government bureaucracy
7 GDP (gross domestic product)
8 unemployment rate
9 foreign investment
10 balance of trade

a) total value of goods and services produced in a country
b) percentage increase in prices
c) cost of borrowing money
d) price at which one currency can buy another
e) percentage of people without jobs
f) the number of people working
g) low taxes to encourage business activity
h) money from overseas
i) official rules/regulations/paperwork
j) difference in value between a country's imports and exports

B **Try to complete this economic profile without looking back at the terms in Exercise A.**

The economy is stable following the problems of the past two years. By following a tight monetary policy, the government has reduced the inflation rate[1] to 2%. For borrowers, after going up dramatically, the i........... r........... [2] is now down to 8%. The last six months have seen a slight improvement in the e........... r........... [3] against the dollar. For the country as a whole, the G........... [4] has grown by 0.15%. Exports are increasing, and the b........... of t........... [5] is starting to look much healthier.

In terms of jobs, the u........... r........... [6] continues to be a problem, as it is still 16%. In order to stimulate the economy and attract f........... i........... [7] from abroad, the government is offering new t........... i........... [8], as well as making a renewed effort to reduce g........... b........... [9] and red tape. Finally, a large skilled l........... f........... [10] means there could be attractive investment opportunities over the next five years.

C 🔊 CD2.1 **Listen and check your answers to Exercise B.**

D **Think about some of the economic terms you looked at above in relation to your own country. Which do you think are going up / going down / staying about the same? Also consider the following:**

- consumer prices (the price of things in the shops)
- public spending (the money the government spends)
- consumer spending (the money people spend)

E **What do you think are the biggest economic problems in your country at the moment? What do you think the government's priorities should be? Talk to a partner about your ideas.**

*See the **DVD-ROM** for the i-Glossary.*

F **Write a short paragraph about the economic profile of your country.**

New business

Abdirashid Duale

A 🔊 CD2.2 **Abdirashid Duale is the Chief Executive Officer of Dahabshiil, a global money-transfer company. Listen to the first part of the interview and answer these questions.**

1 How many countries does the company transfer money to?

2 Dahabshiil helps four types of people or organisations. What are they?

B 🔊 CD2.3 **Listen to the second part and complete these notes.**

All successful new businesses have to:

- have a .... [1]

- have a .... [2]

- know how they are going to .... [3] that vision

- motivate their .... [4]

- keep their customers .... [5]

- maintain their .... [6] with their customers

- make sure that the customers are happy with their .... [7]

- manage the difference between their income and their .... [8]

Susan Barratt

Watch the interviews on the DVD-ROM.

C 🔊 CD2.4 **Susan Barratt, the CEO of Nature's Way Foods, talks about the advice she would give to anyone starting their own business. Listen and complete this extract from the audio script.**

I hope they've got lots of .... [1]. I think it is difficult and quite hard .... [2], and needs a significant level of commitment. I think it's really, really important to make sure you understand the .... [3] and who your customers are going to be. And how you differentiate yourself, or make yourself different, from any of your .... [4] in that marketplace.

People will only go to you and buy your .... [5] or your service if they feel it is added .... [6] over and above what they can get elsewhere, or something they can't get elsewhere.

So, for me, understanding the market and the .... [7] is absolutely critical to the success of the business. The other key thing is that you've got sufficient .... [8].

D **In groups, discuss these questions.**

1 What sort of problems do new businesses face?

2 What advice would you give to someone starting their own business in your country?

New business ideas

A **Which new business has impressed you most in the last six years? Why did it impress you?**

B **Work in pairs. Student A, read Article A on the opposite page. Student B, read Article B. Make notes in this chart.**

	Article A	Article B
name of new business		
name of founder		
age of founder		
age of business at time of writing		
location of new business (city and country)		
number of employees		
what the new business is/does		

A

FT

Internet whiz-kid's discount idea makes billions in two years

by Jonathan Birchall

Andrew Mason studied music at university, where he dreamt about making his riches as a rock star. Instead, the 29-year-old decided to set
5 up an Internet business that offers discounts on everything from restaurant meals to hair transplants and yoga classes. The big idea is about to turn him into the latest web billionaire.
10 Google is preparing to buy Groupon, his two-year-old company, for $5.3 billion, according to reports. The proposed deal will put Mr Mason in a group of young Internet billionaires
15 including Mark Zuckerberg of Facebook and the Google founders, Larry Page and Sergey Brin.

The site offers vouchers named "Groupons" that can be spent at
20 participating retailers. Every user gets a discount offer based on his or her location and profile, but these huge discounts expire unless enough people sign up. The trend, described
25 as "social buying", has spread rapidly across the Web, and Groupon was described by Forbes as "the world's fastest-growing company".

Its explosive growth and healthy
30 profits have convinced Google to dig into its deep pockets. It is believed to have started its bidding at $3 billion, a price that has been steadily rising over the past few weeks.
35 Mr Mason appears to be a man who knows his worth. In April, it was reported that he turned down a $2 billion offer from Yahoo, because the valuation was too low.
40 Groupon employs about 1,000 people, mostly based in Mr Mason's home town of Chicago. It is active in more than 80 countries
45 and is growing at the rate of 10 per cent a week by adding new
50 users through Facebook and Twitter.

B

Help with exports

by Peter Marsh

Scattered around the world are many thousands of "micro-manufacturers" of craft items such as jewellery and handbags, often offering high standards of
5 design and quality. Most, however, have little idea of how to sell their products in international markets.

At the same time, retail outlets are eager to get their hands on products
10 that look new and different – but find it difficult to discover them.

Just over a year ago, Sandra Felsenstein, a 27-year-old former industrial engineer, decided to start a
15 business that would try to link these two groups. Her approach was to find a series of high quality manufacturers in her native Argentina – a country with a good reputation for
20 design, yet poor connections to the rest of the craft trade worldwide – and link them with shops and distribution companies elsewhere.

Dinka, the four-person company
25 she founded in Buenos Aires, is now showing signs of success. Ms Felsenstein has organised links with 30 Argentinian companies that have agreed to let Dinka promote
30 their goods in export markets. Under these deals, Dinka will find buyers for their products and handle shipments and customs formalities in exchange for a proportion of sales
35 revenues.

She has laid the foundations, too, for establishing a network of retail outlets in other countries, arranging connections with retailers in Chile,
40 Peru and Ecuador as a first step, while signing up a distributor in Austin, Texas, that she hopes will help them enter the potentially large US market.

Ms Felsenstein says she is also
45 "exploring several opportunities" for finding retailers in Europe – particularly in Spain, Italy, Germany and Switzerland – where she thinks sizeable sales could be established
50 for Argentinian-made goods.

C Note down two other interesting pieces of information about your article.

D Give your partner an oral summary of your article, then take notes as you listen to your partner's summary.

E Work in groups of three or four. Think about a business you could start as a group. Consider these questions.

1 What kind of business would it be?

2 Which country and city would you like to locate your new business in? Think of the factors mentioned in Starting up, Exercise A.

3 What do you already have as a group? Think about skills, experience and contacts.

4 What other strengths do you have? What about your gaps?

5 What difficulties do you think you may face? How will you overcome them?

LANGUAGE REVIEW
Time clauses

Time clauses provide information about actions and events in the past, present and future.

1 We often use *when* to introduce time clauses.
*She remembers **when** she first started her business.* (past time)
***When** you fly first class, you get more leg room.* (present time)
***When** I'm in Geneva, I'll review all the start-up costs.* (future time)

2 We can also use *while, before, after, until* and *as soon as* to introduce time clauses.
*He looked at our business plan **while** we were waiting.*
*We need to have a solid business plan in place **before** we launch our online business.*
***After** we finish this project, we'll look at new markets.*
*He waited **until** she finished speaking.*

3 When we use a time clause to talk about the future, the verb in the time clause is in the present tense or the present perfect tense.
*We'll deliver **as soon as** they **pay** their last bill.*
***When** we**'ve finished** the report, we'll e-mail it to you.*

➡ *Grammar reference* page 147

A **Match the sentence halves to make appropriate sentences.**

1 Could you check the departure time
2 As soon as interest rates rise,
3 We need to stay
4 The Finance Director needs to speak to you
5 She will move to Frankfurt
6 We won't open our new office
7 I think you should save some money
8 We can set up in that country

a) until the meeting has finished.
b) as soon as you get to the office.
c) until we've saved enough money.
d) while you are still working.
e) when the conditions are right.
f) when she finds a good job.
g) before we leave for the airport.
h) the economy will slow down.

B **Complete these sentences with *when, while, before, after, until* or *as soon as*. More than one answer may be possible in each case.**

1 We won't buy anything new .... we've paid off all our debts.
2 They'll start the meeting .... the manager arrives.
3 I was finishing the report............ my boss went out with clients.
4 It's urgent, so I'll phone you .... I get home.
5 Can you check the figures .... you go home?

C **Birgit Scheider is writing to her previous boss, a successful American businesswoman. Read her questions about starting a new business and choose the most appropriate option in each case.**

I remember *before / as soon as / when* [1] I first thought about quitting my job and you advised me to gain some experience *as soon as / while / before* [2] I started a new business. I need to earn some profit *until / as soon as / before* [3] possible, as I don't have much spare cash. Or do I have to accept that I won't have much money *as soon as / until / while* [4] I'm starting up my new business? Do I need to have some savings *when / while / as soon as* [5] I get my new business off the ground? I'm just not sure how I'll survive *as soon as / when / until* [6] my company starts earning money.

Please advise me *before / as soon as / while* [7] you can.

D ◀)) CD2.5 **Listen and check your answers to Exercise C.**

SKILLS

Dealing with numbers

A ◀)) CD2.6 **Say these numbers. Listen and check after each group.**

1 a) 362   b) 1,841   c) 36,503   d) 684,321   e) 4,537,295

2 a) 3.5   b) 2.89   c) 9.875

3 a) 3/4   b) 1/8   c) 6/7   d) 1/2   e) 2/3

4 a) 15%   b) 50%   c) 97%   d) 100%

5 a) £80   b) $5,800   c) €150,000   d) €20,000

B **Try to answer these questions.**

1 What is the population of your a) country? b) city?

2 How many people work for your company / study at your institution?

3 What is the average salary in your country?

4 What is the current inflation rate?

5 Approximately how many people are unemployed?

6 What is the interest rate for savings?

7 What fraction of their income do you think people spend on living costs?

8 What percentage of your income do you spend on transport?

C ◀)) CD2.7–2.10 **Listen to four extracts from a radio business-news programme. Underline the numbers you hear.**

1 a) Inflation rate: 2.0% / 1.2 %
   b) Unemployment: 1,258,000 / 1,800,000

2 a) Profits increase: $1.8 billion / $1.8 million
   b) Sales increase: 80% / 18%

3 a) Job losses: $1/3$ / $1/4$
   b) Workforce reduction: 15,000 / 5,000

4 a) Interest rate reduction: 0.5% / 1.5%
   b) Economic growth: 2.8% / 1.8%

D **Work in pairs. You work for a marketing department, which is launching a new range of mobile phones in an overseas market. You are gathering statistical information.**

Student A: Turn to page 135.   Student B: Turn to page 140.

1 Ask each other questions to complete your charts.

2 Discuss which are the best markets to launch the new range of phones in.

USEFUL LANGUAGE

SAYING LARGE NUMBERS

912,757,250 =

912 = nine hundred and twelve million,

757 = seven hundred and fifty-seven thousand,

250 = two hundred and fifty

FRACTIONS

$5/7$ = five-sevenths $2/5$ = two-fifths
$1/2$ = a half $1/4$ = a quarter

BRITISH AND AMERICAN ENGLISH DIFFERENCES

320 = three hundred and twenty (BrE)
     three hundred twenty (AmE)

0 = nought/oh (BrE) / zero (AmE)

DECIMALS

1.25 = one point two five

0.754 = nought point seven five four (BrE)
     zero point seven five four (AmE)
     point seven five four (BrE/AmE)

PERCENTAGES

65% = sixty-five per cent

CURRENCIES

£3,000,000 = three million pounds
€16,000 = sixteen thousand euros

71

Case study 7

TAKA SHIMIZU CYCLES

An expanding business wants to begin production outside Japan

Background

Taka Shimizu Cycles (TSC) is based in Nagoya, Japan. Its brand is well known in Japan and in the United States. The company sells four models of bicycle:

- **road bicycles** for the non-enthusiast, general user. Price: US$100–$300

- **touring bicycles** for serious cyclists who travel long distances. Price: US$600–$3,000

- **racing bicycles** for professional cyclists. Price: US$1,000 upwards

- **mountain bicycles** for energetic, adventurous, keep-fit cyclists. Price: US$100–$250

Note: The company is about to launch a new bicycle for children, which has great sales potential.

In the next 10 years, TSC plans to expand in Europe and South-East Asia so that it becomes a global company. To do this, it has decided to build its own factory in an overseas country. The factory will have approximately 2,000 workers, who will produce the frames for the cycles locally. Other components, such as saddles, gears, chains, tyres, etc., will be imported.

Workers will be recruited locally and trained, if necessary, at a special school set up for that purpose.

The company is considering four countries as a location for the factory. There is some information about each country on page 73. They are code-named A, B, C and D.

Sales revenue of cycle models as a percentage of turnover

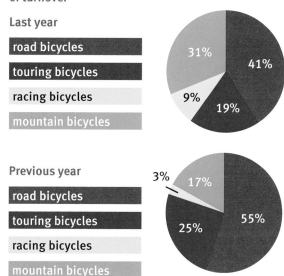

Last year

road bicycles
touring bicycles
racing bicycles
mountain bicycles

41%
31%
9%
19%

Previous year

road bicycles
touring bicycles
racing bicycles
mountain bicycles

3% 17%
55%
25%

Task

You are members of the planning committee, which must choose a location for the new factory.

1 Work in pairs. Discuss the advantages and disadvantages of each location.

2 Work in small groups. Discuss the four countries and rank them in order of suitability as a location.

3 Meet as one group, with one of you leading the discussion. Decide which is the most suitable location for the new cycle factory.

COUNTRY A (EUROPE)

Population 120–150 million (exact figure not available)
GDP per capita* US$21,100
Geography A variety of physical features + climate changes
Economy
- Growth rate (last year): 2%
- Inflation rate: 7.2%
- Interest rate: 6.5%
- Unemployment rate: 8.25%

Taxes
- Business tax on annual profits: 22%
- Import tax on cycle components: 8%

Transport
- Good rail network, but poor roads (frequent traffic jams)
- New international airport
- Sea ports not very efficiently run

Labour
- Unskilled labour available; a lot of training needed for cycle workers
- Wage rates: rising in major cities

Comments
- Political problems: people in some southern provinces want to become independent.
- The government will contribute 30% towards the cost of a new factory.

COUNTRY B (EUROPE)

Population 4.6 million
GDP per capita* US$65,800
Geography No mountains, few hills; very flat land
Economy
- Growth rate (last year): 1.9%
- Inflation rate: 1.6%
- Interest rate: 2.2%
- Unemployment rate: 3%

Taxes
- Business tax on annual profits: 12%
- Import tax on cycle components: 18%

Transport
- Has a fully integrated road and rail network
- International airport
- Two modern seaports; high charges for handling goods

Labour
- Not much skilled labour available
- Wage rates: high

Comments
- The country has a stable government.
- There are strict new laws on pollution.
- There are generous tax credits for building new factories.

COUNTRY C (ASIA)

Population 110 million
GDP per capita* US$3,800
Geography Several mountains in the north, flat in coastal areas
Economy
- Growth rate (last year): 8.9%
- Inflation rate: 7.25%
- Interest rate: 7.8%
- Unemployment rate: 6.9%

Taxes
- Business tax on annual profits: 15%
- Import tax on cycle components: 35%

Transport
- Good transport around the main seaports
- Small but well-managed airport
- Road network needs a lot of investment

Labour
- Plenty of skilled labour available
- Wage rates: low but rising fast

Comments
- About 70% of the population in major cities are under the age of 30.
- There is a strong protest movement against international companies.

COUNTRY D (ASIA)

Population approximately 262 million
GDP per capita* US$3,580
Geography Mountains, hills and flatlands
Economy
- Growth rate (last year): 4.6%
- Inflation rate: 8.7%
- Interest rate: 8%–12%
- Unemployment rate: 7.1%

Taxes
- Business tax on annual profits: 28%
- Import tax on cycle components: 5%

Transport
- Several modern, well-run airports; low rates for handling cargo
- Road and rail network needs investment
- Government has a five-year programme to improve transport system

Labour
- Large supply of unskilled workers who are used to working long hours
- Unions in cycle industry
- Wage rates: average

Comments
- A lot of paperwork is required for new businesses.
- There are serious problems with air and water pollution.
- Profits are tax free for the first three years after a factory has been built.

* GDP per capita = Gross Domestic Product per person (the value of goods produced per person in a country during a period of time)

*Watch the Case study commentary on the **DVD-ROM**.*

Writing

Write an e-mail to the Head of the Chamber of Commerce of the country you have chosen. You should introduce Taka Shimizu Cycles and suggest a possible meeting in order to discuss the proposal further.

➡ *Writing file page 126*

STARTING UP

A 'The four Ps' form the basis of the 'marketing mix'. If you want to market a product successfully, you need to get this mix right. Match the Ps (1–4) to their definitions (a–d).

1 product
2 price
3 promotion
4 place

a) the cost to the buyer of goods or services
b) informing customers about products and persuading them to buy them
c) where goods or services are available
d) goods or services that are sold

B ◀)) CD2.11–2.14 Listen to four consumers talking about different products. Decide which of the four Ps each speaker is discussing: product, price, promotion or place.

C Think of some products you have bought recently. Why did you buy them? Which of the four Ps influenced your decision to buy?

D Tell your partner about a marketing campaign that impressed you.

VOCABULARY
Word partnerships

A For each group of words below (1–5):

- fill in the missing vowels to complete the word partnerships;
- match each of the three word partnerships to the correct definition (a–c).

1 market   r e s e a r c h   a) the percentage of sales a company has

      s _ g m _ n t   b) information about what customers want and need

      s h _ r e   c) a group of customers of similar age, income level and social group

2 consumer   b _ h _ v _ _ _ r   a) description of a typical customer

      p r _ f _ l _   b) where and how people buy things

      g _ _ d s   c) things people buy for their own use

3 product   l _ _ n c h   a) introduction of a product to the market

      l _ f _ c y c l _   b) length of time people continue to buy a product

      r _ n g _   c) set of products made by a company

4 sales   f _ r _ c _ s t   a) how much a company wants to sell in a period

      f _ g _ r _ s   b) how much a company thinks it will sell in a period

      t _ r g _ t   c) numbers showing how much a company has sold in a period

5 advertising   c _ m p _ _ g n   a) a business which advises companies on advertising and makes ads

      b _ d g _ t   b) an amount of money available for advertising during a particular period

      _ g _ n c y   c) a programme of advertising activities over a period, with particular aims

B ◄)) CD2.15 **Mark the stress on the word partnerships in Exercise A. Listen and check your answers.**

example: 'market re'search

C **Choose a well-known brand for each of these categories.**

- car/motorbike *Mercedes*
- mobile phone / camera
- clothing/perfume
- food/drink
- magazine/newspaper
- computer / electronic goods

For each brand, think about these questions.

1 What is the product range of the brand? *The range includes cars, vans and trucks.*

2 Which market segment is it aimed at in your country?

3 What is a typical consumer profile for the brand? Include the following:

   • age   • gender   • job/profession   • income level   • interests/hobbies
   • other products the consumer might buy

D **Work in pairs. Choose one of the brands you looked at in Exercise C. Discuss what sort of advertising campaign you could have for it in your country. How else could you try to increase the sales figures of the brand?**

*See the **DVD-ROM** for the i-Glossary.*

E **Exchange your ideas with another pair.**

Marketing pharmaceuticals

Richard Turner

A 🔊 **CD2.16 Richard Turner is the European Marketing Manager for a pharmaceutical company. Listen to the first part of the interview and answer these questions.**

1 What is very important when you market to doctors?

2 How much time do marketing people usually have with doctors?

3 What are 'rational' advantages?

4 What are 'emotional' advantages?

B 🔊 **CD2.17 Richard talks about 'the regulatory environment'. This is where the authorities have official powers to control the production and safety of drugs. Listen to the second part and complete this audio-script extract.**

I think the biggest ....¹ for us is the regulatory environment. The laws that we need to follow are quite ....² – and quite rightly so. We in the pharmaceutical industry have the same interests as the doctor. We want to help ....³ lead better lives.

We have to present the data in a ....⁴ and balanced way, not to overstate the advantages of our ....⁵. Because we're often trying to develop ....⁶ which are consistent across many different countries across Europe ... it's often a challenge ...

C 🔊 **CD2.18 Listen to the third part and say if these statements are true (T) or false (F). Correct the false ones.**

1 The key to good marketing is being able to speak directly to patients.

2 Marketing people are gaining from all the benefits of the Internet and new communication methods.

3 Companies are starting to look at using technology such as the iPad when presenting data to doctors.

*Watch the interview on the **DVD-ROM**.*

D 🔊 **CD2.19 Listen to the final part and put these stages in the correct order.**

a) Peak sales

b) Clinical trials

c) Present data to the doctor

d) Scientist comes up with an idea

E **What can you say about the different product lifecycles of these things?**

• pharmaceutical drugs • computer software • cars • English-language textbooks
• Rubik's cubes • skateboards • football shirts of a famous team

Adidas and the Chinese market

A **Discuss these questions in pairs.**

1 Who do you think is the biggest manufacturer of sports goods in a) Europe, and b) China?

2 What do you know about Nike, Adidas and Li Ning?

B **Before you read, match these questions (1–6) to the answers (a–f).**

1 Why is Adidas expanding in China?

2 How many stores does Adidas have in China at the time of writing?

3 Who is Christophe Bezu?

4 How did Li Ning get its name?

5 What is Li Ning hoping to do?

6 Who is the market leader for sports goods in China?

a) 550

b) It is planning to focus on low prices.

c) Adidas

d) He is the Chief Executive of Adidas.

e) It comes from the President of the Beijing Olympics Committee.

f) Because it wants to become the market leader in China.

C **Read the article below and correct all the answers (a–f) in Exercise B.**

FT

Adidas targets the Chinese interior

by Patti Waldmeir

Adidas, Europe's biggest sports-goods maker, will open 2,500 stores and expand its sales network to 1,400 Chinese cities, in an effort to regain
5 market share lost to foreign and domestic competitors in one of the world's most rapidly growing retail markets.

The German company is one of
10 many consumer-goods multinationals that have recently decided to shift their focus from near-saturated cities like Shanghai and Beijing to target smaller cities and less wealthy
15 consumers, where they believe growth potential is higher for foreign brands.

Adidas plans to reach far into the Chinese interior to open the new
20 stores. Initially, this will be in urban areas with as few as 500,000 people and then, by 2015, in cities with a population of just over 50,000, company officials said in Shanghai
25 on Tuesday.

"We will be in much smaller cities by 2015," said Christophe Bezu, Adidas Managing Director for Greater China. At present, the company has
30 5,600 stores in 550 cities.

The product mix in smaller cities will be chosen so that the entry price for consumers would be 15 per cent less than in Adidas's existing shops in
35 larger cities, he added. The company would be targeting consumers with an average disposable income of Rmb5,000 ($753) a month.

Herbert Hainer, Adidas Chief
40 Executive, predicted that the strategy would allow the German group to regain the number-two market position that it recently lost to Li Ning, the Chinese sportswear manufacturer.
45 Li Ning, named after the Olympic gymnast who lit the flame at the opening ceremony of the 2008 Beijing Olympics, recently announced plans to take its brand
50 upmarket to compete more directly with foreign brands like Adidas and the market leader, Nike.

Li Ning's move up to second position could prove a key moment.
55 Retail analysts see it as one of the first signs in the retail field that Chinese products can rebrand themselves as not just cheap but desirable.

Li Ning has strong sales and distri-
60 bution networks in the lower-tier cities that Adidas hopes to penetrate.

Mr Hainer dismissed Adidas's recent problems in China as temporary, related to overstocking in the
65 run-up to the Olympics. Mr Hainer predicted double-digit sales growth in China over the next five years.

D **Match these words and phrases (1–7) to their definitions (a–g).**

1 market position   a) the combination of products that a company has to offer

2 upmarket   b) a market filled so completely that no more products can be
                       added
3 product mix   c)
                    d) expensive compared to other products of the same type
4 penetrate
                       alter a product or service to change the way that people think
5 disposable   about it
  income   e)
                    f) start selling goods or services in a new market
6 rebrand
                       money that is available to spend after paying for essentials like
7 saturated   taxes, food and housing
                    g)
                       the ranking of a company or brand against its competitors in
                       terms of its sales

E **Complete these sentences with some of the words/phrases from Exercise D.**

1 The Beatles were able to .... the US market.

2 During the economic crisis, people had less ....

3 Smaller banks are struggling to compete in an already .... market.

4 We are trying to lose our cheap image and move .... with more expensive products.

5 Coca-Cola decided to .... Diet Fanta in the UK, to fit in with the rest of Europe.

Questions

- In questions which we can answer with either *yes* or *no*, we put an auxiliary verb before the subject.
  '***Do*** *you trust this market-research survey?*' '*No, the sample size wasn't large enough.*'
  '***Is*** *the market going to crash again?*' '*No, not in the near future.*'
  '***Have*** *you finished the marketing report?*' '*Yes, I printed it out earlier.*'

- To ask for more information, we use question words like *what*, *why*, *where*, *when* and *how*. We put the question word before the auxiliary verb.
  When do *you want the sales figures?*
  How should *we promote it?*
  How many are *we expecting to sell?*

➡ *Grammar reference* page 148

A **Correct the grammatical mistakes in these sentences.**

1 What means *market position*?   *What does 'market position' mean?*

2 How much it cost?

3 Why you don't sell it on eBay?

4 When the cars must be recalled?

5 Did you went to the farmers' market last week?

6 Is coming your boss tomorrow?

B **The letter below is part of an authentic consumer survey on wines.**

1 Write the words in the questions in the correct order.

EXAMPLE: *1 Which group do you belong to?*

2 Answer the questions.

Dear Mr Paz-Andrade

We are conducting a consumer survey on international wines.
We place great value on your personal opinion and, therefore, request your support.

	QUESTION	ANSWER
1	group / you / do / belong / to / which / ?	self-employed ☐ employed ☐ retired ☐
2	you / old / how / are / ?	under 30 years ☐ 30–50 years ☐ over 50 years ☐
3	which / do / you / prefer / wines / ?	white ☐ red ☐ rosé ☐
4	how / do / you / drink / often / wine / ?	seldom ☐ occasionally ☐ once a week ☐ often ☐
5	do / you / spend / usually / how / much / of / wine / on / a / bottle / ?	up to €6 ☐ €6–€8.50 ☐ more than €8.50 ☐
6	do / have / you / a / cellar / at / personal / wine / home / ?	no ☐ yes: small ☐ yes: large ☐
7	many / bottles / of /wine / how / you / have / bought / during / the / last / year / ?	fewer than 36 bottles ☐ more than 36 bottles ☐
8	you / know / do / wine-growing / areas / which / ?	Chianti ☐ Nahe ☐ South Australia ☐ Rioja ☐ Burgundy ☐ Bordeaux ☐ Rheinhessen ☐
9	when selecting wine, / you / do / the various / growing areas / take into account / ?	yes ☐ no ☐ occasionally ☐
10	taste / which / you / prefer / do / ?	white wine: dry ☐ medium dry ☐ sweet ☐ red wine ☐

C **Work in pairs. Ask each other the questions.**

D **Work in groups. Think of a product and prepare a similar consumer survey for it. Then form new groups. Use your consumer surveys to find out about each others' buying habits.**

SKILLS

Telephoning: exchanging information

A 🔊 CD2.20 **Listen to four people giving some numbers, phone numbers and addresses. Tick the correct ones.**

1 a) 30,456   b) 13,456

2 a) 0033 2399 0324   b) 0033 3299 0342

3 a) v.artin@sawlna.com   b) v.altin@sawslan.com

4 a) 128/16 Rattanatibarth Road   b) 128/60 Rattanatibeth Road

B **Write down some numbers and addresses you know. Dictate them to a partner. Check that your partner has written the numbers correctly.**

C **Work in pairs. Say the international spelling alphabet.**

Alpha, Bravo, Charlie, Delta, Echo, Foxtrot, Golf, Hotel, India, Juliet, Kilo, Lima, Mike, November, Oscar, Papa, Quebec, Romeo, Sierra, Tango, Uniform, Victor, Whisky, X-ray, Yankee, Zulu

🔊 CD2.21 **Check each other's pronunciation. Then listen to the recording.**

D **Choose an e-mail address and dictate it to your partner. Spell each word when you dictate, then check your partner's answer.**

E 🔊 CD2.22 **Listen to the first part of a phone conversation between a sales director, Martin, and his manager, Fiona. Answer these questions.**

1 Did they meet their sales targets?

2 How has their market share changed?

3 What were their total sales?

4 How much did they spend on shampoo advertising?

F 🔊 CD2.23 **Now listen to the second part and note down this information.**

1 customer's name   4 e-mail address

2 nationality   5 meeting day and date

3 telephone number

G 🔊 CD2.22, 2.23 **Listen to the whole conversation again. Tick the phrases in the Useful language box below that Martin uses to check information, ask for information and finish the conversation.**

H **Role-play a telephone call between the Marketing Director and the European Sales Manager of a coffee-machine manufacturing company. They are talking about a focus group for the company's new range of coffee machines.**

Student A: Turn to page 140.   Student B: Turn to page 139.

USEFUL LANGUAGE

CHECKING INFORMATION	ASKING FOR INFORMATION	FINISHING A CONVERSATION
Sorry, did you say …?	Could you give me a few details?	OK, I think I've got all that.
Sorry, I didn't catch that.	What about the new range?	Thanks very much. That was very helpful.
Could you repeat that, please?	Did she say when she'd like to meet?	I should go now. Let's speak again soon.
Let me read that back to you.		Right, I think that's everything.

8

Wincote International

An outdoor-clothing company's key product range has not achieved its sales target

Background

Wincote International is an outdoor-products company based in Colorado, US. Eighteen months ago, it launched a range of jackets and boots for men and women. The company believed that the market for these products was not saturated. The clothes were aimed at mountaineers, hikers, snowboarders and anyone participating in extreme sports or outdoor activities. The brand name of the range was XWS (Extreme Winter Sports).

The launch

Following the product launch, the boots sold well, but the jacket fell below its sales target. Few people seemed to know that there was a new jacket on sale made from a new all-weather material. This was very disappointing, as the jacket was considered to have great sales potential. The management decided therefore to relaunch the product and change their approach to marketing it.

Read the information below about the jacket and how it was marketed. Study the charts opposite. Why do you think sales have been so poor?

Product
- The two-layer jacket is for men and women. It is a versatile, all-weather garment.
- It is offered in two sizes: medium and large.
- Colours: black for men; black and red for women.
- The outer shell of the jacket is made from a special new material. As a result, it is lightweight, hard-wearing, very warm and weatherproof.
- The lining is removable, making the jacket suitable for all seasons.
- The jacket has a removable hood, 14 pockets, and a wide zipper down the centre.

Price
Men's and women's jacket: $110

Promotion
- Full-page advertisements in magazines for people with outdoor and sports interests
- Half-page advertisements in newspapers; posters and point-of-sale advertisements
- Product demonstrations at exhibitions
- Slogan: 'A jacket for all seasons'

Place
The jacket was sold in outdoor-product stores (e.g. camping-equipment shops), sports-goods outlets and upmarket department stores.

Chart 1 Comparison of the price of the Wincote XWS with four other top-selling outdoor jackets

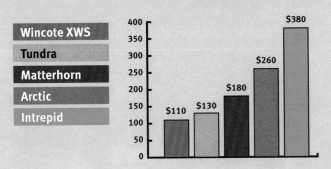

Wincote XWS
Tundra
Matterhorn
Arctic
Intrepid

$110 $130 $180 $260 $380

Chart 2 Market share of outdoor jacket brands

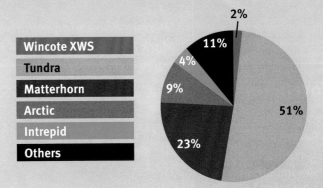

Wincote XWS
Tundra
Matterhorn
Arctic
Intrepid
Others

2% 11% 4% 9% 51% 23%

◀)) **CD2.24–2.28** The Marketing Department did some research with focus groups to get opinions about the jacket. The group participants' ages ranged from 16 to 60. Listen to their comments and make notes.

Summary of a consultant's report on the Wincote XWS

The market for outdoor jackets is highly competitive. Because of its unique qualities, the Wincote XWS jacket could achieve its sales target with a new marketing approach. It needs to be relaunched as a stylish jacket for younger people in the 16–30 age group, and appeal to people living and working in cities as well as to outdoor enthusiasts.

It should be promoted as a 'must-have' item of clothing for younger people.

Changes must be made to the product and its marketing. The jacket should be relaunched as soon as possible.

Task

1 Work in groups. Each group is a team in the marketing department. Hold a meeting to discuss what you should do to improve sales of the Wincote XWS. Use the questions in the box on the right as a guide.

2 Present your ideas to the other teams in the marketing department.

3 As a whole department, hold a meeting and decide what the company must do to improve the sales of the Wincote XWS.

Questions

• **Product:** How should the product be changed? Think about colour, sizes, changes to its design, specifications, etc.

• **Price:** Is the price correct? If not, what should it be? Should there be a different price for the men's and women's jackets?

• **Promotion:** Was it promoted the correct way? Is the Wincote XWS targeted at the right segment of the market? Does it need a new slogan? If so, what? What kind of advertising campaign should be used to relaunch the product?

• **Place:** Is it being sold in the right places?

Watch the Case study commentary on the DVD-ROM.

Writing

As Marketing Director, write an e-mail to the Chief Executive Officer (CEO) of Wincote International, summarising the changes that you will make to the product and its marketing when the jacket is relaunched.

To: CEO

From: Marketing Director

At a meeting on … , we discussed the changes we want to make when relaunching the Wincote XWS. They are as follows:

• Product: …

• Price: …

• Promotion: …

• Place: …

➡ *Writing file page 126*

81

UNIT

9 Planning

'People don't plan to fail. They fail to plan.'
Mark McCormack (1930–2003), sports agent and founder of IMG

STARTING UP

A **What do you think about when you plan these things?**

1   a holiday

2   a special family occasion, for example a wedding

3   an ordinary working day/week

4   your career

B **Which of the following do you use to plan your day or week? Which do you prefer? Why?**

- desk or pocket diary   • electronic organiser   • writing on your hand   • memory
- asking someone (e.g. your PA) to remind you   • wall chart   • smartphone
- notes stuck on board, desk, fridge, etc.   • computer program (e.g. Google calender, iCal)

C **Discuss these statements.**

1   Making lists of things to do is a waste of time.

2   You should plan your retirement from an early age.

3   If you make a plan, you should stick to it.

4   There are some things you can't plan for.

Making plans

A Match the verbs in the box to the nouns below (1–5). Each word partnership describes a way to plan effectively. Use a dictionary to help you if necessary.

| collect   consider   do   ~~estimate~~   forecast |

1   *estimate* costs

2   .... sales

3   .... research

4   .... information

5   .... options

B Match the verbs in Box A to the nouns in Box B. Make as many word partnerships as you can.

example: *write/implement a plan*

A

| arrange   implement   keep to   meet   prepare   rearrange   write |

B

| a budget   a deadline   a meeting   a plan   a report   a schedule |

C A managing director talks about the planning of a new sales office in the United States. Complete this text with nouns from Exercises A and B. One noun is used twice.

Recently, we decided to open a new sales office in New York. First, I arranged a *meeting*[1] with the finance department to discuss the project. We prepared a ....[2] with details of the various costs involved. Then we collected ....[3] about possible locations for the new office. We considered two ....[4] – one in Greenwich Village and the other near Central Park. After doing some more ....[5], I wrote a ....[6] for the Board of Directors.

Unfortunately, we made a mistake when we estimated the ....[7], as the exchange rate changed, so we didn't keep within our ....[8]. We overspent by almost 20 per cent. We had to rearrange the ....[9] for moving into the building because the office was not redecorated in time. The Board of Directors was unhappy because we didn't meet the ....[10] for opening the office by December 15. It finally opened in January. However, we forecast ....[11] of at least $1,000,000 in the first year.

D ◀)) CD2.29 Listen and check your answers to Exercise C.

E Choose one of these events and tell your partner how you will plan it. Try to use some of the vocabulary from Exercises A–C above.

1   A team-building weekend for your department / sports club

2   An event to mark your company's/organisation's 100th anniversary

3   A party to celebrate the return of a close friend after two years abroad

4   The opening of a new store

*See the **DVD-ROM** for the i-Glossary.*

How important is planning?

Ian Sanders

A ◀)) CD2.30 **Ian Sanders is a business consultant and the author of** *Unplan your business.* **In the first part of the interview, he answers the question 'How far ahead should businesses plan?'. Listen and complete these notes.**

- Depends on ....¹.
- Three-year contracts should have a plan for ....².
- Three years is a long time for ....³ businesses and new businesses entering the market in the field of ....⁴.
- Ian likes the idea of a ....⁵ plan, because it's very ....⁶.
- Problem with business planning: it can sometimes be business ....⁷.

B ◀)) CD2.31 **Listen to the second part and complete this audio script.**

I think the best business plans are ones that are ....¹ and ....² enough to take into account changing markets and changing situations. Any plan that is too ....³ or too set in ....⁴ becomes very unwieldy, because it can't accommodate economic changes, market changes, ...⁵ changes.

C **Which word in Exercise B refers to the ability to change easily, and which two words or phrases refer to the opposite?**

D ◀)) CD2.32 **Listen to the final part and answer these questions.**

1 What is it important for entrepreneurs to do?

2 Ian talks about an entrepreneur he met recently. What business had the entrepreneur set up?

3 Why did the entrepreneur eventually succeed?

*Watch the interview on the **DVD-ROM**.*

E **What are the advantages and disadvantages of writing a business plan?**

To plan or not to plan

A **Which of these would you normally find in a business plan?**

1 business aims	3 management team	5 staff holidays
2 opening hours	4 financial forecast	6 assessment of the competition

B **Read the article on the opposite page and complete this chart.**

name	job/position	company	type of company	location
Dan Scarfe				
David Hieatt				
Rajeeb Dey				
Paul Maron-Smith				

C **Read the article again and answer these questions about the four people in Exercise B.**

1 How many people did not write a business plan for their present companies?

2 Who thinks that setting fixed aims involves too much time and is not valuable?

3 Who says that some plans don't work because we don't know what will work?

4 Who thinks that planning often leads to doing nothing?

5 Who provided the finance for the companies themselves?

6 Which of the four is not against business plans?

When there's no Plan A

by Jonathan Moules

Dan Scarfe, Chief Executive of Windsor-based software development company Dot Net Solutions, says that he has never written a business plan for the company he founded in 2004.

Now, it is one of Microsoft's five key partners in the UK and a leading player in the hot new area of cloud computing – and to Scarfe, that is proof that setting fixed objectives is a complete waste of time.

"Writing software, or starting a new business, is incredibly difficult to plan for," he says. "You're effectively trying to second-guess exactly what you may want down the line, based on marketing conditions and varying customer demand." Whilst short-term business budgeting and strategy is vital, long-term business plans are less so. Twitter, Facebook and cloud computing were not even concepts a number of years ago, Scarfe notes, so there would be no way he could have planned for them.

David Hieatt, co-founder of Howies, the ethical-clothing manufacturer based in Cardigan, claims that a business plan is really just a guess.

"There are some brilliant business plans written, but they fail because the customer wants to do business differently," he says. "The awful truth is we don't know what will work."

He claims that the secret is to be flexible – although this often takes a lot of courage. For example, in 2001, Hieatt phoned up all of Howies' retailers and said he was going to introduce organic cotton. The initial effect of this spur-of-the-moment act was disastrous.

"We lost all our wholesale accounts overnight because they said nobody

would pay £27 for a T-shirt," he recalls.

Hieatt and his colleagues managed to rescue the situation by launching a catalogue to sell products. It proved to be a turning point for Howies. "Losing all your shop accounts in one day is not great for business, but it's probably the best thing we did," Hieatt concludes. Now, the company sells 80 per cent of its products through this medium.

Others argue that business planning is often a reason for inaction. Rajeeb Dey launched Enternships, a student internship matching service. "I never wrote a business plan for Enternships, I just started it," he says – although he admits that it is easier for Internet-based businesses to do this.

Perhaps unsurprisingly, Dey and Scarfe have entirely self-financed their businesses. Venture capitalists and private investors do not usually approve of this casual attitude to planning.

To Paul Maron-Smith, Managing Director of Gresham Private Equity, a business plan is rather like a car's dashboard, guiding the entrepreneur along the road to success.

But even he admits that problems can arise when business plans become too fixed. "The aim of a business plan is to give the stakeholders a good idea of where the business is heading," he says. "Sure, there are going to be some forecasts in there that are not going to be accurate, but they are a best guess at the time."

D   **Discuss these questions.**

1   In which sectors is it difficult to plan?

2   How far ahead should you plan?

3   How often should you review plans?

4   What reasons are given for and against having business plans?

5   What is your opinion of business plans? How useful do you think they are?

LANGUAGE REVIEW
Talking about future plans

- We can use verbs like *plan, hope, expect, would like* and *want* to talk about future plans.
  *Coca-Cola **is hoping** to more than double its number of bottling plants in China over the coming decade and **would like** to triple the size of its sales to China's middle class.*

- We often use *going to* to talk about more definite plans.
  *We**'re going to** open a new dealership this summer.*

- We can also use the present continuous to talk about definite plans and arrangements.
  *I**'m meeting** the accountants on Tuesday.*

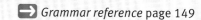 *Grammar reference* page 149

A **The CEO of a large supermarket chain is talking to her managers about the group's future plans in relation to the World Cup. Underline the plans that she mentions.**

'Well, as you all know, we are hoping that the World Cup spirit will get more customers through our doors. We are planning a wide range of activities to capitalise on our football links and are expecting to sell more televisions, food and drink. We are also going to sell official merchandise before and during the tournament. We would like to get some big-name endorsements and want to sell stickers and trading cards. Then we are going to launch a digital site to promote our association with football legends. We are hoping to be the supermarket of choice for our country's football fans.'

B **Match the verbs (1–3) to their meanings (a–c).**

1 hope
2 expect
3 plan

a) believe something will happen
b) decide in detail what you are going to do
c) wish something would happen

C **A salesperson is talking about the end-of-year bonus. Complete this conversation with the verbs from Exercise B in the correct form.**

I'm ....[1] to get a bonus at the end of the year, but I haven't met all my sales targets, so I'm a little worried. My colleague Jan has met all her targets and she is ....[2] to get a good bonus. She is already ....[3] to go on an expensive holiday abroad and has got lots of travel brochures.

D **Tell each other about your plans and expectations for 1–6 below.**

example: A: *What are you going to do after this lesson?*
  B: *I'm hoping/planning to ... What about you?*
  A: *Oh, I'm hoping to ...*

1 after this lesson
2 tomorrow
3 this weekend
4 on your next holiday
5 in your career
6 when you retire

Meetings: interrupting and clarifying

A 🔊 CD2.33 **Listen to a meeting in which members of a planning group discuss relocating their head office. In which order are these points mentioned?**

a) the cost of moving ☐

b) when to move ☐ 1

c) the advantage of using a specialised firm ☐

d) whether to use their own transport department ☐

e) how to communicate with staff ☐

f) which transport company to use ☐

B **Look at these extracts from the planning meeting in Exercise A. Decide whether each expression in *italics* is a) interrupting, or b) clarifying.**

1 B: I think July would be the best time. It's very quiet then, isn't it?

　　A: *You mean*, we don't do too much business then?

2 C: *Could I just say something?*

3 C: In my opinion, we should do it department by department.

　　B: *How do you mean exactly?*

4 B: We've contacted two companies, National Transport and Fox Removals.

　　A: *Sorry, could I just comment on that, Mark?*

5 B: You know, there's another possibility. We could get our own people to do the moving.

　　A: *What? You think our transport department could do the job?*

C **Role-play this situation. A group of international VIPs is going to visit your company/organisation for three days. You need to plan the programme for the visit. Discuss these questions with other managers in the department.**

1 Where will the VIPs go, and what will they see? (e.g. inside the company/organisation, local sights, etc.)

2 Who do they need to meet?

3 Where will they stay?

4 How will they move around? (e.g. transport)

5 What sort of farewell event/dinner will you have on the final evening?

　　a) Will you have food? What? (e.g. snacks? a meal?)

　　b) Will there be a speech? Who will make it?

　　c) Who will attend? (e.g. special guests?)

　　d) Will there be any entertainment?

6 What sort of gifts will you give the visitors?

7 What else do you need to plan? (e.g. the itinerary – will they have any free time?)

USEFUL LANGUAGE

INTERRUPTING	DEALING WITH INTERRUPTIONS	CLARIFYING
Could I say something?	If you'll just let me finish …	How do you mean exactly?
Could I just comment on that?	Just a moment, please.	What exactly do you mean by …?
Hold on a minute.	I'd like to finish if I may.	Are you saying …?
Sorry to interrupt, but …		So what you're saying is that …

9

EUROPEAN PRESS AND MEDIA CORPORATION

A media company plans to launch a new health-and-fitness magazine

Background

European Press and Media Corporation (EPMC) is a large media company which produces magazines, and radio and television programmes. It has decided to bring out a new magazine for people interested in health and fitness. The magazine will be launched in the UK, then sold in overseas markets if it is successful. It will be supported by an online website.

Several teams within the company are preparing a plan for the new magazine. The team with the best ideas will receive a substantial cash prize.

Planning

Work in groups to compete for the cash prize.

- Think of ideas for topics that you could include in a new health-and-fitness magazine. For example weight loss, tips on fitness, etc. Write down the list of topics under the heading in the chart below.

- Evaluate the topics by ticking the appropriate column of the chart.

Chart 1   Interest in possible topics for the new magazine

topic	very interesting	quite interesting	not interesting

Consider these questions and note your answers.

1 What are the aims of the new magazine?

2 Who is the target consumer?

3 What will be the magazine's name? number of pages? cover price?

4 How often will it appear? (once a week? twice a month? once a month?)

5 What will be the proportion of content to advertising? 80%/20%? more? less?

6 Will it have any special design features?

> ◄)) **CD2.34** Now listen to two senior managers, who will choose the best plan for the new magazine. Note down the key points they discuss.

The marketing department is considering these promotions for the first issue of the magazine. In your groups, discuss the promotions and decide which is the best one for the first issue. Suggest other ways of promoting the new magazine.

- Include a free 20-page supplement with four healthy diets.

- Sell the first issue at half price.

- Add a mini magazine with diet and fitness plans.

- Offer a 25% discount for an order of six issues.

- Give a full refund if a customer orders 30 issues but is not happy at the end of that period.

- Send a selection of body lotions and eau de cologne if a customer orders 30 issues.

Task

Work in your groups. You are all members of the EPMC planning team.

1 **Agree on a plan for the first issue. Use the key questions below to help you.**

2 **Present your plans for the first issue and for the new magazine as a whole to the other groups.**

3 **Choose the best plan for the new magazine. Take a vote if necessary.**

Key questions

- What sections and topics will the first issue include?

- What special features will it have?

- What will the front page of the first issue look like?

- How will the magazine be promoted?

- What will be on the website? Will the website be free?

*Watch the Case study commentary on the **DVD-ROM**.*

Writing

As the Editor of the new health-and-fitness magazine, write a letter to a famous person asking them for an interview. At the start of the letter, introduce yourself and give brief details of the new magazine and its aims.

> Dear …
> I am writing to you as Editor of EPMC's exciting new health-and-fitness magazine.

➡ *Writing file page 128*

3 International conference calls

A **Discuss these questions.**

1 Do you enjoy using the phone? Why? / Why not?

2 What is a conference call? How is it different from a regular phone call?

3 Have you ever been involved in a conference call? How successful was it?

4 What do you think are the differences/ similarities between conference calls and face-to-face meetings?

5 What do you think the biggest problems are?

B ◀)) CD2.35–2.40 **Listen to six short extracts from conference calls. What do you think is the problem in each situation?**

C ◀)) CD2.35–2.40 **Listen again and match the extracts (1–6) to these types of problem (a–f).**

a) getting cut off ☐

b) background noise ☐

c) speaking too fast ☐

d) unknown speaker ☐

e) leaving the main topic ☐

f) interrupting / stopping a speaker talking ☐

D ◀)) CD2.41 **Listen to the first part of a talk by an expert on international conference calls.**

1 Which of the problems in Exercise C are mentioned?

2 According to the expert, what is the biggest / most common problem?

E ◀)) CD2.42 **Listen to the second part of the talk and complete these tips for participants.**

1 Make sure you are in a q_ _ _ _ p_ _ _ _ .

2 Avoid e_ _ _ _ _ and d_ _ _ _ _ _ _ .

3 Prepare for the call in a _ _ _ _ _ _ .

4 When speaking, stay on t_ _ _ _ .

5 Signal or label what you s_ _ .

6 Try not to i_ _ _ _ _ _ _ _ .

7 Wait to be invited to c_ _ _ _ _ _ .

F **Read these notes made by another participant on the final part of the talk and decide whether the sentences below are true (T) or false (F).**

> *Call leaders*
>
> • *Make sure everyone knows when call will be — send e-mail reminder and numbers or passwords*
>
> • *Pay attention to time zones for international calls — very early or very late not popular with all!*
>
> • *Like meetings, make sure you have agenda and goals, so everyone is clear about purpose*
>
> • *Conference-call meetings take longer than face-to-face meetings — not too many agenda items*
>
> • *Need to open and close call + important for the call leader to begin on time and welcome participants*
>
> • *Do a roll call at the start. Get people to introduce themselves — helps to build relationships*
>
> • *Signal the move from introduction to actual talk*
>
> • *Begin with: 'We're ready to go. I've heard from John, Katja and Marina. Have I missed anyone?'*
>
> • *If a lot of people / big meeting, tell those not speaking to go on mute, to reduce noise*
>
> • *End with summing up + reminder of action points*
>
> • *Set date and time of next meeting*

1 The times of conference calls are important.

2 An agenda is not important for conference calls.

3 Conference calls tend to be slower than face-to-face meetings.

4 The call leader should introduce everyone at the start.

5 A summary of the main points by the call leader is important.

Task

You are managers in a multinational company which needs to reduce costs and is looking at ways to do this.

1 **Work in groups of four. Look at the agenda below. Turn to the correct page and study your role card. Prepare for the conference call.**

Student A: Turn to page 134.   Student C: Turn to page 137.
Student B: Turn to page 132.   Student D: Turn to page 139.

Hold the call and discuss the points. Decide what to do.

2 **Following your call, in pairs write some tips on how to participate effectively in international conference calls.**

Do:

Don't:

Be careful of:

Compare your tips with another pair.

Agenda

1 **Introduction of regular conference calls**

2 **Timing of calls**

3 **Training courses**

4 **AOB**

7 New business

Complete the sentences below with the words in the box.

balance domestic exchange foreign government
inflation interest labour tax unemployment

1 China's gross .... product is about $5 trillion.

2 The .... rate has decreased because people have gone back to work as the economy recovers.

3 Companies are worried about paying pensions as the .... force grows older.

4 The government has offered .... incentives to new companies in hopes of boosting the economy.

5 Businesspeople say that .... bureaucracy makes starting a new business difficult.

6 It's common for companies to spend money overseas, but some people think that too much .... investment in their country is a bad idea.

7 Exports have increased recently, which makes the .... of trade much healthier.

8 Borrowers are enjoying the low .... rate, but savers hope it increases soon.

9 Travellers from Britain to the Eurozone are enjoying a good .... rate this year.

10 The .... rate has dropped to 1%, thanks to the government's monetary policy.

Choose the best word or phrase to complete each sentence.

1 *As soon as / Until* the contract was signed, everyone cheered.

2 Can you please come to my office *when / after* the meeting?

3 Larissa said she'd phone *as soon as / while* she arrives in London.

4 Martin checked the projector carefully *when / before* he started his presentation, then began right on time.

5 Olga can't sign the contract *until / while* she gets Andre's approval.

6 Pierre learned to speak some Japanese *as soon as / while* he was working in Tokyo.

7 *Until / After* the delivery is confirmed, we won't release the payment.

8 We have to improve the sales forecasts *before / after* we can approve the project.

9 We went out *when / after* the meeting to celebrate the merger we'd agreed.

10 *When / While* I first started out as a manager, I made a lot of mistakes.

11 Yusuf got to know Peter *when / as soon as* they worked together for three years in Saudi Arabia.

12 Zeynep was able to write the report *until / while* he was waiting for his plane.

You have recently become the European distributor for ChuTools, a new Chinese power-tool manufacturer. You want H&G, a big DIY chain, to sell ChuTools. Write an e-mail (80–100 words) to Alan Sykes, Purchaser at H&G, introducing ChuTools and asking for a meeting to discuss a deal. You have worked with Alan before and you know him well.

ChuTools

- Based in Shenzen
- Produces a range of DIY power tools – drills, saws and garden tools
- Mid-range price
- Very high quality for price – have received excellent reviews in trade press
- Company wants to support retailers with marketing and promotion, including prizes and special offers

8 Marketing

Cross out the word in each group that does not form a word partnership with the word in bold.

1   **advertising** share / campaign / budget / agency
2   **consumer** behaviour / profile / launch / goods
3   **market** goods / research / share / segment
4   **product** launch / lifecycle / range / segment
5   **sales** forecast / range / figures / target

A   Put these words in the correct order to make questions.

1   market / the / research / Is / complete / ?
2   it / do / want / to / When / you / do / ?
3   at / to / website / Do / the / you / new / have / look / time / ?
4   survey / Did / read / you / the / ?
5   figures / the / Have / sales / seen / you / ?
6   model / How / we / should / describe / new / the / ?

B   Match each question from Exercise A (1–6) to one of these answers (a–f).

a)   Yes, I did. The results were interesting.
b)   Yes, it is. We finished last week.
c)   No, I haven't. Is there any good news?
d)   Next Monday.
e)   I don't know, but let's not say it's *new and improved*.
f)   Yes, I do. I really want to see it.

Complete the phone conversation below with the phrases in the box.

| Could you give me | Did they say when | I didn't catch | I should | I'll e-mail you to |
| Sorry, did you say | Thanks very much | What about | | |

A: How did your meeting with H&G go?

B: Really well. They've placed an order totalling £50,000 over the next year.

A: ....¹ £15,000?

B: No, £50,000!

A: That's great! ....² a few details?

B: Sure. Basically, they want to buy up everything in the old range.

A: ....³ the new range?

B: After they sell the old range through, they'll start buying the new one.

A: Which part numbers?

B: They really like AC5959 and AC4536.

A: Sorry, ...⁴ that.

B: I said, they really like AC5959 and AC4536.

A: ....⁵ they'd like the first delivery?

B: Next week! ....⁶ confirm.

A: ....⁷ for the great news.

B: My pleasure. ....⁸ go now. Let's speak again soon.

9 Planning

Complete the e-mail below with the verbs in the box in the correct tense.

| arrange | consider | do | estimate | forecast |
| implement | keep | meet | prepare | write |

To: | Tomas@hcc.com
From: | Jamal@hcc.com
cc: | Leanna@hcc.com
Subject: | Project update

Hi Tomas,

Here's a brief project update. We've ....¹ a meeting with the design team for next Monday. Before that meeting, Leanna is going to ....² a schedule to show how we can ....³ the December 1 delivery deadline. We've already spent about €15,000, so I'm sure we aren't going to ....⁴ within the budget. After the Monday meeting, we can ....⁵ the options for Plan B, because obviously Plan A has already failed. If we ....⁶ more research, we may be able to ....⁷ higher sales and increase the budget. Also, when we ....⁸ costs last year, we were expecting to manufacture here in Europe; however, we've found a factory in China that can do it cheaper, so we'll save some money there.

After the meeting next week, I'll ....⁹ a formal report which will explain how we can ....¹⁰ Plan B.

All the best,

Jamal

Match the halves of these expressions.

1 If you'll just   a) comment on that?

2 Just a   b) to finish if I may.

3 I'd like   c) let me finish …

4 Could I say   d) saying is that …

5 Could I just   e) do you mean by …?

6 Hold on   f) moment, please.

7 Sorry to   g) saying …?

8 How do you   h) mean exactly?

9 What exactly   i) interrupt, but …

10 Are you   j) a minute.

11 So what you're   k) something?

Cultures 3: International conference calls

Put the words in order to make tips for international conference calls.

1 time / on / Be / for / call / the / .

2 are / sure / in / place / Make / quiet / you / a / .

3 possible / If / , / call / use / the / a / for / headset / .

4 when / Use / you / the / are / 'mute' / not / button / speaking / .

5 conference call / Avoid / eating, drinking or / chewing gum / while / a / on / .

6 to / the / 'mute' button / use / If / you / to / really need / have a drink, / remember / .

7 advance / in / Prepare / the / for / call / . / you / what / Plan / to / need / say / may / .

8 may / you / need / hand / Have / to / any / documents / close / .

9 call leader / carefully / Listen / and / to be / by / invited to comment / the / wait / .

10 speak / you / When speaking, / each time / it / are / can be helpful / to / say / you / who / .

11 stay / topic / When / on / speak, / you / .

12 long/ Make / speeches / short / rather / contributions / than / .

13 not / Try / interrupt / to / speaking / when / people / are / they / .

14 as typing will / be / for / noisy / the other participants / Avoid / taking notes / on a computer / , / .

Telephoning

Objectives

Speaking

- Can introduce themselves on the phone and close a simple call.
- Can answer simple work-related questions on the phone using fixed expressions.
- Can ask for repetition or clarification on the phone in a simple way.

Lesson deliverable

To plan, prepare and participate in a telephone conversation in a business context and write a short follow-up document.

Performance review

To review your own progress and performance against the lesson objectives at the end of the lesson.

A SPEAKING 1

1 Think about when you make a phone call. What information do you need to ask for or give on the phone in these situations?

1 telephoning a restaurant
2 checking a hotel reservation
3 placing an order

2 Make a list of five things you have to do when you are on the telephone. Then discuss the questions.

1 What do you find difficult to do?
2 What do you find easiest to do?
3 What do you do if you don't understand?

3 Work in small groups. Compare and discuss your answers to Exercise 2. Do you all have the same problems on the phone in English?

4 Write three top tips for holding a successful telephone conversation.

B LISTENING

1 🔊 BSA3.1.10 ExtractaJuice is an American brand of luxury juicers. In the UK, it sells its products through demonstrations in department stores. Ewan Riley from the UK office phones the Head Office in Boston. Listen to the conversation and look at the notes. Are they correct (✓) or incorrect (✗)?

1 sales up 40% ☐
2 total sales: 57 units ☐
3 hire demonstrators for stores in Glasgow and Manchester ☐
4 training: 16th and 17th this month ☐
5 trainer: Sheila Thomson ☐
6 hotel needed for three nights ☐

2 Work in pairs. Look at these phrases from the call and try to work out what the missing words are.

1 ..... Sorry ....., ... not ..... forty, fourteen. One, four.
2 Sorry, I .... the name of the first place.
3 .... her first name, please?
4 And Thomson is T-H-O-M-S-O-N, I ....
5 No, ... a P in the middle.
6 No, P .... Papa. T-H-O-M-P-S-O-N.
7 OK, I .... it.
8 So the accommodation is for the 14th, 15th and 16th. Is ....?

3 🔊 BSA3.1.10 Listen again and check your answers. Then write the phrases in the correct part of the table.

Explaining a communication problem	
Asking someone to spell something	
Correcting somebody	*Sorry, not forty, fourteen. One, four.*
Checking information	
Using the international spelling alphabet to clarify spelling	
Showing you have understood	

C PRONUNCIATION

Turn to page ix. Look at the international spelling alphabet and practise spelling these names from the conversation.

1 ExtractaJuice
2 Janice Bell
3 Harold Taylor
4 Ella Bright

D SPEAKING 2

Work in pairs. Role-play a conversation similar to the telephone call between Janice Bell and Ewan Riley. Follow this plan and use the phrases in the table in B to help you.

Alex: Answer the phone.

Sam: Identify yourself and say who you want to speak to.

Alex: Identify yourself and tell Sam you can deal with the call.

Sam: Explain the sales figures and the company's plans.

Alex: Ask for clarification and spelling if necessary.

Sam: Explain and correct if necessary.

Alex: Tell Sam about the trainer who is going to the UK.

Sam: Ask for clarification and spelling if necessary.

Alex: Explain and correct if necessary.

Both: End the call.

Task

Part 1: Preparation

1 Group A

Context: You work for a chain of shops that sells fashion accessories. You are going to make a call to arrange an appointment for your manager to visit a company which supplies you with a range of fashion jewellery.

Complete these notes before you pick up the phone. You will use this information during the call to introduce yourself, your company, and to explain the reason for your call.

Before you make the call you need to:
- Create a profile for your company: choose a company name and agree on the kind of jewellery you sell.
- Decide why your manager wants to visit the supplier, e.g. new ranges, special offers, business expansion.
- Plan how you are going to introduce yourself and the reason for your call.

Complete the notes below. You will use this information during the call.

Your name:
Your company:
What your company does:
Your manager (who wants to visit the supplier):
His/Her name:
Reason for his/her visit:
Dates he/she will be there:
What he/she needs (accommodation, transport, directions, etc.)

2 Group B: you are going to receive a call from Group A. Turn to page ix to read and complete the details on your role card.

Part 2: Making and receiving calls

1 Work in A/B pairs to role-play the telephone conversation. Think about the tips you produced in A to help you.

Student A: Show the information on your role card to Student B. When he/she is ready, make the call. Use your notes from Part 1. Check understanding during the telephone call.

Student B: Look at your role card. Answer the call. During the call, write down (a) the caller's name, (b) any other important names, (c) any important dates or other points. Check understanding during the telephone call.

2 Now swap roles and role-play. Student B's phone call. Student A takes notes.

E PEER REVIEW

1 Look at the notes your partner made during the call. Are the details and spelling correct? Is all the important information there? Give your partner feedback.

2 Now talk about your telephone conversations with another pair. Think about the lesson objectives and discuss these questions.

1 What was good about the calls?

2 What was not so good?

3 Can you suggest some tips to help with the problem areas?

F SELF-ASSESSMENT

Think about the calls you made, the lesson objectives and the feedback from your colleagues. Complete these sentences.

1 When I was the caller, I performed (well/badly) because ...

2 When I answered the call, I performed (well/badly) because ...

3 The spelling in the notes I wrote afterwards (was/was not) correct.

4 I (included/did not include) all the important details in my notes.

G PROFESSIONAL DEVELOPMENT AND PERFORMANCE GOALS

Write two or three sentences about ways you can improve your telephone skills.

Next time I make a call in English, I will ... before I make the call.

Next time I receive a call in English, I will ...

During calls I make or receive in English, I will ...

Objectives

Writing
- Can use appropriate openings and endings in simple informal e-mails.
- Can write a simple e-mail requesting work-related information.
- Can write a basic informal e-mail/letter of invitation with simple, key details.

Reading
Can understand standard e-mails on work-related topics.

Lesson deliverable
To write simple e-mails in a business setting.

Performance review
To review your own progress and performance against the lesson objectives at the end of the lesson.

A SPEAKING 1

1 Discuss this statement with a partner:

It's always better to call someone than to send an e-mail.

2 Test your e-mail language. Write five phrases you can use to begin an e-mail and five phrases you can use to end an e-mail. Which phrases can you use in the same e-mail?

B LISTENING

1 ◀》 BSA3.2.11 Listen to Bob and Maribel discussing Maribel's e-mail and answer the questions.

1 Why is Maribel worried?
2 What advice does Bob give to Maribel?
3 What does Bob offer to do?

2 ◀》 BSA3.2.12 Listen to Bob giving Maribel some advice and answer the questions.

1 In Bob's opinion, which phrases can we use at the beginning and end of e-mails?
2 What does Bob say is very important for all e-mails? Why? Do you agree?

3 Look at Maribel's e-mail. Bob has underlined the parts that need attention. Can you correct them?

Subject: Project Capri – PMO Update 05.06.2015

Dear Jan,

I hope you are well. I am writing to give you a briefly update on Project Capri, as requested in your e-mail last week.

All three workstreams have reported to me that they are in time with everything. Peter's waiting for an important information from Accent, the IT supplier, but he said me yesterday that he is not worried. Please find attached an updated and actual project report with all information.

If you have any questions, do not hesitate to contact me.

BR,

Maribel

4 ◀》 BSA3.2.13 Listen to Bob talking to Maribel about her e-mail and answer the questions.

1 What changes does he suggest?
2 What advice does Bob give about e-mail style?

C READING

Maribel is organising a trip to meet the team members in London. Read Jan's e-mail about the trip and complete Maribel's to-do list.

Dear Maribel,

I'm just writing to check a few details regarding your forthcoming visit to London.

Can you confirm arrival details – flight number, arrival time and terminal – for you and the rest of the team? I will arrange for a driver to meet you at the airport and take you to your hotel.

On the second evening of the workshop, I'd like to invite everyone to dinner. Can you let me know if there are any special dietary requirements and if everyone wants to go? I'm playing safe and going for a little Italian restaurant I know.

If you need any further support, just let me know.

I'm really looking forward to finally meeting you and the rest of the Spanish team in person, rather than on Skype!

Very best wishes,

Jan

To do
1 Send arrival details:
___
___
___
2 Check dinner:
___
___
___

D SPEAKING 2

1 **Maribel said she was worried about making mistakes in e-mails. Work in pairs. Look at the dos and don'ts below and follow these steps.**

1 Discuss in your pairs: which points do you agree with? Which do you disagree with?

2 Join another pair and agree on five 'rules' for writing e-mails.

3 Share your ideas with other pairs and decide on the best three ideas.

The seven golden dos and don'ts for e-mail at work

A new research study highlights best practice for writing e-mail. The findings are sometimes surprising.

- **Language:** Always ask a native speaker to check your grammar.

- **Speed:** Always reply to an e-mail within 24 hours.

- **Politeness:** Never start an e-mail without *Dear.*

- **Length:** Never write more than five lines in the body of an e-mail.

- **Purpose:** Always state the objective of your e-mail.

- **Timing:** Don't e-mail people when they are on holiday.

- **Send list:** Only copy people into an e-mail if they have to read it.

Task

E-mail 1

Context: You met a potential customer at an international trade fair recently. You want to invite him/her and his/her colleagues to your company. You think this could be a good business opportunity.

1 **Work in two groups. Decide:**

- the name of your company and what it produces
- the name of the potential customer and a profile for his/her company
- a clear objective for the visit
- a timing and agenda for the visit.

2 **Now form pairs within your group and write an e-mail. Think about:**

- how to start the e-mail and explain its objective
- how to communicate clearly, professionally and politely to this potential customer.

3 **Give your e-mail to a pair from the other group.**

E-mail 2

1 **Read the e-mail you received and write a reply. Decide:**

- how to start the e-mail professionally
- how to accept the invitation politely
- how to end the e-mail.

2 **When you have finished, pass your e-mail back to the pair who sent it.**

E-mail 3

1 **Write a different reply which accepts the invitation but declines the specific date mentioned. Include:**

- a positive opening
- a polite sentence to say why you cannot visit
- a suggestion for a visit on another date
- a positive close to the e-mail.

2 **When you have finished, pass your e-mail back to the pair who sent it.**

E PEER REVIEW

Look back at the lesson objectives. In small groups, answer these questions to see how well your e-mail writing meets the objectives.

1 Which parts of the e-mails were effective? Why?

2 Which parts of the e-mails were less effective? Why?

3 What can you do better?

F SELF-ASSESSMENT

Look at the e-mails you wrote in this lesson. How good are you at:

1 understanding work e-mails?

2 beginning and ending work e-mails correctly?

3 inviting, accepting and declining invitations?

G PROFESSIONAL DEVELOPMENT AND PERFORMANCE GOALS

Look at the last ten e-mails in your Sent box. Think about the progress you have made in this lesson and what you can improve. Complete these sentences to create an action plan.

1 One thing I will do to improve further is to ...

2 Another thing I can do is ...

3 Finally, I will try to avoid ...

UNIT 10 | Managing people

'A boat can't have two captains.'
Akira Mori, Japanese businessman

OVERVIEW

VOCABULARY
Verbs and prepositions

LISTENING
Managing people

READING
Management and motivation

LANGUAGE REVIEW
Reported speech

SKILLS
Socialising and entertaining

CASE STUDY
Ashley Cooper Search Agency

STARTING UP

A **What qualities and skills should a good manager have? Choose the six most important from the list. Discuss your ideas with a partner.**

To be a good manager you need to:

1   be an expert.
2   like people.
3   focus on tasks, not people.
4   enjoy working with others.
5   give orders.
6   listen to others.

7   make suggestions.
8   judge people's abilities.
9   plan ahead.
10 be good with numbers.
11 make good presentations.
12 be older than your staff.

B **If you are managing people from different cultures, what other personal qualities and skills do you need?**

examples: *personal qualities: flexibility*
                  skills: good at languages

C **Talk about the good or bad qualities of managers/bosses you have had.**

96

VOCABULARY
Verbs and prepositions

A ‘Verb + preposition’ combinations are often useful for describing skills and personal qualities. Match the verbs (1–7) to the prepositions and phrases (a–g).

A good manager should:

1 respond

2 listen

3 deal

4 believe

5 delegate

6 communicate

7 invest

a) *in* their employees’ abilities.

b) *to* a deputy as often as possible.

c) *to* employees’ concerns promptly.

d) *with* colleagues clearly.

e) *with* problems quickly.

f) *in* regular training courses for employees.

g) *to* all suggestions from staff.

B Which do you think are the three most important qualities in Exercise A?

C Some verbs combine with more than one preposition.

*He **reports to** the Marketing Director. (to someone)*

*The Sales Manager **reported on** last month’s sales figures. (on something)*

Say whether these combine with *someone*, *something* or both.

1 a) report to   *someone*
  b) report on

2 a) apologise for
  b) apologise to

3 a) talk to
  b) talk about

4 a) agree with
  b) agree on

5 a) argue about
  b) argue with

D Complete these sentences with suitable prepositions from Exercise C.

1 I agreed ..*with*.... her that we need to change our marketing strategy.

2 I talk .... my boss every Monday at our regular meeting.

3 We argued .... next year’s budget for over an hour.

4 He apologised .... losing his temper.

5 We talked .... our financial problems for a long time.

6 The Finance Director argued .... our Managing Director over profit sharing.

7 I apologised .... Paula for giving her the wrong figures.

8 Can we agree .... the date of our next meeting?

E Write three questions using some of the ‘verb + preposition’ combinations from Exercises A and C. Then work in pairs and ask each other the questions.

EXAMPLE: *Who do you communicate with every day?*

*See the **DVD-ROM** for the i-Glossary.*

F Join up with another pair. Compare your answers to Exercise B above and Starting up Exercise A. What is your ideal manager like? Are they male or female?

LISTENING
Managing people

Laurie Mullins

A 🔊 CD2.43 **Laurie Mullins is the author of** *Management and organisational behaviour.* **Listen to the first part of the interview and answer these questions.**

1 Who was the first manager that impressed Laurie?

2 How do you spell his name?

3 What was his job?

4 What three things did he emphasise?

B 🔊 CD2.44 **Listen to the second part and complete these notes.**

Anita Roddick

- founded The Body Shop in ....[1]
- displayed a genuine ....[2] towards staff
- strong belief in:
  - environmental and ....[3] issues
  - feminist principles
  - practical ....[4] to Third World countries
- not possible to provide ....[5] and social support without making a profit
- was in business to make a ....[6]

Richard Branson

- founded the ....[7] brand in ....[8]
- over ....[9] companies
- famous for combining a true ....[10] spirit with a genuine ....[11] for people

C 🔊 CD2.45 **Listen to the final part and complete this summary.**

All three managers have or had a genuine belief in effective ....[1]; involvement and ....[2] for their staff; ....[3] so that staff can see them, ...[4] them; and they were able to have immediate ....[5] with them.

All either did or do engender a genuine ....[6] from members of their staff. All three had or have a genuine belief in creating a climate of mutual consideration, ...[7] and ....[8] with their staff.

Watch the interview on the DVD-ROM.

D **In pairs, tell each other which manager you would like to work for. Why?**

READING
Management and motivation

A **What would you do if you were a director of your company or school and had the power to change anything?**

B **Douglas McGregor, a US psychologist, argued that managers hold one of two theories about the people they have to deal with. Read this extract about the two theories and say which you prefer, and why.**

Theory X is based on a fairly negative view of human nature. It says that people are essentially lazy and uncomfortable with the idea of having too much responsibility for anything. They only turn up to work for the pay. Employees have to be managed in a strict way, otherwise nothing will get done.

Theory Y, on the other hand, suggests people may be capable of something more positive – that they will seek out responsibility and try to get better at their jobs, from which they can get significant personal satisfaction. Theory Y managers have high expectations of their people. They are also much more likely to develop a truly motivated workforce.

C Read the article below. Say which theory is probably supported by the management of Ruby's company, and which by the management of Geraldine's company.

FT

Share the power

by Stefan Stern

What does employee engagement look like in practice? John Smythe, from the Engage for Change consultancy, offers two situations to illustrate it.

Imagine two different employees, called Ruby and Geraldine, who work for different businesses. In the first situation, Ruby is invited to attend a morning meeting titled "Help our recovery".

"The invitation states that all parts of the company have performed badly, and that its parent company is unable to provide more cash for investment. It says that fast action must be taken to stabilise the situation," Mr Smythe explains. "But it also says there are no secret plans for extreme action. It says: 'We want to communicate openly. We also want you and your colleagues to take ownership with management to solve the crisis, recognising that unpleasant options will have to be on the table.'"

Ruby is both concerned and flattered. She arrives at the meeting feeling like a player rather than a spectator.

A two-month timetable is laid out in which she and her colleagues are invited to use their knowledge to find achievable cost savings without damaging key business areas.

In this process, Mr Smythe says, there are three good questions employees can be asked. What would they do if they:
- had a free hand in their day job?
- were a director of the company?
- had to propose important changes?

In this way, employees can feel part of the decisions that are necessary. They don't become demotivated.

The alternative scenario, which concerns Geraldine, is less appealing. She is also invited to a meeting described as a "cascade briefing". Rumours have been spreading, directors are hard to find, and there has been hardly any communication from the company.

"At the 'cascade', her fears are confirmed when, in a PowerPoint presentation, the full extent of the terrible state of the business is revealed for the first time," Mr Smythe says. "Detailed manage-

ment plans for restructuring and efficiencies are revealed. The focus is all on reduction, with no hint of new business opportunities. Geraldine feels less like a spectator and more like a victim. To varying degrees, her colleagues leave the meeting in shock."

"When have you felt most engaged and most valued and in a successful project or period at work?" he asks. "Absolutely none of us is going to report that it was more like Geraldine's experience."

D Read the article again and say if these statements are true (T), false (F) or the article doesn't say (DS).

1 Ruby and Geraldine were both invited to a meeting.

2 Ruby felt part of the decision-making process.

3 Ruby and Geraldine both left their meetings in shock.

4 The companies that Ruby and Geraldine work for are both having problems.

5 Geraldine enjoyed her meeting more than Ruby.

6 Communication was better in Geraldine's company than Ruby's.

7 After the meeting, Ruby was invited to a staff party.

8 Geraldine's company focused on reduction.

9 Geraldine is looking for another job.

E In pairs, tell each other about:

1 when you have felt most engaged and most valued at work, or in a sports team, or in your daily life;

2 the best way to communicate bad news;

3 any other theories of managing people that you know.

Reported speech

There are a number of ways to report what people say.

1 When we report things that have just been said, we often use the same tense as the speaker.
   'I want to see Pierre.'
   *'Pierre, Susan has just phoned and says she **wants** to see you.'*

2 When we report things said in the past, we usually make these changes.
   • The verb goes back one tense (for example from present simple to past simple).
   • Nouns and pronouns may change.
   'My new sales team is difficult to manage.'
   *He said (that) **his** new sales team **was** difficult to manage.*

3 We often use *say* and *tell* to report speech.
   'The new job is challenging.'
   *She **said** (that) the new job was challenging.*
   We use *tell* with an object.
   'The new job is challenging.'
   *She **told her boss** (that) the new job was challenging.*

➡ *Grammar reference* page 150

A **Complete these sentences with the correct form of *say* or *tell*.**

1 He ...*said*... that I was late.

2 He .... me that I was late.

3 She .... him to work harder.

4 She .... they would never agree.

5 Nobody .... me that she was the CEO.

6 She .... that she worked for Toyota.

B **Rewrite these sentences in reported speech, changing the tenses. Begin *He/She/They said*.**

1 Hamza: 'I'm not enjoying my job very much.'

2 Adela: 'I want to listen to my staff more.'

3 Susan and Sharon: 'We need to invest in the development of staff.'

4 Pierre: 'I'm feeling under pressure at work.'

5 Justin: 'The company has been performing badly.'

6 Eleanor: 'I'm going to look for a new job.'

C ◀)) CD2.46 **The HR Director couldn't attend this morning's meeting. Listen to the meeting and take notes on what was said and who said it. Then write a short e-mail to the HR Director.**

EXAMPLE: *Anna said the level of absenteeism had gone up over the month. She said we needed to monitor sickness levels more closely.*

Socialising and entertaining

A **Socialising is an important part of good management. When socialising for business in your country, how important are the following?**

1 being on time

2 the way people dress

3 what people are interested in, e.g. fashion, football, etc.

4 how you address people (first names or family names?)

5 giving gifts

6 shaking hands / kissing / hugging / bowing

B ◀)) CD2.47 **Paul is on a business trip to Syria. Mohammed is a Syrian business contact. Listen to their conversation, then answer these questions.**

1 What does Mohammed invite Paul to do?   2 Does Paul accept?

C **Complete this extract from the conversation in Exercise B.**

Paul: Mmm, ...¹ to invite me, Mohammed, but I think I'd prefer to stay in the hotel, ...². I'm really tired at the moment. It was a long flight, and I feel a little jet-lagged. I need an early night.

Mohammed: OK, Paul, I............³. Perhaps we could meet Abdullah at the weekend.

D ◀)) CD2.48 **Paul is being entertained by Abdullah and Mohammed. Listen to their conversation. Below are the answers to three questions. What were the questions?**

1 Well, we like the same things as Western people.

2 I generally watch TV with my wife.

3 I like to go out to restaurants.

E ◀)) CD2.49 **Listen to another part of the conversation between Paul and Abdullah. Why has Paul come to Damascus? How can Abdullah help him?**

F ◀)) CD2.49 **Listen again. In which order do you hear these sentences?**

a) I do know someone who might help you. ☐

b) Would you like me to give him a call first? ☐

c) Can you recommend anyone? ☐

d) Hold on a minute, I've got his business card. ☐

e) I'm looking for a company to supply carpets for my store. ☐ 1

f) He specialises in traditional designs. ☐

G **Role-play this situation.**

You meet a business contact in a foreign country. Find out this information.

a) how they spend their weekends   c) what they do in the evenings

b) where they go for their holidays   d) what kind of hobbies and sports they like

Also, you want to find an agent for your firm's products. Ask him/her if they can help.

USEFUL LANGUAGE

MAKING EXCUSES

I'm afraid I already have plans to ...
I'd like to take it easy if you don't mind.
It's very kind of you, but another time perhaps.

SAYING GOODBYE / THANKING

Thanks very much for your hospitality.
I really enjoyed the meal.
Thanks for showing me round the city.
I'll be in touch soon.
Goodbye. All the best.

MAKING CONVERSATION

What do you like to do in your spare time?
How do you spend your evenings/ weekends?
What's your favourite hobby/pastime?
Where are you going for your holiday this year?
Can you tell me about any interesting places to visit?
What/How about you?
What do you usually do after work?

NETWORKING

I'm looking for ...
Can you recommend anyone?
Do you have any contacts in ...?
I could make some enquiries for you.
I might be able to help.
Can I mention your name?
Would you like me to give them a call first?
Let me give you their business card.

ASHLEY COOPER
Search Agency

Tensions within the team are damaging operations at a property company

Background

The Ashley Cooper Search Agency (ACSA) specialises in finding top-class properties for wealthy clients from all over the world. It charges clients a fee based on the value of the property. Its London office finds properties in the UK, France and Germany for its clients. The agency has a database, which needs building up, and many contacts with upmarket estate agencies in the three countries.

The London branch has six relationship consultants who are multilingual. It is their job to find suitable properties, meet clients, arrange viewings and complete the purchase on their behalf. They only search for properties which are worth more than €1 million.

What advantages do you think clients gain by using ACSA to find a property?

Staff payment system

At present, relationship consultants are paid a salary, depending on their length of service, and an end-of-year bonus. The manager decides the amount of the bonus for each consultant. The company is reviewing this system, because it is not popular with some members of the team. The management is likely to cancel the bonus and adjust the salaries of the consultants.

What is your opinion of this proposal? Do you think it is a good idea?

Briefing the new manager of the London office

◀)) **CD2.50** Because of poor health, the present manager, Jim Driscoll, is leaving at the end of the month. He will be replaced by Diana Bishop. Listen to the conversation between them. Jim is briefing Diana about two of the consultants, Adriana and Ahmed.

Make notes about the two consultants.

Summary of recent appraisal interviews with relationship consultants

Read the summary notes on the other four consultants that Jim Driscoll has provided for Diana Bishop. Study the sales chart below and think about the payment system. Working individually, identify the problems Diana may have to deal with when she becomes manager of the team. Make a note of your main points.

Daria

- Good sales performance, especially in Germany – a difficult market.
- Excellent reports/paperwork.
- Always contributes well in meetings.
- Popular with her colleagues.
- Thinks we treat her unfairly because she's female. Says we always allocate the best clients to male consultants.
- Is not happy with the present payment system.

Klaus

- Sales have fallen sharply in the last three years, but still brings in the second biggest proportion of the total sales revenue.
- Not very innovative or creative.
- Does not have many ideas for increasing sales.
- Best contributor to building up the property database.
- Very good at encouraging team spirit and cooperation.
- Is happy with the present payment system.

Jackie

- Excellent sales performance.
- Is very good at closing deals – best negotiator in the team.
- Outstanding presentation skills.
- Not very popular with colleagues – too direct, lacks social skills.
- Very critical and outspoken in meetings.
- Is not happy with the payment system – thinks she should get a much bigger bonus.

Peter

- Sales have fallen in the last three years, but still brings in the biggest proportion of the total sales revenue.
- Does not like change or new technology.
- Has not contributed at all to building up the property database – one of the company's key objectives.
- Has missed several monthly meetings. Reason: 'too busy'.
- Submits poor sales reports – they lack detail.
- Is very happy with the present payment system.

Consultants' sales as a percentage of total sales revenue (three-year period)

consultant (years of service)	last year	previous year	three years ago
Peter (12)	28	34	40
Adriana (1)	8	–	–
Klaus (9)	22	30	38
Daria (6)	14	11	10
Jackie (5)	17	15	12
Ahmed (2)	11	10	–

Task

You are a director of ACSA. You have been asked to give Diana Bishop some informal advice about how to improve the performance of the relationship consultants so that they work more effectively as a team and are more motivated.

1 Working in small groups, discuss these questions.

- What are the main problems that Diana will have to deal with when managing the team?

- What solutions do you propose?

- Should the payment system be changed? If so, how?

2 It is very likely that Diana may soon be asked by head office to make one consultant redundant, in order to cut costs. If this happens, which consultant do you think she should ask to leave? What changes might Diana have to make as a result of her decision?

Watch the Case study commentary on the **DVD-ROM.**

Writing

As a director of ACSA, write the recommendation section of a report on the staff problems and your proposed solutions. The report is for the CEO of ACSA.

 Writing file page 129

UNIT 11 Conflict

'The aim of argument, or of discussion, should not be victory, but progress.'
Joseph Joubert (1754–1824), French moralist and essayist

OVERVIEW

VOCABULARY
Word-building

LISTENING
Resolving disputes

READING
Conflict management

LANGUAGE REVIEW
Conditionals

SKILLS
Negotiating: dealing with conflict

CASE STUDY
Herman & Corrie Teas

STARTING UP

How good are you at managing conflict? Answer the questions in this quiz. Then turn to page 135 to find out your score. Compare with a partner.

1 You are in a meeting. People cannot agree with each other. Do you:
   a) do nothing?
   b) intervene and propose something new?
   c) take sides with those you like?
   d) suggest a 10-minute break?

2 Your two closest friends have an argument and stop speaking to each other. Do you:
   a) behave as though nothing has happened?
   b) bring them together to discuss the problem?
   c) take the side of one and stop speaking to the other?
   d) talk to each one separately about the situation?

3 You see two strangers. One begins to hit the other. Do you:
   a) pretend to be an off-duty police officer and ask them what is going on?
   b) call the police?
   c) shout at them to stop?
   d) walk away quickly?

4 Your neighbours are playing very loud music late at night. Do you:
   a) ask them to turn it down?
   b) do nothing?
   c) call the police?
   d) play your own music as loudly as possible?

5 You are in the check-in queue at an airport. Somebody pushes in. Do you:
   a) ask them to go to the back of the queue?
   b) say nothing?
   c) complain loudly to everyone about people jumping queues?
   d) report them to an airport official?

6 A colleague criticises your work. Do you:
   a) consider carefully what they say?
   b) ignore them?
   c) get angry and criticise them?
   d) smile, but wait for an opportunity to take revenge?

104

VOCABULARY
Word-building

A Complete the 'noun' and 'adjective' columns of this chart with the correct word forms. Use a dictionary to help you if necessary.

	noun	adjective	opposite adjective
1	'patience	'patient	....
2	calmness	....	nervous
3	weakness	....	strong
4	flexibility	....	....
5	emotion	....	....
6	consistency	....	....
7	sympathy	....	....
8	....	formal	informal
9	enthusiasm	....	....
10	....	creative	....

B ◀)) CD2.51 Mark the stress on the noun and adjective forms in Exercise A. The first one has been done for you. Practise the pronunciation with a partner. Then listen and check your answers.

C Opposite adjectives are formed in one of three ways:

a) using a prefix such as *un-, in-* or *im-*: *formal* ▢ *informal*

b) using a different word: *weak* ▢ *strong*

c) using a paraphrase: *friendly* ▢ *not (very) friendly* (= *unfriendly*)

Complete the right-hand column of the chart in Exercise A with the opposites of the adjectives.

D Complete these sentences with one of the adjectives from Exercise A or its opposite.

1 He gets very angry if people are late for negotiations. He is very ..*impatient*...

2 She always has ideas and easily finds solutions to problems. She is a very .... person.

3 He never shows anger, enthusiasm or disappointment during a negotiation. He is totally ....

4 He usually agrees with the things his negotiating partner suggests. He is ....

5 I told him I was feeling really bad, and all he asked was 'Will you be able to meet the deadline?' How can anyone be so .... ?

6 He likes people to feel comfortable and relaxed during a negotiation. He's a very .... person.

7 He let the other side have everything they wanted in the negotiation. He was very ....

8 She is very .... She keeps changing her mind all the time, which makes her very difficult to negotiate with.

E Look again at the adjectives and their opposites. Choose what you think are the best and worst qualities for a negotiator. Then compare your ideas with a partner and try to reach an agreement.

*See the **DVD-ROM** for the i-Glossary.*

F Following your discussion in Exercise E, which of the qualities do you think you and your partner possess / don't possess? Discuss your ideas.

LISTENING
Resolving disputes

Eileen Carroll

A 🔊 CD2.52 **Listen to the first part of an interview with Eileen Carroll, from the Centre for Effective Dispute Resolution, and answer these questions.**

1 When was the centre founded?

2 Where is it located?

3 What does it do?

4 How many mediators has it been involved in training?

B 🔊 CD2.53 **Listen to the second part, where Eileen talks about the commonest causes of conflict at work, and complete this extract from the audio script.**

The key problem is inappropriate ....[1] or no ....[2]. So I would say, avoidance, so that managers are not ....[3] with their employees as effectively as they might.

There's a lot of European legislation now around the areas of sex discrimination and ....[4] work practices, and this does lead to a lot of controversy in the ....[5].

I think other areas are: clash of personalities, ...[6], different belief systems, and interestingly, I think a lot of ....[7] feel that their workloads can be very oppressive.

C 🔊 CD2.54 **Listen to the final part and complete these notes on how to resolve business disputes.**

1 Have an early ....

2 Recognise there is a ....

3 Have a good ....

4 Get key decision-makers to allow enough ....

5 Have a good ....

6 Make sure difficult issues are ....

7 Bring together parts of different groups to improve levels of ....

8 Work on problem-solving to find a ....

Watch the interview on the DVD-ROM.

D **In pairs, talk about an example of conflict you have had and how you resolved it. How many of the methods in Exercise C did you use?**

READING
Conflict management

A **When does joking or teasing become bullying?**

B **In pairs, think of as many sources of conflict at work as you can.**

examples: *poor time-keeping, interrupting people in meetings*

C **Read the article on the opposite page quickly and see how many of your answers to Exercise B are mentioned.**

D **Read the article again and answer these questions.**

1 What should managers do when teasing starts to become hurtful?

2 Why should managers note examples of inappropriate behaviour or language?

3 Why should managers get involved as soon as conflict develops?

4 What happens if managers ignore conflict and poor behaviour?

5 What are the advantages of return-to-work interviews?

Intervening quickly in cases of conflict

Managers should be sensitive to when teasing starts to become hurtful. They should be prepared to step in and have a quiet word with the team members
5 involved. The manager should inform those involved that, while plenty of communication is encouraged, it's important that there is respect for other people and that certain standards of
10 behaviour are expected at work. The manager should have noted examples of the types of behaviour or language that have been used that are inappropriate at work, so that those involved
15 will understand what is unacceptable.

It's much easier to have this conversation as soon as a manager starts to have concerns about behaviour or early signs of conflict – to prevent
20 habits from being formed and to ensure that the manager is taken seriously. It's much more difficult to be respected if a manager appears to accept certain behaviour by letting a situation
25 continue for weeks or months.

Dealing with conflict directly
Taking action to manage conflict can appear quite worrying to some managers, but it's an essential part
30 of their role and responsibilities. If managers ignore unacceptable behaviour, problems will get worse until the disciplinary process has to be used or a formal complaint is made, by
35 which time it will be much harder to achieve a successful resolution.

Some potential sources of conflict at work are obvious, such as:
• too much personal use of the Internet
40   or e-mail;
• poor attendance and time-keeping;
• any form of bullying behaviour;
• any form of discrimination
   (e.g. sexism);
45 • unacceptable language;
• theft;
• drink or drug problems.

However, frequently it is the less obvious behaviour that over time, if
50 not confronted, will lead to workplace disputes. Examples of less obvious types of dispute include:
• taking credit for other people's
   work or ideas;
55 • interrupting people in meetings;
• not inviting team members to social
   evenings or events;
• not covering for people when they
   are sick;
60 • not taking messages for people;
• using someone else's contacts
   without permission;
• not including people in group
   e-mails;
65 • ignoring people or being impolite;
• poor personal hygiene.

Managers should not ignore problems that are developing in their teams. It's vital that line managers
70 have regular, informal, one-to-one conversations with the people they manage, so that these kinds of issues can be discussed naturally where possible.
75 However, managers must also be prepared to begin informal discussions if they think a problem is starting to develop. Conflict at work can lead to absences, so return-to-work interviews
80 are also a good opportunity for managers to ask questions about any conflict issues that might be worrying employees.

with permission of the publisher, the Chartered Institute of Personnel and Development, London, www.cipd.co.uk

E **Find words in the article that mean the opposite of these words.**

1 appropriate   2 acceptable   3 polite   4 formal

F **Discuss these questions.**

1 Have you ever been involved in any of the examples of conflict listed in the article? How did/would you feel?

2 What behaviour at work do/would you find inappropriate or unacceptable?

3 How would you deal with these problems?

Conditionals

- **First conditional**
  if + present simple, *will* + infinitive without *to*
  This describes a possible situation and its probable result.
  *If he **bullies** anyone again, he**'ll lose** his job.*
  *If sales **increase**, we**'ll make** more profit.*

- **Second conditional**
  if + past simple, *would* + infinitive without *to*
  This describes an unlikely situation and its probable result.
  *If he **made** more eye contact, he**'d be** a better negotiator.*

- **Conditionals and negotiating**
  Conditionals are often used when negotiating. We use conditionals for offers.
  *If you **sign** the contract today, we**'ll give** you a 10% discount.* (firm offer)
  *If you **ordered** 100 cases, we**'d give** you a larger discount.* (less firm offer)

➡ *Grammar reference page 151*

A **Correct the grammatical mistakes in these sentences.**

1 If you pay in dollars, we would deliver next week.

2 If I would have his number, I would phone him.

3 If the goods will arrive tomorrow, I'll collect them.

4 If the cars would be more reliable, more people would buy them.

B **Combine phrases from Columns A and B to make conditional sentences. More than one answer is possible in each case.**

example: *If you place an order today, we'll offer a large discount.*

A	B
1 offer more flexible payment conditions	a) offer a large discount
2 pay all the promotion costs	b) give you 90 days' credit
3 place an order today	c) make you an exclusive agent
4 pay in dollars	d) give you a signing-on bonus
5 place firm orders in advance	e) despatch immediately
6 provide good technical support	f) accept the deal
7 offer us a unit price of $22	g) reduce the price by 20%
8 sign the contract now	h) increase the order

C ◀)) CD2.55 **Listen to two people negotiating. Look at the audio script on page 164 and underline the sentences in which the speaker makes an offer, but is not sure it will be accepted.**

Now circle the sentences in which the speaker makes a *firm* offer.

D **Discuss these questions in pairs.**

What would you do if:

1 your boss asked you to move abroad? *I would ask for a raise.*

2 you saw a colleague bullying another colleague?

3 you saw a colleague stealing something?

4 your boss took credit for your ideas?

5 you saw two colleagues having an argument?

SKILLS

Negotiating: dealing with conflict

A **Which of these are good ways of dealing with conflict in a negotiation?**

1 Avoiding eye contact.

2 Smiling a lot.

3 Sitting back and appearing relaxed.

4 Stopping the discussion and coming back to it later.

5 Saying nothing for a long time.

6 Saying 'I see what you mean'.

7 Finding out why the other side is unhappy.

8 Focusing on the issues, not on personalities.

9 Saying something humorous.

10 Speaking calmly and slowly.

B ◀)) CD2.56 **Rachel, an American executive, works in a sales office in Geneva, Switzerland. She is negotiating a salary increase with Scott, a director of the company.**

1 What do these figures refer to? **a)** $60,000 **b)** $120,000

2 List the arguments that:

    a) Rachel uses to get an increased salary;

    b) Scott uses to avoid paying her the salary she asks for.

3 What solution do they finally agree on?

C ◀)) CD2.56 **Listen again and complete these extracts.**

1 I think I'm .... a lot more than that to the company. My work's greatly undervalued at the moment.

2 I've done really well in the last two years. I've exceeded my .... by almost 40% ...

3 Put yourself in our shoes. We're facing a difficult .... situation, you know that.

4 OK, I understand what you're .... I can see your point of ....

5 Let me suggest a .... How about if we give you an increase to, say, $80,000 now and promise to review your salary in six months' time?

6 I'm pleased to hear it. I think we've .... everything.

D **Identify the key phrases in the extracts in Exercise C and write them under the appropriate heading in the Useful language box below.**

E **Work in pairs. Role-play this situation.**

A marketing executive meets the General Manager to discuss an overseas posting. The marketing executive has not been chosen for the position and is very unhappy.

Student A: Turn to page 133.   Student B: Turn to page 139.

USEFUL LANGUAGE

EXPRESSING YOUR POINT OF VIEW

I've got an excellent sales record.

I've always met my sales targets.

I believe I should be paid more.

CALMING DOWN

Well, I know/see what you mean.

Why don't we come back to that later?

Let's have a break and come back with some fresh ideas.

CREATING SOLUTIONS

I'd like to make a suggestion.

What if ...

Let's look at this another way.

Another possibility is ...

CLOSING A NEGOTIATION

Let's see what we've got.

Can I go over what we've agreed?

Let's go over the main points again.

We've got a deal.

Fine. / Right. / That's it, then.

HERMAN & CORRIE TEAS

A well-established company in the Netherlands must decide whether it wishes to become part of a large multinational

Background

Herman & Corrie Teas was founded by Herman and Corrie Van Etten in Rotterdam in 1888. The firm is privately owned. It imports and packages tea, selling its products mainly in Europe, the US and Australia. A large multinational drinks company, Universal Cola Corporation (UCC), has recently made an offer to buy Herman & Corrie Teas. The management must decide whether to recommend the shareholders to accept the offer.

🔊 **CD2.57 Listen to a business report on Radio Europe.**
The presenter is talking to Joan Knight, an expert on the tea industry. Joan describes Herman & Corrie Teas as a 'green company' and talks about its values and ethical principles.

How might Herman & Corrie Teas benefit from the sale?

Conflict

Read this e-mail from the Chief Executive of Herman & Corrie Teas to a senior manager in the company. Note down the key points.

| To: | Simon Marsh |
| Subject: | UCC offer |

We'll be deciding whether to recommend UCC's offer at our Board of Directors' meeting next Tuesday. I intend to invite our two major shareholders to attend, as well as a staff representative and a senior manager from within the company.

I want to hear all the arguments for and against the offer before we make a decision.

I haven't made up my mind yet, nor have my colleagues on the Board. We accept that profits have not been impressive in the last three years. We also know that we have a limited range of suppliers and products, which has attracted criticism in the financial press. Finally, it's true that we've had problems recently attracting top-class executives to fill management positions.

I hope we will have a good discussion, which will enable us to make the right decision.

Task

1 You are members of the management meeting. Work in groups of five. Choose a role and prepare for the meeting.

Student A (Chief Executive):   Turn to page 136.
Student B (Shareholder A):   Turn to page 137.
Student C (Shareholder B):   Turn to page 140.
Student D (Staff Representative):   Turn to page 135.
Student E (Senior Manager):   Turn to page 138.

2 Hold the meeting. The Chief Executive leads the discussion. Give your opinion about whether or not the Board should recommend accepting UCC's offer. Present your arguments strongly and try to persuade the others to accept your point of view.

3 Decide whether or not to recommend the offer to all shareholders. Take a vote if necessary.

Watch the Case study commentary on the DVD-ROM.

Writing

As Chief Executive of Herman & Corrie Teas, write a letter to the shareholders, giving your reasons for recommending or not recommending UCC's offer to purchase the company.

Dear Shareholders,

The multinational drinks group Universal Cola Corporation has made an offer to purchase the company. Our reasons for accepting / not accepting their offer are as follows:

 Writing file page 128

UNIT 12 Products

'When the product is right, you don't have to be a great marketer.'
Lee Iacocca, US businessman

STARTING UP

A Describe some of your favourite products. Why do you like them? What do they say about you? Which of these products could you not do without?

B What product would you most like to own? Why? Which product would make your life easier?

C Do you agree or disagree with these statements? Give reasons for your answers.

1 It is better to pay a bit more for products which are made in your own country.

2 'Organic', 'energy-saving' or 'green' products are overpriced and often not as good as the alternatives.

3 Companies spend far too much on launching and promoting new products.

4 Multinationals which manufacture in developing countries help the world economy.

5 Modern technology-based products do not improve people's lives.

VOCABULARY

Describing products

A Check that you know the meaning of the adjectives below. Think of a product that matches each word. Compare your ideas with a partner. How many were the same?

- attractive • comfortable • economical • efficient • expensive • fashionable
- healthy • popular • practical • pure • reliable • safe

B Complete this chart with adjectives with the opposite meanings to those in Exercise A.

un-	in-	im-
unattractive		

C Complete the sentences below with the words from the box.

best   hard   ~~high~~   high   high   long   well

1 IBM manufactures *high*-tech computer products.

2 Timberland makes a range of ....-*wearing* footwear.

3 Hermes produces ....-*quality* fashion accessories.

4 Coca-Cola and Pepsico both developed ....-*selling* soft drinks.

5 Duracell sells ....-*lasting* alkaline batteries.

6 Levi jeans are a ....-*made* clothing product.

7 Ferrari make ....-*performance* sports cars.

D Use the adjectives in Exercise C to describe other companies and products.

example: *Nestlé makes many of the world's best-selling food products.*

E Look at this list of products. Which of the adjectives from Exercises A, B and C (including opposites) could you use to describe them?

- bottled water
- an MP3 player
- soap
- a pair of jeans
- a four-wheel-drive car
- a perfume
- a fast-food product
- a laptop computer

F Match the verbs (1–8) to their meanings (a–h). Then put the verbs into a logical order to show the lifecycle of one of the products from Exercise E.

1 launch   a) to stop making

2 test   b) to build or make

3 promote   c) to introduce to the market

4 manufacture   d) to change in order to improve

5 modify   e) to try something in order to see how it works

6 discontinue   f) to make a plan or drawing

7 design   g) to increase sales by advertising, etc.

8 distribute   h) to supply to shops, companies, customers

See the DVD-ROM for the i-Glossary.

listening

Favourite products

James Wallman

A 🔊 CD2.58–2.61 **Four people were asked the question 'What is the best thing you have ever bought?'. Listen and, for each speaker, note what the product is, and why they think it was a great buy.**

B 🔊 CD2.62 **James Wallman is Editor of LS:N, a lifestyle news network which follows trends and innovations in the retail and technology sectors. Listen to the first part of the interview and complete his notes for answering the question 'What makes a product great?'.**

1 It should be easy to ....

2 It should solve a .... or fulfil a .... (example: ....).

3 It should be ...., ... and make your life .... and make things ....

C 🔊 CD2.63 **James was asked which product of recent years has been the most exciting. Listen to the second part and correct the three mistakes in this summary of what he says.**

It's the Tesla Roadster. This is the new gas vehicle which goes from 0 to 60 mph in 34 seconds. I drove one from Paris to Cannes, and it was very exciting. The response from the accelerator is instant.

D 🔊 CD2.64 **Listen to the third part and answer these questions.**

1 What product does James expect to see in the near future?

2 What does he sometimes not like about driving?

3 Where does he not like driving?

4 Which companies are mentioned?

5 What is the comparison with the 747 plane?

E 🔊 CD2.65 **Listen to the final part and complete this information about James Wallman.**

his favourite product

the colour of this product

his job

what he is writing

uses Skype to talk to friends in which places?

F 🔊 CD2.65 **Listen to the final part again and complete these extracts.**

It connects me to ....[1], because obviously I have ....[2] at home. When I go to a ....[3] I have Wi-Fi, I take it with me when I go on ....[4] and I go to places that have Wi-Fi.

So for me, my ....[5] and its connection to the ....[6] and its connection to ....[7] around the world, makes it invaluable and makes my life more ....[8] and more ....[9].

*Watch the interview on the **DVD-ROM.***

READING

Launching new products

A **Discuss these questions.**

1 Which countries are strong in the consumer electronics industry?

2 Which companies do you know in that industry?

3 What is the best electronic product you have bought, and why?

4 What Casio products do you know?

B **Read through the article below quickly to find this information.**

1 three examples of problems for the Japanese consumer-electronics industry

2 four examples of Casio's products

3 two examples of major players in professional photography

4 two of Mr Kashio's favourite expressions

5 three examples of rivals to Japan's electronics industry

FT

A path to salvation through innovation

by Robin Harding

Kazuo Kashio has led Casio, the Japanese consumer-electronics company that he founded with his three brothers, for 20 years.

Whatever problem is put to him, whether it is the yen's strength, the economy's weakness or the collapse in Japanese mobile-phone sales, the energetic executive has a single answer: launch new products.

"For us as a manufacturer, whether conditions are good or bad is all decided by our products, and our strategy is to make sure as many of them as possible are new," he says. Casio plans to replace 50 per cent of its products in the second half of the year.

That strategy amounts to an attempt to maintain sales by taking a larger share of a shrinking market. Challenged as to whether that is possible, given that rivals are not only racing to launch new products but also cutting prices, Mr Kashio argues that Casio's products are unique enough to do it.

This confidence in his products is typical of Mr Kashio. He often says

that his long years of selling make him a keen judge of whether a new product will succeed. He perks up considerably when given the chance to praise his gadgets, such as radio-controlled watches that pick up a broadcast signal to set the time, and the toughened G-Shock brand, which redefined watch design.

A source of pride at the moment is Casio's family of high-speed "burst" digital cameras, which can take up to 60 shots a second after the photographer presses the button. With such a camera, Mr Kashio says, a photographer can catch the precise moment at which a batter hits a baseball and judge instantly whether a runner was safe or out. The product has taken Casio into the professional photography market, which is dominated by Canon and Nikon.

Two of Mr Kashio's favourite phrases sum up the family's approach to research and development. One is to resist "preconceived ideas" of what a device should do and how it should do it; the other is "from zero to one", to describe how Casio creates something that did not exist – such as the electronic calculator that started it all in 1957 – from scratch.

Mr Kashio argues that Japan's electronics industry can stay ahead of its rivals in Taiwan, China and South Korea if it keeps innovating.

His hopes for the future are those of a family company: to maintain Casio's stability and to keep the new products coming.

C **Read the article again. Then decide whether (according to the text) these statements are true (T), false (F) or not mentioned (NM).**

1 The Casio Tower is located in the Shinjuku district of Tokyo.

2 Mr Kashio's answer to the problems he faces is to launch new products.

3 Casio's rivals are focusing mainly on cutting prices.

4 Mr Kashio is confident about the company's financial position, as it has no debt.

5 Mr Kashio says he is good at deciding whether a new product will succeed, because he has a lot of experience of selling.

6 Mr Kashio is proud of Casio's high-speed 'burst' digital cameras.

7 Casio dominates the professional photography market.

8 Mr Kashio's main hope is that Casio will make more and more profits.

D **Work in groups of three or four. You have a very large budget to launch a product of your choice in your country. How would you launch the product?**

Passives

- We make passive verb forms with the verb *be* + past participle.
  *The Casio G-Shock GW-5000 **is made** in Japan.*

- We often choose a passive structure when we are not interested in, or it is not necessary to know, who performs an action.
  *This lens **is** often **used** in skateboarding photo shoots.*

- If we want to mention who performs an action, we can use *by*.
  *The professional photography market **is dominated by** Canon and Nikon.*

- We can use the passive to describe a process, system or procedure.
  *Finally, all Casio products **are tested** before shipping.*

➡️ *Grammar reference page 152*

A **Use this chart to make passive sentences. Then make similar sentences about products from your own country.**

example: *Diamonds are mined in South Africa.*

Diamonds Microchips	produce	Poland Kuwait Japan
Semiconductors	manufacture	the United States
Electronic goods Coffee	make	Finland Switzerland
Leather goods Oil Rice	refine	Malaysia Brazil
Watches Coal	grow	Spain South Africa
Mobile phones	mine	Zambia China

B **Change these active sentences into the passive so that they sound more natural.**

1 Somebody opened the Channel Tunnel in 1994.

   The Channel Tunnel was opened in 1994.

2 They have chosen the new design.

3 Thousands of people see this website every day.

4 The employers asked the staff for their opinions.

5 A mechanic is repairing my car at the moment.

6 Somebody has found the missing file.

7 Somebody made this watch in Switzerland.

C **This article describes how a glass-making company produces some of its products. Complete it with passive forms of the verbs in brackets.**

Our first glass products ....[1] (*launch*) 30 years ago, and for the last 20 years, our production ....[2] (*control*) by computers. Some of the operations ....[3] (*perform*) by robots. This keeps our prices competitive, because unit costs ....[4] (*reduce*), as we gain from economies of scale. In the last five years, some of our products ....[5] (*manufacture*) in China.

We produce a special type of glass, which ....[6] (*design*) to have a fire-polished finish and to be distortion-free. At the start of the process, the raw materials such as sand, soda, ash and limestone ....[7] (*weigh*). Then they ....[8] (*blend*) and ....[9] (*feed*) continuously into a melting furnace. Recycled glass ....[10] (*also feed*) into the furnace in order to reduce waste.

The raw materials ....¹¹ (*melt*) inside the furnace. The molten glass ....¹² (*cool*) and then it ....¹³ (*test*) for stress. Customer orders ....¹⁴ (*feed*) into the computer, and sizes ....¹⁵ (*modify*) to suit the needs of the customers. Finally, the glass ....¹⁶ (*cut*), the panes of glass ....¹⁷ (*load*) into lorries and then they ....¹⁸ (*distribute*).

Our new self-cleaning glass ....¹⁹ (*promote*) recently by some of the biggest names in the building industry at the recent Wonderful Homes exhibition.

SKILLS

Presenting a product

A ◀)) CD2.66 **Listen to a sales manager presenting a product to some buyers. Which of these adjectives does she use?**

| attractive | elegant | energy-saving | fashionable | flexible | high-quality | popular |
| practical | reliable | robust | sturdy | stylish | user-friendly | versatile | well-designed |

B ◀)) CD2.66 **Listen again to the presentation. How does the sales manager describe the product? Complete these words and phrases with between one and three words in each gap.**

1 It has several special ....

2 As you can see, it's stylish, ... and elegant.

3 It's made of .... and is very sturdy.

4 It weighs approximately 12 kilos, but it's very strong and ....

5 What about its main .... ?

6 Well, it's very .... in terms of power and exceptionally quiet ...

7 Now, a word or two about its .... for the user.

8 And because the machine's so .... , it can make cubes of different sizes.

9 It's fairly .... compared with other models. The .... is around €320.

10 It comes with a full five-year .... on parts and labour.

C **Work in small groups.**

1 Think of an innovative new product you would like to launch. (You can use the product you discussed in Reading Exercise D.) Prepare a short presentation about the product. Consider its main features and benefits for the user. Use the headings in the Useful language box below to help you structure your talk.

2 Form new groups and present your products to each other. Answer any questions that you are asked about them.

USEFUL LANGUAGE

INTRODUCING THE PRODUCT

This is our new product.

I'm going to tell you about our new product.

DESCRIBING THE PRODUCT

Let me tell you about its special features.

It's made of leather/wood/steel/aluminium.

It weighs approximately 16 kilos.

Its dimensions in centimetres/metres are: ...... high ...... wide ...... deep.

It comes in a wide range of colours.

STATING THE PRODUCT'S USES

It's ideal for travelling.

It's designed to be used with any type of material.

It's for people who like giving parties.

It's perfect for making different sizes of ice cubes.

LISTING SELLING POINTS

What about its main selling points?

It has several special features.

It has a unique design.

It's economical/quiet/energy-saving.

It's great value for money.

REFERRING TO BENEFITS

It saves people time/money.

It's easy to use.

It makes the user look good/professional.

INVITING QUESTIONS

Does anyone have any questions?

Would anyone like to ask a question?

Any questions?

The George Marshall Awards

A competition is held each year to find the most innovative new consumer products

George Marshall Award Nominations

We invite you to nominate your product
for this year's Best New Product Awards.
For entry forms, write to …

Background

The George Marshall Awards will shortly be announced at a ceremony in Melbourne, Australia. The awards, which are given by the George Marshall Foundation, are an annual event. They are designed to recognise innovation and creativity in developing, marketing and launching new products. Companies from all over the world enter the competition.

The top five companies receive a badge from the Foundation, which they are able to put on their winning products. The badge is a guarantee that the product is truly innovative and of high quality. It appeals to consumers and boosts sales of the product.

There are five prizes for the selected companies. The best product has five stars on its badge, and the product in fifth place has one star. The badges are also colour-coded.

◀)) **CD2.67** Recently, two senior members of the Selection Committee, Hugh Davis and Chika Nakamura, were discussing the sort of qualities they were looking for in the winning products. Listen and note down the key points.

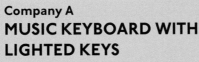

Company A
MUSIC KEYBOARD WITH LIGHTED KEYS

- Keys light up when you play tunes.
- A simple teaching system is provided.
- You learn which note goes with which key.
- The keyboard plays 200 songs.
- An LCD display guides you with the fingering you need for each song.
- Two speakers are built into the keyboard.
- You learn to play the keyboard quickly and easily.
- Price: US$280

Company B
PASSWORD MEMORY FILE

- Generates and protects your passwords.
- Keep up to 100 different logins or key codes safely.
- Use any combination of letters, symbols or figures that you wish.
- Passwords are limited to 20 characters.
- You press buttons to put in passwords.
- You can view your passwords on the LCD screen.
- It will generate passwords for you if you wish.
- Price: US$70

Company C
KEY FINDER

- You put a small device on your keys.
- You keep the credit-card-sized transmitter in your pocket or purse.
- When you need to find your keys, you press a button on the transmitter.
- The transmitter sends a signal to the device on the keys.
- Your keys make an audible noise.
- The keys also give out a flashing light.
- The key finder can locate lost keys up to 60 metres away.
- Price: US$19.99

Company D
BUSINESS-CARD SCANNER

- The scanner is small and portable.
- It enables you to scan business cards into your computer.
- It solves the problem of lost or difficult-to-find business cards.
- When you receive a business card, you simply feed it into the small scanner.
- The scanner stores it directly on your computer.
- The images on the card can be changed into text.
- The scanner saves you time, because you don't spend hours looking for cards.
- Price: US$95

Company E
WATCH ALARM FOR CHILDREN

- Has a range up to two kilometres.
- Helps you to keep an eye on your child.
- Warns you if your child is in danger.
- It has two buttons and an alarm. When the child presses the buttons, the watch gives out a flashing light and also makes a loud noise.
- The noise continues for three hours and cannot be turned off, unless the code is known.
- The watch has an attractive design for young children aged 5–10.
- Young children can operate it easily. They only need to press two buttons.
- Price: US$45

Task

1 Work in small groups. Choose one of the companies above and prepare a presentation of its product. (Or, if you prefer, think of another product which the company is about to launch.) Invent any information you wish.

2 Form new groups and present your products. Try to persuade your audience that your product is the most innovative and creative. When you are not presenting, play the role of a member of the Selection Committee and ask questions about the products.

3 After all the presentations, discuss which product is the most exciting and innovative.

Watch the Case study commentary on the DVD-ROM.

Writing

As a member of the Selection Committee, write a short report on one of the products which you saw presented. The report will be published on the Foundation's website.

➡ *Writing file* page 129

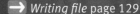

4 Preparing to do business internationally

A Discuss these questions.

1 Which countries share a border with your country or are your near neighbours?

2 How is their culture different to yours?

3 Thinking about the rest of the world, which cultures do you think are most different to your own? In what ways?

B Do this culture questionnaire. Compare your answers with a partner.

IN YOUR CULTURE ...

1 **What time is the most important meal of the day?**
a) 12:00–14:00   b) 18:00–20:00
c) 20:00–22:00   d) another time

2 **How do you greet business contacts or colleagues when meeting?**
a) with a handshake   b) with a kiss/hug
c) with a bow   d) another way

3 **Which of the following do you or would you use in business situations?**
a) first names   b) surnames
c) titles and first names   d) titles and surnames

4 **You have a business meeting at 2.30 p.m. What time do you arrive?**
a) a little before – say 2.20   b) exactly on time
c) some time later – say 2.45

5 **In a meeting, do you expect:**
a) everyone to try and speak?
b) everyone to listen while each person speaks in turn?
c) only some people to speak?

6 **When you are making important business decisions, what is it most important to consider?**
a) what we did before
b) what we are doing now
c) what we are going to do in the future

7 **How should decisions be made?**
a) by the boss alone   b) by everyone together
c) by the boss, but after asking for opinions

8 **If you do a job well, who should be rewarded?**
a) only you   b) all the people in your team
c) the whole company

C After you have completed the questionnaire, discuss these questions with your partner.

1 Do you think other people from your culture would answer in the same way?

2 Which aspects of your culture are important for business visitors to know about?

D Look at the comments below (1–7) made by people doing business in other cultures. Match them to the aspects of culture in the box (a–g).

> a) age/status   b) body language
> c) entertaining   d) humour
> e) showing emotion   f) socialising   g) time

1 Everything went very, very slowly, and a lot of people arrived late. There was a lot of tea drinking and chatting, but nothing seemed to happen. I wanted to make some decisions.

2 I tried to make a joke at the start of my presentation, to break the ice and make people feel relaxed, but nobody laughed. Everybody was so serious. Nobody asked any questions either. But we got the contract!

3 I'm not sure I was taken very seriously, as I'm quite young. It was a bit strange. There were four people at the meeting with us, but only one person – the oldest one – spoke. He asked me when the boss was arriving, even though I told them I was there to make the deal.

4 At the presentation, I couldn't really tell them about the products properly, as they kept interrupting all the time. There was a lot of shouting. Nobody seemed very serious. It was all much too noisy for me.

5 There was a lot of nodding when we were making our offer and we seemed to have a deal. But then suddenly we didn't. It was all very unusual to me. I thought nodding meant 'yes, we agree'.

6 At the drinks reception, I tried to keep the conversation going, but they didn't seem interested. They just looked bored. Maybe they were shy. It was a bit awkward, really – just too quiet for me. In my country, we like a lively conversation. Perhaps they just didn't like me!

7 We had a very stressful meal. After I finished each course, more and more food arrived. I didn't want to be rude, but the more I ate, the more they brought. Some of my colleagues couldn't eat some of the more 'unusual' dishes.

E Discuss these questions.

1 Do any of the situations in Exercise D seem familiar to you?

2 Which situation would make you feel the most/least comfortable?

F You are going to listen to a talk given by a cross-cultural expert. Food is one example of a visible aspect of culture. What other examples can you think of?

G ◀)) CD2.68 Listen to the first part of the talk and check your ideas. What other examples are given?

H ◀)) CD2.69 Listen to the second part and answer these questions.

1 What does the speaker say about the following, and how they affect doing business in other cultures?

a) the structure of society

b) building relationships

c) decision-making

d) time

e) status

2 What general advice does she give for doing business in other cultures?

Task

Work in pairs / small groups.

1 Each person should prepare a short talk giving some advice for foreign businesspeople coming to your country. The title of the talk is:

'Aspects of my culture that a business visitor might find unusual or difficult.'

Decide where the visitors are coming from and what will be useful for them to know. Look back at some of the earlier sections, and try and include some different aspects of culture. Think about attitudes, habits and behaviour.

2 Listen to your partners' talk(s) and ask three questions.

3 Write some dos and don'ts for business visitors to your partners' country.

10 Managing people

Complete this text with *in*, *to*, *with*, *about* and *for*.

I work in a small company, so I report directly ....[1] the owner of the business. I respect her a lot. I think she deals ....[2] her employees firmly but fairly. When we need to talk ....[3] a work issue, she's available, and she really listens ....[4] us. She really believes ....[5] her employees and has invested a lot ....[6] our professional development. That makes us feel loyal to her. But it doesn't mean we always agree ....[7] her. We recently argued ....[8] the best way to supply a customer's order. But even when we were arguing, she communicated ....[9] us clearly about why her way was the best – and she was right, in the end. But when she does make a mistake, she apologises ....[10] it and we move on.

Choose the best word(s) to complete each sentence.

1 'I want to start the meeting at 10 o'clock.'
  She says *she wants* / *she's wanted* to start at 10 o'clock.

2 'Our new offices are fantastic.'
  He said that their new offices *have been* / *were* fantastic.

3 'The back-up software is working very well.'
  She said the back-up software *will be* / *was* working very well.

4 'My new job has been a lot of fun.'
  She told her boss that her new job *had been* / *was* a lot of fun.

5 'The company's shares have been performing badly.'
  The newspaper said that the company's shares *had been* / *were* performing badly.

6 'We need to invest in a new intranet server.'
  She said *we needed* / *we'd need* to invest in a new intranet server.

Match each sentence (1–8) to an appropriate response (a–h).

1 Would you like to join us for dinner?

2 What do you like to do in your spare time?

3 Where are you going for your holiday this year?

4 Can you tell me about any interesting places to visit?

5 Can you recommend a good technical writer?

6 Can I mention your name?

7 Thanks very much for your hospitality.

8 Goodbye. All the best.

a) Do you know Henry Haynes? He's very good.

b) I play tennis a lot.

c) I'll be in touch soon.

d) It's very kind of you, but another time perhaps.

e) It was my pleasure.

f) You should try Croatia. It's fantastic.

g) I'm going to Paris.

h) Sure. Tell him I met you at the Motor Trade Show.

11 Conflict

VOCABULARY

Choose the best word in each case to complete the text.

> **Gaining confidence**
>
> When I first started this job a year ago, I felt very *calmness / calm / nervous* [1] giving presentations. In the past six months, I have learned to be *calmness / calm / nervous* [2] while presenting, even in front of large groups. My main worry a year ago was that audiences would think I was *credibility / credible / not credible* [3] because of my inexperience and also that audience members might turn my presentation into an argument. I really appreciate the *patience / patient / impatient* [4] of my manager, who helped me to understand first of all that most audiences are *sympathy / sympathetic / unsympathetic* [5], and also that giving a very serious, *formality / formal / informal* [6] presentation scares most people. It isn't a sign of *weakness / weak / strong* [7], it's just a natural response to a challenging situation. As a result of the training I've received, the positive feedback on my presentations has been *consistency / consistent / inconsistent* [8].

CONDITIONALS

Complete each of these sentences with the correct form of the verbs in brackets.

1   If you .... (*offer*) us more flexible terms, we'll consider placing a bigger order.

2   If you sorted out the reliability problem, we .... (*start*) ordering again.

3   If you .... (*deliver*) on time, we'll pay on time.

4   If you paid today, we .... (*give*) you an extra discount.

5   If he .... (*speak*) more slowly, he'd be easier to understand.

6   If you sign the contract today, we .... (*start*) work tomorrow.

7   If you .... (*order*) 2,000 or more, we'd give you a discount.

8   If you give me a better price, I .... (*place*) the order today.

SKILLS

Complete the conversation below with the phrases in the box.

> I believe   I know   I'd like   I've always met   I've got
> Let's have   let's look   Why don't

A: ....[1] I should be paid more.

B: ....[2] we come back to that later?

A: We need to talk about it now. ....[3] an excellent sales record.

B: Well, ...[4], but …

A: And ....[5] my sales targets.

B: Yes, but ....[6] at this another way. The fact is, the business is in trouble.

A: What do you mean 'in trouble'?

B: Cashflow. I'd like to pay you more, Tom, but the money isn't there. We've got serious financial problems.

A: ....[7] to make a suggestion. Why don't you tell me exactly what's going on? I had no idea the business was in trouble!

B: ....[8] a break and come back. I'll tell you everything.

12 Products

Complete the sentences below with the words in the box. Use the negative form where necessary.

best-selling economical fashionable hard-wearing high-performance high-tech long-lasting uncomfortable unreliable unsafe

1 The challenge is to design .... spectacle frames – ones that make the wearer feel 'dressed up' – that won't seem old-fashioned next season.

2 If a car model is .... and often needs repair, it will get bad reviews and people will stop buying it.

3 Shoes made for construction workers are tested extensively to make sure they're .... and will protect workers' feet from injury on site.

4 Owners complained that the driver's seat was ...., so we've modified it. The new seat can be adjusted to suit the driver.

5 The new .... motorcycle was launched at a motorsport trade event in Qatar. It's currently one of the fastest bikes consumers can buy.

6 We've solved the manufacturing problem, but we can't find an .... way to distribute the product, because it's so large and heavy.

7 Users of .... products like smart phones and tablets expect them to be well made and attractive.

8 Our .... product is so popular that we no longer need to promote it. Word-of-mouth advertising means that sales increase every month. Of course, we're very pleased.

9 When we found out the product was .... after someone was hurt, we discontinued it immediately.

10 One of the most popular features of our new MP3 player is its .... battery, which can go up to **50** hours between recharges.

Complete each gap in this text with the appropriate passive form of the verb in brackets.

The first pair of Doc Martens shoes ....[1] (*make*) in Germany in the late **1940**s, and in the early **1950**s, the first Doc Martens shoe factory ....[2] (*open*) in Munich. The shoes were so successful in Germany that in **1959**, Doc Martens ....[3] (*market*) internationally for the first time. Almost right away, the patent rights ....[4] (*buy*) by a British shoe manufacturer, and on **1** April, **1960**, the now-famous Doc Martens boot with AirWair soles ....[5] (*launch*). Practical and hard-wearing, the shoes ....[6] (*wear*) mainly by factory workers and postmen at first, but by the late **1960**s and early **1970**s, Doc Martens became a fashion accessory for teenagers – and adults – all over the world.

In **2003**, when sales were declining, Doc Martens' manufacturing ....[7] (*move*) from the UK to China and Thailand. However, in **2007**, some production returned to the UK. Today, more than **50** years after the launch of the AirWair sole, Doc Martens shoes and boots ....[8] (*love*) around the world.

Think of a product you use and like. Imagine that you work for a shop that could sell that product. Write an e-mail (100–120 words) to your manager, Sanjay Singh, describing the product and suggesting that it would be a good item to sell in your shop.

Describe the:

- material
- weight
- approximate dimensions
- colours.

State the product's uses, selling points and benefits.

Cultures 4: Preparing to do business internationally

A Match the sentence halves.

1 The most important thing when doing business with other cultures is to be more aware of

2 What is normal for you may seem strange to

3 Be sensitive, to try and notice

4 You can't hope to cover everything, but with a little bit of research, an open mind and

5 Attitudes to time are also important,

6 Status may be linked to age or connections rather than simply

7 You may try to use humour to make people feel relaxed,

8 You may want to make decisions, but in some places,

a) things and be flexible in your approach.

b) not only in relation to things like deadlines, but how long- or short-term the thinking is.

c) people arrive slowly and are often late. There may be a lot of tea drinking and chatting.

d) talent or ability.

e) but sometimes it doesn't work.

f) your own culture.

g) people from other cultures.

h) an awareness of your own culture, you can go far.

B Complete the sentences below with the words and phrases in the box.

body language   emotion   meals out   personal space
relationships   risk-taking   socialising

1 .... can be very stressful, especially if you're served 'unusual' foods.

2 You may find that people show more .... than you expect, for example interrupting and shouting. There may be a lot of noise.

3 .... can be very different. You may try to keep the conversation going, but the people you're talking to may not seem interested.

4 The idea of '............' includes how close people stand, and can also include gestures with the hands and touching.

5 '............' refers to nodding or shaking of the head, gestures with hands and facial expressions.

6 Building .... and developing trust over a period of time are much more important in certain cultures than getting instant results.

7 .... may be seen in a different way in another culture, so it may take longer than you expect to make decisions.

Negotiations

Objectives

Speaking
Can use simple language to convey the basic facts about a negotiating position.

Listening
Can recognise when speakers agree in a conversation conducted slowly and clearly.

Grammar
Can describe possible outcomes of a future action or situation.

Lesson deliverable
To participate in a business negotiation practising language for negotiating price and quantity with present or future outcomes.

Performance review
To review your own progress and performance against the lesson objectives at the end of the lesson.

A SPEAKING

Discuss the questions.

1 Do you have to do business with people or companies you don't like? Give examples.

2 What do you think this expression means? *Keep your friends close, but your enemies closer.*

3 Do you think it is useful to use small talk before a difficult negotiation? Why?/Why not?

B LISTENING

1 ◀))) BSA4.1.14 **Match the questions (1–5) to the answers (a–e). Then listen to the first part of a conversation between Pete and Miguel and check your answers.**

1 So, how was your journey?

2 And how's your job going?

3 And you? Any plans to retire?

4 So, what can I get you?

5 Can I try one before I buy?

a) It depends on the price.

b) Of course!

c) Great. When you travel, you meet interesting people.

d) Not bad, thanks.

e) Not yet!

2 ◀))) BSA4.1.15 **Listen to the second part of the conversation. Who says these things? Pete (P) or Miguel (M)?**

1 How much are the bananas?

2 They're a bargain.

3 I'll take 200 kilos at 400 pesos.

4 I usually get a discount when I order large quantities.

5 I'll give you 200 kilos of bananas for 450 pesos.

6 That's an extra ten per cent!

7 And then I had some trouble with my business partner, Harry.

8 I didn't trust that man. He never gave me eye contact.

3 **What price and quantity do Pete and Miguel agree to for each product? Do you think it's a fair deal for them both?**

4 ◀))) BSA4.1.16 **Listen to the final part of the conversation and answer the questions.**

1 Why does Pete need a partner?

2 What's on Grey Rock Island?

3 What's the final agreement between Miguel and Pete? Do you think it's a fair deal?

4 What's going to happen when Pete comes back?

Task

Pre-task: Context

You have heard there is hidden treasure on Grey Rock Island. Unfortunately, you do not have everything necessary to find the treasure on your own. You need to go into partnership to share your resources. What will you need to find the treasure?

Part 1: Preparation

Work in groups of three (A, B and C). Form pairs within your group. You have arranged to meet other treasure hunters and you need to work together to find the treasure.

- Look at your map and read your information card. Plan with your partner before you start the negotiation.
  Group A: Turn to page xi.
  Group B: Turn to page xiii and page xiv.
  Group C: Turn to page xiii.
- Prepare questions to find out what resources the others have and what their strengths and weaknesses are.
- Make sure you know what you want from the negotiation (e.g. 50 per cent of the treasure).

Look at Conditionals on page 108 and the Useful Language box on page 109.

Part 2: Negotiation stage 1

Work in groups of three (A, B and C). You meet at the local tavern. Hold the first part of the negotiation so that you get to know each other.

- Make some small talk.
- Ask questions to find out what resources the others have (e.g. only one person knows where the treasure is).
- Try to avoid any conflict at this stage.

Part 3: Consolidation

Return to your group (A, B or C) and work in pairs.

- Discuss your position and do a SWOT analysis: make notes about your strengths and weaknesses, the opportunities and threats or difficulties in the partnership(s).
- How can you work together? What do they have that you need? What do you have that they need?
- Discuss your aims for the next part of the negotiation. Will you search for the treasure with one partner or two?

Part 4: Negotiation stage 2

Hold the final stage of the negotiation. You will need to bargain and make any necessary concessions. The aim of the negotiation is to decide:

- how to get to the island
- the division of labour – who will do what?
- what resources each party brings to the deal
- how the 150,000 pesos of treasure will be divided between the parties.

Part 5: Reporting back

When you have finished, choose one person in each negotiation group to summarise your deal to the rest of the class. Make sure you include the following information:

- how to get to the island
- the division of labour
- how the treasure will be divided.

Look again at Conditionals on page 108 and the Useful Language box on page 109.

◎ **EXTRA PRACTICE: DVD CLIP AND WORKSHEET 6**

C PEER REVIEW

Find a partner from another group and give him/her feedback at the end of the task. Think about these points.

1 Did you achieve a win-win situation? Why/Why not?

2 Did everyone understand the same division of labour and share of the treasure?

3 Is it a balanced partnership? Why/Why not?

4 Did you trust the other parties? How did you deal with any conflict?

D SELF-ASSESSMENT

Look back at the lesson objectives and think about the feedback from your teacher and colleagues. Write a sentence for each of these questions.

1 Which learning objectives did you achieve?

2 What useful language did you use from Section B or from page 109?

3 What do you need to improve when negotiating price, quantity and resources?

E PROFESSIONAL DEVELOPMENT AND PERFORMANCE GOALS

Think of opportunities to practise and improve your negotiation skills in your place of work/study. What kinds of things do you negotiate in your daily life? Choose a situation for a simple price negotiation, then practise and record it with a colleague.

Objectives

Speaking

- Can make simple, direct comparisons between two people or things using common adjectives.

- Can give a short, rehearsed personal presentation and cope with limited questions.

Listening

Can follow the main points of extended discussion around them if in standard speech.

Lesson deliverable

To plan, prepare and give a presentation about a new product.

Performance review

To review your own progress and performance against the lesson objectives at the end of the lesson.

Ⓐ SPEAKING 1

1 Do you give presentations in your job? On what topics?

2 Which presentation structure do you prefer, A or B? Why?

A

Introduction: setting the context

Problem 1 – Solution 1

Problem 2 – Solution 2

Problem 3 – Solution 3

Ending

B

Introduction: setting the context

Problems

Solutions

Ending

Ⓑ LISTENING 1

1 Work in pairs. Look at the table opposite which compares two packing box designs. Try to predict the information for the new, improved box.

	Single-walled brown shipping box	New Rapid Packing Box
Assembly time	40 seconds	*under five seconds*[1]
Weight	120 g	...........[2]
Cost	£0.83–1.09 per unit	...........[3]
Recycling	customer can't return	customer ....[4]

2 🔊 BSA4.2.17 Alan Palmer works for a large packing company. Listen to him discussing the boxes with Maria, a colleague, and check your ideas from Exercise 1.

3 Work in pairs. Look at the table again and take turns to describe the Rapid Packing Box.

4 🔊 BSA4.2.18 Alan is presenting the benefits of the Rapid Packing Box to customers in Madrid. Listen to the introduction. Which structure from Exercise A2 does he say the presentation will follow?

5 🔊 BSA4.2.18 How does Alan organise the information in his introduction? Number these points in the correct order. Then listen again and check.

a) the reasons for the new box design ☐

b) the main purpose of his talk ☐

c) a comment about Madrid ☐

6 🔊 **BSA4.2.19 Listen to the rest of Alan's presentation and complete the table.**

Problems	Solutions

7 🔊 **BSA4.2.19 Listen again and complete the language Alan uses to organise the information in his presentation.**

- There are three .... [1] with the current box.
- Firstly, ...
- The .... [2] problem is ...
- The .... [3] thing we need to think about is ...
- To .... [4] these problems, we're ...
- So, ... [5], the three key benefits are ...

C SPEAKING 2

Work in pairs. Practise presenting another product.

Student A: Turn to page xiv.

Student B: Turn to page xii.

D LISTENING 2

1 🔊 **BSA4.2.20 Listen to how Alan answers customers' questions at the end of his presentation. What technique does he use?**

2 🔊 **BSA4.2.20 Work in pairs. Look at the audio script on page v. Practise asking and answering the customer's questions.**

Task

Pre-task: Preparation

1 **You are going to present a new product at an international design conference which is better than anything else on the market. Think and make notes about possible products. It could be a product you know or have heard about.**

2 **Work in pairs or groups and discuss your ideas. At then end of your discussion you should agree on one product to present. If necessary, refer to the products on pages xii and xiv.**

Part 1: Planning

In your pairs or groups, prepare a five-minute presentation. Think about these points:

Structure:
- Introducing the presentation: Welcome the audience. Explain the main purpose of the talk. Indicate the structure of the talk.
- Main part of the presentation: Decide which structure to use from Exercise A2 on page A15. Describe problems. Introduce the new product and present solutions.
- Ending: Summarise the key benefits of the new product. Invite questions.

Techniques and language:
- Use comparative adjectives and structures to describe the product (e.g. *cheaper than ...*, *the same as ...*, *less ...*).
- Use phrases to organise the information (e.g. *Firstly, ...*, *To solve this problem*, ...).
- Answer questions clearly by repeating the main information in the question.

Part 2: Presentation

Give your presentation.

Presenters: Use the structure in Part 1 to give your presentation.
Audience: Make notes on the problems and solutions while you listen. Think of a question to ask about the product.

⊙ **EXTRA PRACTICE: DVD CLIP AND WORKSHEET 7**

E PEER REVIEW

Think about another presentation. Give feedback.

1 Did the presentation successfully compare two products?

2 Did the presenter cope with questions well?

3 What good techniques/ language did the presenter use?

4 What could the presenter improve?

F SELF-ASSESSMENT

Look back at the lesson objectives and complete the sentences.

1 As the presenter, I performed well because ...

2 As the presenter, one thing I did less well was ...

3 As the audience, I made notes on .... percent of the information.

4 As the audience, I *asked/didn't ask* a good question.

G PROFESSIONAL DEVELOPMENT AND PERFORMANCE GOALS

Think about the job you do/would like to do. What problems are there to deal with? Write three sentences about how you could use the skills in this lesson to offer solutions.

Writing file

E-mails

To:	tony.randall@pricerise.aus
From:	alison.mcdermott@hasbro.com
Subject:	Cooperation agreement

Dear Tony,

To celebrate the signing of the agreement between our two companies, we would like to invite you to participate in our annual sales meeting, which is taking place this year in Honolulu, June 7–10.

Please feel free to bring another person with you as our guest if you would like to join us.

I hope this will be possible. Please let us know.

Best wishes
Alison

Alison McDermott
Product Manager
Has Bro Equipment nc.
Box 28
Chicago IL 60644

Phone: 001 312 555 4176
e-mail: alison.mcdermott@hasbro.com

This semi-formal style is similar to a standard business letter, but less formal and usually shorter. The ending is *Best wishes* rather than *Yours sincerely*. This style is best used when you are sending an e-mail to somebody who is outside your company, or whom you do not know very well. The focus is on giving or asking for information quickly.

The informal style is most suitable for e-mails within your company and for people whom you know well. The greeting is often *Hi*, *Hello* or even *How are you*? *Cheers* is a common ending, or sometimes the ending is omitted. Sometimes the writer won't use capital letters. The style is much closer to spoken than to written English.

To:	tony.randall@pricerise.aus
Subject:	Goodbye party!

Hi Tony

It's my last day in the office on Friday, and I'm giving a small goodbye party, 16.30 in room 122. Hope you can come.

CU

Jenny

Sometimes people use abbreviations if they want to save time:

CU = see you

thx = thanks

RUOK? = are you OK?

Proposals

The introduction gives useful background information for the proposal.

Introduction

Lyddisa Cosmetics is a successful brand in the European market. The company is now ready to move into other international markets.

The objectives say what you want to achieve.

Objectives

To enable the company to become an international brand, we propose an investment of €4 million over the next two years.

This section gives details about the plan and the reasons why the actions are necessary.

Options and benefits

The Board of Directors has agreed the following investment plan.

- Market research needs to be carried out in Asia and the USA to identify the best country to move into.
- Research and development is necessary because we are developing a new range of cosmetics for the international market.
- An international marketing campaign is needed to increase awareness of our brand. At the moment, the company is not known outside Europe.

Information about how much money is needed, and how it will be spent.

Cost

Market research	€350,000
Research and development	€1,400,000
Marketing campaign	€2,250,000

This shows the dates when key stages are expected to start/finish.

Schedule

Market research: This will start immediately and be completed by April 14th.

Research and development: The new product range begins development in May (to be completed by October).

Marketing campaign: Online campaign begins in December. An advertising campaign in magazines begins in January and continues until March.

This explains how progress is reported or checked.

Summary

- A presentation to the board of directors on April 19th to discuss target markets.
- Heads of department for market research, R&D and marketing to have monthly progress meetings during the project and present regular reports to the board of directors.

There is no set layout for proposals. It is a good idea to use headings to organise the information in a clear and logical order.

A proposal should answer some of these questions:
- **What** *needs to be done?*
- **Why** *did you choose the options you selected?*
- **How** *much will it cost?*
- **When** *will you start/finish?*
- **Who** *checks progress?]*

Letters

Salutation

When you know the name of the recipient:

Dear Mr/Mrs/Ms/Miss von Trotta

Note: In AmE, *Mr.*, *Mrs.* and *Ms.* include a full stop/period, e.g. *Mr. von Trotta*.

When you don't know the name of the recipient:
Dear Sir or Madam (BrE)
Dear Sir or Madam: (AmE)

Main point

It is a good idea to put the main point at the beginning of the letter. People read the first paragraph carefully, but not always everything else.

Use the pronoun *we* when writing for your company. This is more formal than *I*.

Endings (BrE)

When you know the name of the recipient:
Yours sincerely

When you don't know the name of the recipient:
Yours faithfully

Endings (AmE)

Yours truly,
Sincerely,

Sign the letter with both your first and second names. Then print your name and position under the signature.

Mr Heinrich von Trotta
Schneemans AG
Hapsburger Platz 1
80333 Munich

European *Business* Associates
26 Rue de Glion
1820 Montreux
Vaud Canton
3 May 201–

Dear Mr von Trotta

Re: Invitation to speak at next conference

On behalf of European Business Associates, we would like to invite you to be a keynote speaker at our 'Responsible Technologies for the Global Economy' conference planned for 19–21 October next year.

European Business Associates is Europe's leading business-oriented media production company. We broadcast business programmes for television and radio throughout the European Union, including *Business Tod@y* every morning from 07.00 on CNM.

We would be very pleased if you would present for us at the conference. As Europe's leading manufacturer of environmentally friendly high-tech equipment, we believe you could help many other companies move in the same direction.

We hope this invitation is of interest and look forward to hearing from you.

Yours sincerely

Brigitte Sea

Ms Brigitte Sea
Events Manager

Encs. Conference brochures
cc: Jean Thornett-Smith
    Senior Director

Common abbreviations

Re:	regarding
pp	(on behalf of) when you sign the letter for another person
Enc(s).	documents are enclosed with the letter
cc:	**copies (The names of the people who receive a copy of the letter)**

Reports

The format used here is suitable for formal reports:

- title
- executive summary
- introduction
- findings
- conclusion
- recommendation(s)

A report should be well organised, with information in a logical order. There is no set layout for a report. It will depend on:

a) the type of report

b) the company style.

The *executive summary* is a summary of the main points and conclusion of the report. It gives the reader a quick overview of the total situation.

The *introduction* shows the points that will be looked at.

The *findings* are the facts discovered.

The *conclusion* is what you think about the facts and how you interpret them.

Recommendations are practical suggestions to deal with the situation and ideas for making sure future activities run more easily.

Business Software plc

Product report

Executive summary

We have been contacted by Lenz AG, a German manufacturer of mobile phones, and asked about the possibility of a cooperation agreement. We would adapt our business software for use in their products. Tests show that their product is a very good one and popular with our target market.

Introduction

This report will look at:

- the hardware manufacturer and their equipment
- software that could be used on their mobile phones
- the advantages of working together
- recommendations for action.

Findings

1 Lenz has been developing cheap, small-scale electronic devices for 35 years. In the last five years, they have focused on more expensive mobile phones for businesspeople. These have been very successful. One in four mobile phones for the business market is a Lenz.

2 Our new 'Executive Organiser' software has a lot of attractive features for the travelling businessperson (e.g. address book, e-mailware, voice recorder, street-finder function, etc.).

3 Market research shows that there is a big interest in our products being used on machines apart from computers.

Conclusion

The two companies have products which fit well together.

Recommendation

We should have a meeting with representatives from Lenz as soon as possible to discuss a joint venture between our companies, with the aim of putting our software onto their mobile phones.

Tracy Cruickshank
Research and Development Director
19 October 201–

Investment plans

There is no set layout for an investment plan, but the information should be well organised. The various sections should have a clear heading and be in a logical order.

The rationale gives background information relevant to the reasons for the plan.

The objectives are the goals which your investment will enable you to achieve.

This section gives details of the areas you have chosen to invest in and of the benefits they are likely to provide.

Breakdown of the total amount of money invested.

The timeline shows the period of time during which you expect the various stages of the plan to be reached.

This section gives information about the mechanism you have put in place to assess the progress made.

Tressel Investment Plan

1 Rationale

In recent years, Tressel has become one of Europe's leading brands of sportswear. It is now on its way to becoming a global brand. However, in the last two years, sales have declined, causing a sharp decrease in the profits. This has been caused mainly by three factors: fierce competition in the industry bringing prices down; a fall in demand; production problems.

2 Objectives

To remedy the problems outlined above and make Tressel a more competitive business internationally, an investment of €2.5 million was proposed.

3 Options and benefits

The Board of Directors has agreed the following investment plan.

- Firstly, we need to invest in market research. This should give us a better understanding of our target customers' changing needs and desires, which can then guide product development.

- Product research and development is the second area that we need to develop, as we have relied heavily on the success of our traditional products. While these will probably continue to account for more than 50% of our turnover in the next two or three years, we will not stay ahead of the competition if we do not vary our range.

- Finally, setting up online sales should widen our customer base, increase sales, and make us more competitive.

4 Cost

Investment in market research	€900,000
Investment in research and development	€1,300,000
Setting up online sales	€300,000

5 Timeline

Market research: to be completed in three months' time, i.e. by the end of June.
R&D: ongoing process to be speeded up from July.
Online sales: website up and running by September.

6 Evaluation

The heads of the departments concerned will hand in a monthly progress report. The Board will then meet to assess the progress made in all three areas.

Notices

Notices are used to inform people about changes of plan or to give instructions or warnings.

Notices need a clear heading.

Notices are used to inform people about changes of plan or to give instructions or warnings.

The name and position of the person who wrote the notice and the date must be included.

Drucker and Drucker SOLICITORS

• STAFF NOTICE

On Thursday 29 July, there will be a staff and management meeting to discuss opening a
• New York branch of the company.

We look forward to hearing your suggestions as to how to ask for volunteers for relocation.

• Joanna Grey
Office Manager
26 July 201-

Sales leaflets

Sales leaflets must be clear, simple and easy to understand.

Provide some way for the public to contact you.

Sullivan's Summer Sun Savers

Book your Greek summer holiday before the end of April and save up to 20% on normal prices!

For full information about our range of exclusive
• holidays, call **01807 476 666** for our **FREE** brochure.

Activity file

1 Careers, Skills, Exercise F, page 11

Student A

Role play 1

1 You work at Lochlin plc. You receive a call for your colleague, Jamie Vincent. Jamie is not in the office at the moment. Take the caller's details and say that Jamie will call them back.

2 You are Jamie Vincent. Telephone the person who called about the job advertisement. Offer to send an application form. The closing date for applications is in two weeks' time.

Role play 2

1 You want to attend the computer training course which you saw in the advertisement below. Call and ask for Alex Frantzen.

2 Some time later, Alex Frantzen calls you back. You want to know more about the course and when the next one starts. Also ask about when you need to register for the course.

Career Ladder plc
The training specialists

NEW FOR THIS YEAR:
- Language training courses
- IT training courses
- Sales training courses

Need to improve your skills to get the right job?
Call Alex Frantzen on

0845 32124 3886

---

3 Selling, Skills, Exercise A, page 27

Group A: Negotiating tips

- Be friendly.
- Have clear aims.
- Tell the other side what you want.
- Listen carefully.

- Pay attention to the other side's body language.
- Don't change your plan during the meeting.
- Never be the first to make an offer.
Ask three of your own questions.

Working across cultures 3, Task, page 91

Student B

You are a senior manager based in Europe. You should:
- listen carefully to the call leader – he/she will invite you to speak;
- try not to interrupt others when they are speaking.

- Your opinion is that more conference calls are a good idea. They will save a lot of money. You like talking and have a lot to say.
- You think the technology is very good and getting better all the time. Webcams mean a call is like a real meeting. The company needs to invest in the latest technology.
- Your suggestion is to have international calls at different times each week, because of different time zones.
- Your idea is to save money by not offering any extra training courses.

4 Great ideas, Skills, Exercise E, page 41

Student C

Participant

You have the following opinions concerning The Hipster:

Selling price:	$25 approximately
Target consumer:	Professional people aged 20–40
Special offer for first purchase:	Discount of 20% for orders over 100
Advertising/promotion:	Advertisements in upmarket magazines and TV commercials

5 Stress, Vocabulary, Exercise D, page 45

Advertising executive	7.3	Diplomat	4.8	Banker	3.7
Firefighter	6.3	Hairdresser	4.3		
Sales assistant	5.7	Architect	4.0		

2 Companies, Skills, Exercise G, page 19

MIFG Data	
Head office	Milan, Italy; founded in 1978
Turnover (last year)	€286 million (increase of 10.4% compared with previous year)
Products	Makes and sells clothing, designer shoes, handbags, giftware Target consumer: 20–35-year-olds
Number of stores	28 in Italy, 35 internationally
Workforce	1,800 employees
Reasons for success	Strong brand image; competitive prices; excellent TV advertisements; endorsement by a famous, young Italian model
Mission	To create an exciting lifestyle for its customers
Advertising and promotion	Focuses on TV advertising and on full-page advertisements in fashion magazines

3 Selling, Case study, Task, page 29

Group A

You are directors of Megaluxe. These are the points you need to negotiate, together with your negotiating position on each one.

Negotiating point	Your position
Length of contract	Three years, then re-negotiate
Suite/rooms	You can offer: **Type of room** **Number** **Nights per year** **Location** Platinum Suite 1 30 All countries Gold Standard 20 100 Europe, Asia, but not Latin America* Executive Standard 15 80 All countries * not enough rooms in Latin America
Services	You can offer: Platinum Suite Breakfast, free bar and all facilities and services, except lunch and evening meals Gold Standard Breakfast + no payment for spa, pool, meeting rooms, business centre, sports facilities Executive Standard Breakfast + no payment for pool, meeting rooms, business centre. All other meals and services require extra payments.
Rates	You can offer these discounts on advertised prices: Platinum Suite 10% Gold Standard 8% Executive Standard 6%
Advertising	You want EPJS to include information about your hotels in all its advertising. You will pay 20% of the advertising costs.

11 Conflict, Skills, Exercise E, page 109

Student A

You are the marketing executive. When you joined the company, your boss promised that you would be sent on an overseas posting after one year. He also told you that you would get an excellent bonus and a luxury car for business and personal use. You are very unhappy indeed for these reasons:

- You were not selected for a recent posting to Argentina (a colleague from the Spanish subsidiary was chosen instead).
- You have been given a middle-of-the range car.
- Your bonus was 50% less than you expected.

Persuade your boss that you've been unfairly treated. Try to negotiate a better deal with him/her.

3 Selling, Skills, Exercise D, page 27

Student B

You are Chen. You want:
1 to buy an additional five deluxe four-seater cars. Negotiate on the price. Try to get a 10% discount on the order;
2 four colours for the two-seater cars: black, white, red and blue;
3 after-sales service: visits every three months from a Pulse mechanic; a training course for a local car-repair firm.

4 Great ideas, Skills, Exercise E, page 41

Student A

Chairperson

You will lead the meeting. Ask for the participants' opinions, encourage discussion and help them reach agreement. You must decide these points concerning the marketing of The Hipster.

1 its selling price
2 its target consumer
3 special offers for first purchase
4 advertising

2 Companies, Language review, Exercise C, page 18

Student A

You are the interviewer for the Sales Manager job on page 18. Ask the interviewee questions based on these prompts:
- What / do?
- Where / live?
- What / currently / work on?
- Describe / typical day
- Second interview / next week / what / do / next Tuesday afternoon?

Ask three of your own questions.

6 Entertaining, Skills, Exercise F, page 57

Student A

You are at a conference. You recognise someone you met at a conference two years ago. Introduce yourself and make small talk. Use this information to prepare for the conversation.
- You met Student B two years ago at a conference on Customer Care in Frankfurt.
- You own a small firm which sells office technology.
- It's your first day at the conference – you arrived late last night.
- You haven't seen the city yet.
- You are staying at the Metropol Hotel in the city centre (a good choice: lovely views; the restaurant and the facilities are also excellent).
- You are leaving in three days' time.
- You think the conference will be very interesting.

Add one other piece of information which you think is important.

Working across cultures 2, Exercise A, page 60

1 F (Morocco is in North Africa, but has a border with Algeria, not Egypt.)	4 T
2 T	5 F (Businesses often close on Friday.)
3 F (It is common to use French as the language of international business. Moroccans also use Arabic, English and Spanish to do business.)	6 T
	7 T
	8 T
	9 T
	10 T

Working across cultures 3, Task, page 91

Student A

You are the conference-call leader. You should:

- open the call and welcome each person by name;
- manage the agenda and decide when to move to the next point;
- invite each person to speak in turn and give their ideas and suggestions on each agenda item (make sure they give their names);
- sum up at the end and close the call.

You know the company is keen to save money, but it also wants to improve communication within the organisation.

7 New business, Skills, Exercise D, page 71

Student A

Ask and answer questions to complete the information in these charts.

example: A: *What's the population of Tokyo?*

B: *Thirty-six point seven million OR Thirty-six million, seven hundred thousand.*

Biggest cities (population in millions)		% of households with Internet (2008)			Oldest populations (% aged over 60)			Cars per 1,000 people		
1	Tokyo, Japan	....	1	South Korea	94.3	1	Japan	....	1	Iceland	....
2	Delhi, India	22.1	2	Iceland	87.7	2	Italy	26.7	2	Luxembourg	664
3	São Paulo, Brazil	....	3	Netherlands	....	3	Germany	....	3	New Zealand	656
4	Mumbai, India	20.0	4	Sweden	....	4	Sweden	25.0	4	Italy	....
5	Mexico City, Mexico	19.5	5	Norway	....	5	Finland	24.7	5	Brunei	608
6	New York, US	....	6	Denmark	81.9	6	Bulgaria	....	6	Malta	....

All figures taken from *The Economist: Pocket world in figures*, 2011 edition (Profile 2010)

11 Conflict, Starting up, page 104

Give yourself these marks.

	a)	b)	c)	d)
1	a) 2	b) 3	c) 1	d) 4
2	a) 2	b) 3	c) 1	d) 4
3	a) 3	b) 4	c) 2	d) 1
4	a) 4	b) 2	c) 3	d) 1
5	a) 4	b) 2	c) 1	d) 3
6	a) 4	b) 3	c) 1	d) 2

Add up your score.

6–11 You need to improve your conflict-management skills.

12–17 You are quite good at conflict management in certain situations.

18–22 You are good at conflict management in most situations.

23–24 You are excellent at conflict management. You should be working for the United Nations.

Working across cultures 2, Task 1, page 60

Suggested errors

1 Andrew Morgan should have chosen a pastry, even if he wasn't hungry.

2 Before the meeting, Andrew should have learned something about Karim Bensour's business. Karim was disappointed at Andrew's lack of local business knowledge.

3 Distributing through department stores is not the right strategy, because there are few department stores outside the large cities in Morocco. The company should start by using a local importer, as the distribution system is complicated in Morocco.

4 Andrew did not ask Karim why his company's approach would not work in Morocco. With better information, he might have changed the company's sales strategy.

5 Andrew will probably need more time to achieve his company's aims in Morocco. Decision-making and contact-building may take more time in Morocco compared to some other countries. Also, informal agreements are just as common as written contracts.

6 Andrew's business card should have had Arabic, French and Spanish translations on the back.

11 Conflict, Case study, Task, page 111

Student D

Staff Representative

You strongly believe that the Board of Directors should not recommend acceptance of the offer. These are some of your reasons:

- There will be job losses. Big companies always get rid of staff when they buy another company.
- UCC will probably close down at least one of the company's packaging plants to reduce costs.
- The present Chief Executive will have no power if UCC buys the company. The CE is popular with all the staff.
- The company will lose its family atmosphere. In addition, UCC will probably force all staff to learn English.

Add any other arguments you can think of.

11 Conflict, Case study, Task, page 111

Student A

Chief Executive (Herman & Corrie Teas)

Ask everyone for their opinion and encourage an open, lively discussion. Take a vote at the end of the meeting.

You are undecided whether to accept the offer or not. You are worried about your future role in the company. Would the new owners keep you as Chief Executive? If they do keep you, would you have any real responsibility and decision-making power?

Listen to all the arguments, then vote for or against at the end of the meeting.

1 Careers, Skills, Exercise F, page 11

Student B

Role play 1

1 You want to apply for the job in the advertisement below. Call Lochlin plc and ask for Jamie Vincent.

2 Some time later, Jamie Vincent calls you back. Ask about how you can apply for the job. You also want to know when the closing date for applications is.

Role play 2

1 You work for Career Ladder plc. You receive a call for your colleague, Alex Frantzen. Alex is not available at the moment. Take the caller's details and say Alex will call them back.

2 You are Alex Frantzen. Telephone the person who called about the training courses. Offer to send an information pack. The next course begins at the start of next month (the 2nd). Participants need to register at the latest one week before the start of the course.

Lochlin plc

Sales representatives

Exciting new career opportunities for the right people. Have you got the qualities we need?

Call Jamie Vincent on

020 7946 4021 for more information.

3 Selling, Reading, Exercise B, page 24

The top answer was *honesty*.

2 Companies, Language review, Exercise C, page 18

Student B

You are an interviewee for the Sales Manager job on page 18. Answer the interviewer's questions based on these prompts:
- Sales Manager / small mobile-phone company
- At moment / live / Paris
- Currently / design sales manual / new staff
- Arrive office eight / usually check e-mails first / brief sales staff / deal with difficult customers
- Next Tuesday afternoon / work / but take time off

Make up the answers to any other questions.

3 Selling, Skills, Exercise A, page 27

Group B: Negotiating tips
- Be strong and try to win.
- Prepare carefully before you negotiate.
- Ask a lot of questions.
- Have a lot of options.
- Summarise often the points you agree on.
- Change your strategy during the negotiation if necessary.
- Never show any emotion.

4 Great ideas, Skills, Exercise E, page 41

Student D

Participant

You have the following opinions concerning The Hipster:

Selling price:	$15 approximately
Target consumer:	All age groups from 20 years old upwards
Special offer for first purchase:	5% discount for orders over 50
Advertising and promotion:	Advertisements in national and regional newpapers/magazines

3   Selling, Reading, Exercise C, page 24

How to master the art of selling

1   Selling is an area of business that many people dislike, whether it's telemarketing or face-to-face selling. It takes quite a bit of skill to become an effective salesperson, but through developing a particular mindset and following some important advice, you can begin to master it.

2   One of the most important attributes to have when selling is confidence – you must sound and appear confident. Remember that many of the most confident people aren't inwardly confident, yet they can show confidence on the outside.

3   There's nothing worse than a salesperson who doesn't fully understand what they are selling. Make sure that you know your product, business and industry inside out.

4   Research suggests that you have less than 30 seconds to interact with someone before they form an opinion of you. For face-to-face selling, having a professional appearance is vital. For selling over the phone, the first 15 seconds are vital, so make sure you know what you intend to say. Getting words mixed up or sounding hesitant will result in a bad first impression

5   Rejection will happen, but don't take it personally. Too many people focus on this rejection and often end up making contact with fewer prospects than they otherwise would. You will receive setbacks, but the more people you call, the more leads or sales you'll make. It's a numbers game – hit the high numbers, and success will almost always follow.

6   Don't think that you have to make a sale the first time that you speak to a prospect. Many telemarketers know this and rarely attempt to generate sales, but instead focus on leads. A lead may be anything from obtaining permission to e-mail over some more information to organising a meeting in person.

7   Never call a prospect or attend a sales meeting without knowing how far you'll negotiate. You should know your starting point, the point which you won't drop below and a mid-way point which you'll aim for.

8   Finally, seasoned sellers talk of adopting a 'sales mindset'. Don't approach selling with dread, as an area where rejections are commonplace. Selling should be a challenge. You should enjoy closing deals, making sales, and each rejection should be looked on as a result – you're one step closer to meeting your next customer.

adapted from www.marketingminefield.co.uk

Working across cultures 3, Task, page 91

Student C

You are a senior manager based in Australia. You should:
- listen carefully to the call leader – he/she will invite you to speak;
- try not to interrupt others when they are speaking.

- Your opinion is that more conference calls are a bad idea. The technology often does not work well, and this wastes time.
- You often find it difficult to be on time. You have to leave early on Fridays and you don't work on Mondays.
- Your suggestion is to perhaps have the calls at different times, but you are not sure.
- Your view is that some extra training could be a good idea, although you know it can be expensive.

11   Conflict, Case study, Task, page 111

Student B

Shareholder A

You strongly believe that the Board of Directors should recommend acceptance of the offer. These are some of your reasons:
- UCC will provide money to finance new products and entry into new markets, such as China, Russia and the Middle East.
- Herman & Corrie Teas will benefit from UCC's advanced production techniques and efficient sales teams.
- UCC will encourage innovation, which Herman & Corrie Teas needs in order to become more competitive.
- UCC has offered to pay a very good price for your shares. You will make a big profit by selling them.

Add any other arguments you can think of.

3 Selling, Case study, Task, page 29

Group B

You are directors of EPJS. These are the points you need to negotiate, together with your negotiating position on each one.

Negotiating point	Your position
Length of contract	One year, then re-negotiate if successful, e.g. *We'd like a one-year contract. After that, a longer period if we're happy.*
Suite/rooms	You want to reserve for your clients: <table><tr><th>Type of room</th><th>Number</th><th>Nights per year</th><th>Location</th></tr><tr><td>Platinum Suite</td><td>1</td><td>20</td><td>All countries</td></tr><tr><td>Gold Standard</td><td>10</td><td>50</td><td>All countries</td></tr><tr><td>Executive Standard</td><td>20</td><td>100</td><td>All countries</td></tr></table>
Services	You want: Platinum Suite — All meals + hotel facilities/services Gold Standard — Breakfast + all hotel facilities Executive Standard — Breakfast + pool, spa, business centre
Rates	For each rate, you want: Platinum Suite — 20% discount on the advertised rate Gold Standard — 10% discount on the advertised rate Executive Standard — 5% discount on the advertised rate
Advertising	You will include information about Megaluxe hotels in all your advertising. Megaluxe must pay 40% of the total advertising budget.

3 Selling, Skills, Exercise D, page 27

Student A

You are Martin. You want to:
1 sell Chen some deluxe four-seater models of your cars.
  Price: €20,000; discount of 5% for first order
2 offer only two colours for your two-seater cars: white and black.
  Extra colours will raise the price by 5%.
3 send a Pulse mechanic to China every six months to service the cars.
  You can train local mechanics at a cost of €200 per hour.

11 Conflict, Case study, Task, page 111

Student E

Senior Manager

You strongly believe that the Board of Directors should recommend acceptance of the offer.
These are some of your reasons:
• There will be more opportunities for promotion if UCC buys the company.
• Herman & Corrie Teas needs a lot more investment to grow and enter new markets, such as China and Russia. These have great sales potential.
• The company needs to be more innovative to compete with rival firms.
• The company needs new management, new ideas, more energy and to be more risk-taking.
Add any other arguments you can think of.

4 Great ideas, Skills, Exercise E, page 41

Student B

Participant

You have the following opinions concerning The Hipster:

Selling price:	$10 approximately
Target consumer:	Young people aged 15–25
Special offer for first purchase:	Discount of 10% for orders over 20
Advertising/promotion:	Advertisements in magazines aimed at young people

8 Marketing, Skills, Exercise H, page 79

Student B

You are the European Sales Manager. You want to do the following when you call the Marketing Director.

1 Tell the Marketing Director when and where the focus group takes place. Details are as follows:

Location: Commercial Institute
20 Koninginnelaan 2482 BN
Amsterdam

Date/Time: Thursday, 25 August at 10.00 a.m.

2 Note down the names of two people whom the Marketing Director wishes to invite to the focus group.

3 Answer his or her questions about last month's sales results in France. Details are as follows:

Total sales: €5.6 million

Sales were 9% higher than the same period last year.

6 Entertaining, Skills, Exercise F, page 57

Student B

You are at a conference. You recognise someone you met at a conference two years ago. Introduce yourself and make small talk. Use this information to prepare for the conversation.

- You met Student A two years ago at a conference on Customer Care in Frankfurt.
- You are the Sales Manager for a mobile-phone company.
- You have been at the conference for three days.
- You have visited the city (beautiful old castle, interesting museum, excellent restaurants, but very expensive).
- You are staying at a small hotel outside the city (a bad choice: room is small and noisy, and too far from the centre of the city).
- You are leaving tomorrow.
- The conference is boring – the speakers talk too much and use too many PowerPoint slides.

Add one other piece of information which you think is important.

11 Conflict, Skills, Exercise E, page 109

Student B

You are the General Manager. Your company is going through a difficult financial period. You have been told to keep costs as low as possible. You know that the executive is very unhappy for these reasons:

- They were not chosen for an overseas posting in Argentina.
- They have to use a middle-of-the-range car.
- They received an end-of-the-year bonus which was below their expectations.

Persuade the executive that they have been treated fairly. These are your reasons for the decisions:

- The executive was not fluent enough in Spanish for the overseas posting.
- They need more training in teamwork skills before being posted overseas.
- Only senior executives are given top-of-the-range cars for work and private use.
- All members of staff received small bonuses because of the financial situation.

Working across cultures 3, Task, page 91

Student D

You are a senior manager based in Latin America. You should:

- listen carefully to the call leader – he/she will invite you to speak;
- try not to interrupt others when they are speaking.

- Your view is that you are not sure more conference calls are a good idea. Your experience of conference calls is mixed (some good/some bad).
- Your opinion is that the technology is difficult to use. You prefer e-mail or face-to-face meetings.
- Your idea is that calls should be at the same time of day each week or month, so people do not forget. You prefer the morning.
- Your suggestion is to have a number of training courses for all staff before increasing the number of conference calls.

7 New business, Skills, Exercise D, page 71

Student B

Ask and answer questions to complete the information in these charts.

example: B: *What's the population of Delhi?*

A: *Twenty-two point one million OR Twenty-two million, one hundred thousand.*

Biggest cities (population in millions)			% of households with Internet (2008)			Oldest populations (% aged over 60)			Cars per 1,000 people		
1	Tokyo, Japan	36.7	1	South Korea	....	1	Japan	30.5	1	Iceland	669
2	Delhi, India	....	2	Iceland	....	2	Italy	....	2	Luxembourg	....
3	São Paulo, Brazil	20.3	3	Netherlands	86.1	3	Germany	26.0	3	New Zealand	....
4	Mumbai, India	....	4	Sweden	84.4	4	Sweden	....	4	Italy	609
5	Mexico City, Mexico	....	5	Norway	84.0	5	Finland	....	5	Brunei	....
6	New York, US	19.4	6	Denmark	....	6	Bulgaria	24.5	6	Malta	559

All figures taken from *The Economist: Pocket world in figures,* 2011 edition (Profile 2010)

8 Marketing, Skills, Exercise H, page 79

Student A

You are the Marketing Director. You want to do the following when the European Sales Manager calls you.

1 Note down when and where the focus group meeting will take place.
2 Suggest that these people attend the meeting:
   • Elisavet Efstathiou
     Tel: (812) 275 6381
     E-mail: e.efstat@nimarkt.com
     She is a marketing consultant based in Athens, Greece.

   • Katja Buchholtz
     Tel: (361) 339 4032
     She is Head Buyer for a department store in Munich, Germany.
3 Ask the European Sales Manager about last month's sales results in France.
   Did they increase or decrease?

11 Conflict, Case study, Task, page 111

Student C

Shareholder B

You strongly believe that the Board of Directors should not recommend acceptance of the offer. These are some of your reasons:

• Herman & Corrie Teas will lose its identity and principles if UCC buys it. UCC will only be interested in making money.
• UCC will change the management. This will not please the staff, who like the family atmosphere in the company.
• Many customers will no longer buy Herman & Corrie's products when they find out that a large multinational now owns and manages the company.
• A small, privately owned tea company, FTC, contacted you recently. They would like to merge with your company. They have the same values and principles as Herman & Corrie Teas.

Add any other arguments you can think of.

Grammar reference

1 Modals 1: ability, requests and offers

Form

+ I/You/He/She/It/We/They **can** go.
− I/You/He/She/It/We/They **can't** (= **cannot**) go.
? **Can** I/you/he/she/it/we/they/go?

Uses

1 We use *can* and *could* to:
- *make requests.*

  Can *I make a phone call?*
  Could *you tell me the time, please? (a little more formal)*

- *give or refuse permission.*

  You **can** *use my mobile phone.*
  You **can't** *go in there. It's private.*

- *make an offer.*

  Can *I help you?*
  I **can** *take you to the station if you like.*

- *describe ability.*

  Paola **can** *speak Chinese.*
  When he was younger, he **could** *(= was able to) run a marathon in under three hours.*

- *say that something is possible or impossible.*

  You **can** *make a lot of money if you work hard.*
  I **can't** *get through to them. Their phone's always engaged.*

2 *We also use could to refer to future possibilities.*

   I think we **could** *increase our market share in the long term.*

3 *We use would to:*
- *make requests.*

  Would *you open the door for me, please?*

- *make offers.*

  Would *you like a glass of water?*

- *describe imaginary situations.*

  I **would** *buy a Ferrari if I had enough money.*

2 Present simple and present continuous

Present simple
Form

+ I/You/We/They **work**.
  He/She/It **works**.
− I/You/We/They **don't** (= **do not**) **work**.
  He/She/It **doesn't** (= **does not**) **work**.
? **Do** I/you/we/they **work**?
  Does he/she/it **work**?

Uses

1 We use the present simple to:
   - give factual information about permanent activities.
     *Valentino **makes** luxury chocolates.*
   - describe a state that doesn't change.
     *He **looks** like his father.*
     *Nothing **succeeds** like success.*
   - talk about routine activities, repeated actions or habits. This use of the present simple is associated with adverbs of frequency.
     *We usually **have** our weekly sales meeting on Mondays.*
     *I often **travel** abroad on business.*
     *We sometimes **get** complaints, but not many.*

2 There are verbs that we normally use only in simple tenses, not in continuous tenses.
   For example *believe, belong, depend, know, like, love, mean, own, remember, understand, want*, etc.

   These verbs describe states, not actions.

   It depends on the exchange rate (NOT *It is depending …)
   The premises don't belong to them. (NOT *The premises aren't belonging …)
   What do they want? (NOT *What are they wanting …)

Present continuous
Form

+ I **am working**.
  He/She/It **is working**.
  You/We/They **are working**.
− I **am not working**.
  He/She/It **isn't** (= **is not**) **working**.
  You/We/They **aren't** (= **are not**) **working**.
? **Am** I **working**?
  Is he/she/it **working**?
  Are you/we/they **working**?

Uses

We use the present continuous to:
- describe activities in progress at the moment of speaking.
  *She's **talking** to him on the phone right now.*
- describe temporary situations.
  *The delegation **is staying** at the Hilton until Friday.*
- refer to future arrangements.
  *He's **starting** a new job next week.*
- describe changing situations.
  *We're **developing** a new marketing strategy.*

3 Modals 2: *must, need to, have to, should*

1 We often use *must*, *need to* and *has/have to* to say that something is compulsory or necessary.

*We **must** be patient when our goals are for the long term.*
*Companies **have to** advertise to let consumers know they exist.*
*I **need to** have the figures before next Monday's meeting.*

2 We use *had to* to refer to a past obligation.

*When I lived in Tokyo, I **had to** learn Japanese.*

3 We use *should* and *shouldn't* to give advice or to suggest the right course of action.

*A CV **should** be printed on good-quality notepaper.*
*It **shouldn't** be more than two pages long.*

Should often follows the verbs *suggest* and *think*.
*I suggest/think we **should** aim at the top end of the market.*

4 We use *should* to say that something is likely in the future.

*Interest rates **should** come down soon – that's what the economists are predicting.*

5 We use *don't have to* and *don't need to* if something is not necessary.

*You **don't have to** queue up when you buy online.*
*If you buy now, you **don't need to** pay anything until next year.*

6 We use *mustn't / must not* when things are forbidden or against the law.

*Drivers **must not** park their vehicles by a traffic light.*

Compare the uses of *mustn't* and *don't have to* in this sentence.

*In many companies, employees **mustn't** wear jeans, but they **don't have to** dress formally.*

7 We use *must* to say we are sure of something because of what we know.

*He **must** be very rich – he drives a Ferrari.*

8 *Have to* is more common in questions than *must*.

*Do we **have to** make a decision now?*

4 Past simple and past continuous

Past simple
Form

+ I/You/He/She/It/We/They **worked**.
− I/You/He/She/It/We/They **didn't** (= **did not**) **work**.
? **Did** I/you/he/she/it/we/they **work**?

Uses

1 We use the past simple to refer to states and actions which finished in the past.
   *He **left** for Australia yesterday.*
   *When I was young, I **wanted** to be a pilot.*

2 The action can be short, long or repeated.
   *They **took** a taxi to get here.*
   *The flight **lasted** 10 hours.*
   *I **took** the same train every day.*

3 Remember that some verbs are normally used in simple tenses only (see Section 2, page 140).
   *They **owned** five shops in Madrid alone.* (NOT *They were owning ...*)
   *We **didn't know** the market forecast.* (NOT *We weren't knowing ...*)
   ***Did** our guests **like** the food?* (NOT *Were our guests liking ...*)

Past continuous
Form

+ I/He/She/It **was working**.
   You/We/They **were working**.
− I/He/She/It **wasn't** (= **was not**) **working**.
   You/We/They **weren't** (= **were not**) **working**.
? **Was** I/he/she/it **working**?
   Were you/we/they **working**?

Uses

We use the past continuous to:
• talk about actions that were not yet finished and continued over a period of time.
   *At that time, we **were** still **trying** to solve our recruitment problem.*
   Sometimes this period of time includes another event which is completed.
   *She **had** an accident while she **was driving** to work.*
   *I **was talking** to him on the phone when I **heard** an explosion.*
• refer to situations that were changing over time in the past.
   *During the 1980s, many of the older industries **were closing** down.*
   *At that time, we **were coming** out of recession and things **were improving**.*

5 | Past simple and present perfect

Present perfect
Form

+   I/You/We/They **have worked**.
    He/She/It **has worked**.

–   I/You/He/She/It/We/They **haven't** (= **have not**) **worked**.

?   **Have** I/you/we/they **worked**?
    Has he/she/it **worked**?

Uses

1   We use the present perfect to:
- talk about actions that continue from the past to the present.

  We **have been** in this business for over 50 years. (= We are still in business.)
- talk about past events that have an impact in the present.

  Recently, profits **have fallen** sharply because of strong competition.
  Genova **has had** to cut costs by reorganising the workforce.
- talk about life experiences.

  He**'s worked** in a number of different firms.
  I**'ve been** to London on many occasions.
  She**'s** never **had to** lead a team before. (= in her life up to now)

  Because the time reference includes the present, we use time expressions that refer to both present and past.

  So far, we **have captured** 30% of the market.
  This week, I**'ve written** three long reports.
  Over the last few days, I **have had** too much work to do.

Present perfect versus past simple

1   We use the past simple for completed actions that happened in the past.

    Andrew Mason **set up** Groupon in 2008.

2   Because the time reference is past, we use time expressions that refer to finished past time.

    Last year, we **increased** turnover by 15%.
    Five years ago, we **didn't have** an overseas subsidiary.
    She **joined** the company **three months ago**.

3   The decision to use the past simple or present perfect depends on how we see the event. If we see it as related to the present, we use the present perfect. If we see it as completed and in the past, we use the past simple.

    I**'ve known** Bill for many years. (= We are still in touch.)
    I **knew** Bill when I was at college. (= We don't keep in touch.)

6 Multiword verbs

1 A multiword verb is a combination of a verb and one or two particles (e.g. *at*, *away*, *down*, *in*, *on*, *up*).

2 Types of multiword verbs
- without an object
  *The photocopier has **broken down**.*
  *Something has **come up**.* (= happened)
- with an object – separable
  The direct object can come after the verb or before the particle.
  *Could you **turn on** the coffee machine?* | *Could you **turn** the coffee machine **on**?*
- with an object – inseparable
  *The director cannot **do without** his secretary.* (NOT *The director cannot do his secretary without.*)

3 In many cases, the multiword verb is more informal than its synonym.
  *How did you **find out**?* (= discover the information)
  *We **set off** early.* (= departed)

4 Many multiword verbs are idiomatic; in other words, their meaning is difficult to interpret.
  However, it can help if you understand the meanings of the particles. For example:
- ***away*** (creating distance)
  *I'm **going away** next week.*
  *Don't **run away**. I need to talk to you.*
- ***on*** (continuing)
  ***Carry on** the good work!*
  *The meeting **went on** until seven o'clock.*
- ***over*** (considering)
  *I need time to **think** it **over**.*
  *Come and see me, and we'll **talk** it **over**.*
- ***up*** (completing)
  *Some urgent matters need **clearing up**.*
  ***Drink up**. We've got to go.*

(For further information, consult the *Longman Dictionary of Phrasal Verbs*.)

7 Time clauses

1 We use time clauses to provide information about actions and events in the past, present and future.

*Do you remember **when** you had your first interview?* (past time)
***When** your customers are unhappy, they'll usually tell at least 20 other people.* (true all the time)
***When** I find the missing documents, I'll bring them to you.* (future time)

2 We use a present tense, not *will*, to refer to future time in a time clause.

***Until** inflation **is** under control, planning will be difficult.* (NOT *will be under control*)
***Once** we **finish** the project, we'll have more time.* (NOT *will finish the project*)
*Can you look at this **before** you **leave**?* (NOT *will leave*)
*The share price will rise **as soon as** we **announce** the merger.*
*I'll see you **when** the meeting **finishes**.*

3 Note that:

- a present perfect in a time clause refers to a future situation.

  *I'll get back to you **as soon as** we **have decided** what to do.*
  *She'll write to you **after/when** she**'s spoken** to her boss.*
  *We won't know the results **until** we**'ve received** all the sales reports.*

- *while* means 'during the time that' or 'at the same time as'.

  *I like to listen to music **while** I'm working.*
  *I was working late at the office **while** she was out socialising.*
  ***While** I was in Italy, I went to see Alessandro.*

for/since/during

1 We use both *for* and *during* with periods of time, but *the* is usually used after *during*.

*I haven't seen her **for** a month.* (NOT *during a month*)
*What are you planning to do **during** the vacation?*
*He fell asleep **during** the meeting.*

2 We use *since* with points in time.

*The company has expanded fast **since** it was founded.*
***Since** Martin joined the company two years ago, profits have risen dramatically.*

8 Questions

Yes/No questions

In questions that can be answered with either *yes* or *no*, we put an auxiliary verb before the subject.

Are you coming?	Yes, I am. / No, I'm not.
Can you drive a truck?	Yes, I can. / No, I can't.
Do you know his name?	Yes, I do. / No, I don't.
Did you arrive on time?	Yes, I did. / No, I didn't.
Have you heard the news?	Yes, I have. / No, I haven't.
Will you have time?	Yes, I will. / No, I won't.

Open questions

1 We use question words such as *what, who, where, when, why* and *how* to ask for more information. The question word comes before the auxiliary verb.

To ask about:	We use:
a thing	**What** is the brand name?
	Which door is it?
a person	**Who** is the Chief Executive?
a place	**Where** do you come from?
a reason	**Why** are you putting up your prices?
a moment in time	**What time** did the meeting start?
	When did the goods arrive?
a period of time	**How long** did you stay in Beijing?
the number of times	**How many times** have you been to China?
quantity (with plural nouns)	**How many** cases did you order?
quantity (with uncountable nouns)	**How much** money do you have on you?
the way you do something	**How** do you manage to read so quickly?

2 We use *what* if there are many possible answers and *which* if there are fewer possible answers.

What is their policy?
Which of these cases is yours?

3 If *who* or *what* is the subject of the sentence, the word order is the same as in a statement.

Who looks after the travel arrangements?
What happens when things go wrong?

4 If *who, what* or *which* asks about the object, we put the auxiliary before the subject.

Who shall I get in touch with?
What number did you ring?
Which restaurant have you chosen?

5 The question word *how* can be followed by an adjective or adverb.

How big is the warehouse?
How good is your Spanish?
How well do you speak Spanish?
How far is the hotel from here?
How often do you travel abroad?

9 Talking about future plans

1 We use the present continuous for future arrangements.

   *What **are** you **doing** next weekend?*
   *We**'re visiting** our suppliers next week.*

2 We also use *going to* for arrangements, plans and intentions.

   *What **are** you **going to** do next weekend?*
   *We**'re going to** visit our suppliers next week.*
   *I**'m going to** talk to you today about my company.*

3 But we do NOT use the present continuous to make predictions for the future. Compare:

   *The transport strike **is going to cause** a real problem.* (= This is anticipated for the future.)
   *The transport strike **is causing** a real problem.* (= The strike has started and the effects are present.)

4 Some verbs, like *anticipate, expect, look forward to, hope* and *plan*, automatically refer to the future. These verbs can be used in either the simple or continuous form.

   *I **look forward to** seeing you soon.*
   *I **am looking forward to** seeing you soon.*
   *We **hope** to do better next year.*
   *We **are hoping** to do better next year.*
   *We **plan** to attract more foreign investment.*
   *We **are planning** to attract more foreign investment.*

Other future forms

1 *Will* is very often used for predictions.

   *The forecast says that tomorrow **will** be warm and sunny.*
   *I don't think they **will** complain.*
   *She **won't** like what you've written about her.*

2 We use the contracted form *'ll* to make spontaneous offers.

   *I**'ll** help you write the report if you like.*
   *(= I'll help you **now**, or when you want me to help you.)*

10 Reported speech

We use reporting verbs like *say, tell* and *ask* to report what other people say.

1 Reporting words just said

In this case, the situation is still present.

*The boss **says** she **wants** to see you immediately.*

2 Reporting words said in the past

- Words that are said in one place at one particular time may be reported in another place at another time. Because of the change in time, there may be a change of tense or modal auxiliary. A different pronoun is used to suit the context.

Actual words	Reported words
'We are not going to panic.'	*He said they were not going to panic.*
'I left my briefcase at work.'	*She said she (had) left her briefcase at work.*
'I've already spoken to her.'	*He said he had already spoken to her.*
'We won't know before Friday.'	*She said they wouldn't know before Friday.*
'I can't give you a lower price.'	*He said he couldn't give me a lower price.*

- *Would, could* and *should* do not change.

'I would tell you if I could.'	*She said she would tell me if she could.*
'You should be more careful.'	*He said I should be more careful.*

3 *Say* versus *tell*

- We do not usually use a person object (*me, us*, etc.) after *say*.

  *She **said** she would come later.* (NOT **She said me ...*)

- But after *tell*, we indicate who receives the information.

  *She **told me** she would come later.* (NOT **She told she would ...*)

- We can use *that* directly after *say*, but not directly after *tell*.

  *He **said that** he understood the reason.* (NOT **He told that ...*)

- *Tell* also means 'to inform' or 'to instruct'.

  *He **told** me he was interested in my proposal.*

  *She **told** me to hurry up.*

4 Reporting questions

We use *ask* (with or without an object) to report questions.

Note the word order in the reported question: (1) question word (2) subject (3) verb.

Actual words	Reported words
• in open questions *(When / Why / How / What / etc.)*:	
'When do you want to take your vacation?'	*He asked (him) when he wanted to take his vacation.*
'How long is the conference?'	*He asked (her) how long the conference was.*
• in *yes / no* questions:	
'Do you want to take your vacation in July or August?'	*He asked (him) if / whether he wanted to take his vacation in July or August.*
'Will you be able to attend the conference?'	*He asked (her) if / whether she would be able to attend the conference.*

11 Conditionals

First conditional

(*if* + present simple, *will* + infinitive without *to*)

In these two examples, the speaker feels that there is a real possibility that they will increase their order and that their visitors will be late.

*If we **increase** our order, they'**ll give** us a higher discount.*

*If our visitors **are** late, we **won't be able to** take them to the theatre.*

Second conditional

(*if* + past simple, *would* + infinitive without *to*)

1   When the situation is less likely to happen or be accepted, we use the second conditional.

   *If we **had** more money to spend, we **would be** interested.* (but we don't)

2   Sometimes the condition is logically impossible to fulfil.

   *If he was the Queen of England, he'**d sell** Buckingham Palace.*

Points to remember

1   The position of the *if* clause and the main clause can be changed.

   *I would lend him some money **if** he needed it.*
   If he needed it, I would lend him some money.

2   We cannot use *will* or *would* in the *if* clause.

   *If I ~~will~~ go to Japan, I'll probably go to a tea ceremony.

        knew
   *If I ~~would know~~ the answer, I would tell you.

3   It is possible to use *If I were* rather than *If I was*, especially when giving advice.

   *If I **were** the Minister of Finance, I'd reduce taxation.*
   *If I **were** you, I'd buy those shares now.*

4   Instead of *would*, we can use *might* or *could*, depending on the meaning.

   *If he relaxed more, he **might** enjoy this new challenge.*
   *If he wanted to, he **could** become CEO.*

12 Passives

Form

+ It's **done**. It's **being done**. It **was done**. It **has been done**. It **will be done**.

– It's **not done**. It's **not being done**. It **wasn't done**. It **hasn't been done**. It **won't be done**.

? **Is** it **done**? **Is** it **being done**? **Was** it **done**? **Has** it **been done**? **Will** it **be done**?

Passives can also be formed with modal verbs.

Can it **be done**?

It **can't be done**.

It **should be done**.

It **would be done**.

It **might be done**.

Uses

1 We choose a passive structure when we focus on the action itself rather than who performs the action.

    *Tea **is grown** in Sri Lanka.*
    *Our quality procedures **are** strictly **monitored**.*
    *The new machine **has been** installed.*

2 We can use *by* to mention who performs an action.

    *All her clothes are designed **by** Armani.*
    *The first computer was invented **by** Alan Turing.*
    *G-Shock is a brand of watch which is manufactured **by** Casio.*

3 We often use the passive to describe a process, system or procedure, as in the extract below.

    Naming a new product

    *Before a product **is launched**, focus groups **are set up** and a name **is chosen**. Potential consumers **are asked** to give their impressions, and these **are matched** against the desired brand image. Once the name **has been decided**, it **must be registered** so that it **cannot be used** by other manufacturers.*

4 We often use the passive in impersonal constructions beginning with *it*. These constructions are frequently found in reports and the minutes of meetings.

    *It **was agreed** that the budget should be increased.*
    *It **was decided** to implement the new policy immediately. (or It **was decided** that the new policy should be implemented immediately.)*
    *It **was felt** that an early decision had to be made.*

Audio scripts

UNIT 1 CAREERS

CD1 TRACK 1

PERSON 1

Well, for a long time, I think I was very ambitious – you know, wanting to get to the top and to earn as much money as possible. But then I decided that other things are more important. I recently decided to take a career break, so I'm travelling for a year and doing some unpaid work. I want to see something of the world and look at my options. Everyone at work says it's not a very good career move, but it's what I want to do. All my friends think I'm mad, but I think I have time. I'm only in my thirties, after all.

CD1 TRACK 2

PERSON 2

It's been very difficult, I think – to get a start without much experience, you know. It's the chicken-and-egg situation – you can't get a job without experience, and you can't get experience without a job. The career opportunities everybody talks about are not really happening for me. Maybe the problem is that I don't really have a career path in mind. I'm still not really sure what I want to do in the long term. I've done different things, but they don't seem to lead anywhere. I don't really know where I'm going. Studying at university made a lot of sense at the time, but now I'm not so sure. I don't feel very prepared for my working life.

CD1 TRACK 3

PERSON 3

Well, I suppose I always had a career plan, and for me it seems to have been successful. I first worked for the company part time when I was a student, part of a work placement, which I organised myself. I always wanted to work in this area and only really for one company. They offered me a full-time job, and then I worked my way up the career ladder from trader to associate to manager to director. I'm now a partner. Maybe it's a bit unusual these days to only work for one company, but for me it's all I wanted. It's only been 17 years, but I'm going to take early retirement next year and buy a boat.

CD1 TRACK 4 (I = Interviewer, MF = Melissa Foux)

I: Can you tell us about your job?

MF: I'm currently the Finance Director of CSC Media Limited, Chart Show Channels Group, which is the largest independent television business in the UK. We have a mixture of 16 channels – some are music, some are children's and some are movie channels.

I: What was your previous job?

MF: I was previously the Finance Director of a chocolate-pudding business, so very different from television. But, um, the good thing about being in the finance world is that it's relatively easy to move from sector to sector. The basic skills that you need are, are similar in each case.

CD1 TRACK 5 (I = Interviewer, MF = Melissa Foux)

I: How did you get into finance as a career?

MF: When I was a student, although I was studying chemistry, I thought I would like to do something, er, different afterwards, and I actually did a summer internship with one of the big accountancy firms, um, which was, which was an excellent way to get an understanding of what the job would be like. I started off as an auditor, and it was, it was through that experience that I got my first job.

CD1 TRACK 6 (I = Interviewer, MF = Melissa Foux)

I: Have you had any good advice during your career?

MF: Um, yes, I've had lots of advice during my working career. I think the thing that stands out is, really, not to overcomplicate things. Um, especially in the finance world, people can get bogged down in a lot of detail, and it's important to try and maintain clarity and always be able to see above all the numbers that you're given and all the data, and what is really the key point and the key decision you have to make.

CD1 TRACK 7 (MF = Melissa Foux)

MF: What I found, in coming across people who've applied for positions in the companies I've worked, um, in, is ... the key difference is, people who've done a lot of research on the companies that they've applied to. People have taken the time to, not just read company accounts, but, you know, research on what the company is moving into, and are able to really ask those interesting questions at interview. It makes all the difference. So I say, research is the key.

CD1 TRACK 8

A: Good morning, VTS. Which department, please?

B: I'd like to speak to Corina Molenaar in Human Resources, please.

A: Thank you. Hold on. I'll put you through.

C: Hello. Human Resources.

B: Hello. Is that Corina Molenaar?

C: Speaking.

B: Yes, I'm phoning about your advert in *Careers Now*. Could you send me an application form, please?

C: Certainly. Can I take some details? Could you give me your name and address, please?

B: Yes, sure, it's Sophie Boiteaud, which is B-O-I-T-E-A-U-D. And my address is ...

CD1 TRACK 9

A: Hello. Could I speak to Giovanna, please?

B: I'm afraid she's not here at the moment. Can I take a message?

A: Yes, please. This is Johan from Intec. Could you tell her I won't be able to make the training course on Saturday? She can call me back if there's a problem. I'm on 0191 498 0051.

B: OK. Thank you. Bye.

CD1 TRACK 10 (K = Karl, M = Matt)

M: Hello, Matt speaking.

K: Hi, Matt. Karl here.

M: Oh, hello, Karl. How are you?

K: Fine, thanks. Listen, just a quick word.

M: Yeah, go ahead.

K: Do you think you could let me have the other number for Workplace Solutions? I can't get through to them. Their phone's always engaged.

M: Er, I've got it here. It's 020 9756 4237.

K: Sorry, I didn't catch the last part. Did you say 4227?

M: No, it's 4237.

K: OK. Thanks. Bye.

M: No problem. Bye.

CD1 TRACK 11 (JR = Juana Ramos)

EXTRACT 1

JR: The children will be no problem. I'll probably send them to an international school in São Paulo. My husband's a writer, so he can work anywhere. I've got a career plan; I want to get to the top. I think I can do that and be a good mother as well. You have to be well organised, of course, and be a bit selfish at times.

CD1 TRACK 12 (JR = Juana Ramos)

EXTRACT 2

JR: How can we increase sales in the three markets? Well, I'll be checking the performance of the managers and sales reps carefully. I'll set the reps targets, and if they meet them, they'll get good bonuses. The managers will also have to meet their targets. If they don't, they should start looking for a new job. The main aim of a sales manager is to make money for the company, isn't it?

CD1 TRACK 13 (CF = Chantal Lefevre)

EXTRACT 1

CF: My son is only five, but he'll come with me if I get the job. His father won't be at all pleased, but he can't do anything about it. I could leave my son with his grandparents, but I don't want to do that. I'm sure he'll be all right in a Brazilian school. Children adapt very quickly to new places. It won't be a problem for me or him.

CD1 TRACK 14 (CF = Chantal Lefevre)

EXTRACT 2

CF: What's the best way to improve the performance of the sales teams? Well, I'll work closely with the sales managers, try to get a good relationship with them. And I'll look at the commissions we give the sales reps. Are they high enough to motivate them? I'll check the reps' progress regularly. Also, I'll make suggestions about improving the customer database, that's very important.

CD1 TRACK 15 (JS = JEFF SANDERSON)
EXTRACT 1

JS: What kind of person am I? Well, people often say I'm a loner because I've never married. But I think I'm fairly sociable. I'm definitely a bit of an intellectual. I have many interests – literature, music, um, world cinema, travelling abroad and getting to know other cultures. Perhaps that's why I've never married or had children.

CD1 TRACK 16 (JS = JEFF SANDERSON)
EXTRACT 2

JS: I have the experience and skills to improve our performance in these markets. I'd send the sales teams on team-building courses and have regular meetings with the three sales managers. The job would be a big challenge for me at the end of my career with our company. Of course, I've studied the cultures of the three countries, so I should have no problems working with the sales teams.

UNIT 2 COMPANIES

CD1 TRACK 17

I am pleased to say the parent company has continued its excellent performance. We are changing, growing and doing well at a difficult time for the industry. Turnover was €57.2 million, an increase of 15% on last year, and net profit rose by 5% to €6.4 million.

We are a highly competitive business. We have increased our market share to 20%. Consequently, our share price has risen and is now at an all-time high of €9.6.

Increased production and strong demand have had a positive effect on our cashflow, so we are able to finance a number of new projects. We have successfully moved to our new head office in central London. We are now planning to start full production at the recently opened Spanish subsidiary in October.

Finally, thanks once again to our loyal and dedicated workforce. Our employees will always be our most valuable asset.

CD1 TRACK 18 (I = INTERVIEWER, SB = SUSAN BARRATT)

I: Can you tell us about your company?

SB: Nature's Way Foods is a food-manufacturing company based on the south coast of England. We put chilled product, the majority of which is lettuce and fruit, into various types of packaging for the major retailers and various food-service companies in the UK. Examples of retailers would be Tesco's, Morrison's and Waitrose, and in terms of food-service companies, our biggest customer is McDonald's, which I'm sure most of you will be familiar with.

CD1 TRACK 19 (I = INTERVIEWER, SB = SUSAN BARRATT)

I: What are the reasons for the company's success?

SB: There are various reasons for the company's success. I think one of the major ones is the markets in which we operate. There are some, what we call 'big marketing themes', which are: health, convenience, sustainability and indulgence. We think the products we produce in both leaf and fruit fit a lot of those themes. So a majority of the UK population have a desire to eat healthy products. They tend to be what we call 'time-poor', i.e. they haven't got much time in their lives for creating great food, so they want to be able to buy a convenient product of good, healthy food.

There was also a theme for sustainability, so people want to feel like they are contributing towards a sustainable world, and a lot of our product has a fairly low level of what we call food miles and therefore is fairly sustainable.

Some of our products also have a fairly indulgent feel, so the UK population, er, has a habit of wanting to be indulgent at certain times. So they might diet on a Monday to Friday, but when it gets to Friday night, they will have several pieces of cake and maybe a few drinks. I think the other reason for our success is the way we run our business. We are a high-volume business, so we're producing hundreds of millions of units, so we need to be very efficient in the way we produce them. So we've invested heavily as a business in systems and processes, to make sure we are very efficient in the manner in which we produce the products for our customers.

CD1 TRACK 20 (I = INTERVIEWER, SB = SUSAN BARRATT)

I: When running a company, what have you enjoyed most and least?

SB: I think most is achieving what you set out to achieve. So when you're running a company, one of your key objectives, or key roles, is to set the strategy for the company, and then make sure the building blocks are in place to achieve that strategy. And that I find very satisfying – to set a clear goal for the business and then watch the business, and help the business go and achieve that goal.

I think the other thing which I find very satisfying is creating a team ethic and watching the people grow, and watching people develop and work towards the goals that you set as a business, and work as a team and get enjoyment out of that, and develop as people and as businesspeople within the organisation.

I: And least?

SB: I think least is probably the relentlessness of the role as a chief executive. You're never actually off duty, and a business like ours, which is a food-manufacturing company, it's running 364 days a year, so there's always something to be responsible for and something that's happening within your organisation. So I think that can be quite tiring. And also, the other thing that sometimes can be wearing, is it is quite a lonely life. You know, you have to make decisions, sometimes you can't talk to other people about them, and they have to be your decisions.

CD1 TRACK 21 (I = INTERVIEWER, SB = SUSAN BARRATT)

I: What lessons have you learned from the companies you've worked for?

SB: I've learned a lot of lessons from the companies I've worked for. I think the key thing is that you have to make sure your people in the organisation are engaged with the organisation and have a clear understanding of what that organisation is trying to achieve. If you can get that clarity of direction and enthusiasm from the people within the organisation, then that will help move the business forward in itself.

CD1 TRACK 22 (RP = ROBERT PULLIN)

RP: Good morning, everyone. Thanks for coming to my presentation. My name's Robert Pullin, I'm the Director of Human Resources at DCV Fashions. My purpose today is to talk to you about our company. You can then decide if you'd like to work for us in the future. First, I'll give you some basic information about DCV Fashions. After that, I'll explain why we've been so successful in the fashion industry. Next, I'll tell you about our mission statement. This describes what we're all about, why we're in business. And finally, I'll explain how we communicate with people through our advertising and promotion.

CD1 TRACK 23 (RP = ROBERT PULLIN)

RP: OK, some basic facts. We were founded in Florence in 1990. That's where we're currently based. Since then, we've expanded at a very fast rate and established our brand worldwide. We make and sell clothing and fashion accessories for the 18 to 30 age group. Please take a look at the chart. It shows our financial performance over a five-year period. As you can see, last year, our turnover was over 300 million euros and our net profit approximately 28 million. What's the key to our success? Well, I'd say there are three reasons we've grown so rapidly. We have a very talented team of young designers. Our distribution system is first class. And we're very creative when advertising and promoting our products.

Moving on now to our mission. It's to be a dynamic company, constantly changing but always leading fashion. Fun, youth, action, energy – this is what our brand is all about.

Finally, a word about our advertising and promotion. DCV advertises on all the Italian TV networks, as well as those in other major European markets. It sponsors fashion shows, and its products are endorsed by many celebrities in the world of music and sport.

Well, I hope you'll be interested to learn more about our company. Thanks very much for listening to my presentation. Are there any questions?

CD1 TRACK 24 (PC = PAOLO CONTI, DM = DONNA MARTIN, BK = BILL KINGSLEY)

PC: It's true our results haven't been good, our pre-tax profits have fallen once again. It's all very worrying. Well, we know one of the reasons: our two main competitors have been cutting their prices, so our prices are beginning to look rather high. They've also been increasing their advertising spend to get a bigger market share. But it doesn't explain everything, does it? How do you see things, Donna?

DM: It's not a crisis, Paolo, but we do need to make changes as fast as possible. The way I see it, we don't offer a very wide range of flavours; that's not helping us, and our packaging isn't very exciting. It gives the wrong impression. It could be the reason why our classic product isn't selling as well as it used to.

OK, so what do we need? More products and more outlets. We must reach more than the big supermarkets and our own ice-cream stores. Also, it'd be a good idea to upgrade our equipment and storage facilities … maybe our fleet of trucks as well – they're terribly out of date.

PC: Mmm, plenty to think about there, Donna. How about you, Bill?

BK: Well, I'd say innovation is the key. We need more new products, exciting new products people will want to buy. Don't forget, people are health conscious these days. So how about bringing out some fat-free flavours, 100% fat free, made from natural ingredients, no additives? Another thing, Paolo, we need to be more green, to do more for the environment. You know, recycle our containers, take the fat out of our waste products, then give the pure water to local communities – that sort of thing. Maybe donate money to charities, like a heart or cancer foundation. That'd improve our image for sure.

UNIT 3 SELLING

CD1 TRACK 25
EXTRACT 1

I like shopping for things I'm interested in buying, like clothes, but I really hate going to the supermarket. I just find it really boring, walking round and round looking for things. Supermarkets don't seem very well organised for customers. They have fruit and vegetables near the entrance, but then heavy things are further away and they move things around, which makes it difficult. Often the staff don't know where things are and can't help you!

CD1 TRACK 26
EXTRACT 2

I love the Internet for shopping. I buy lots of things on it. It's just so easy and convenient. Most retailers now work online. You can compare prices and products so easily. I also like the auction sites like eBay – you can get some real bargains. Some people say it's risky to shop this way, things can go wrong, but I've never had a problem. A lot of my friends like shopping malls, but I really hate them. They're always so crowded, and they make me feel tired.

CD1 TRACK 27
EXTRACT 3

I enjoy the experience of shopping – you know, being a customer, being made to feel special. I prefer specialist shops where service is more personal, where people remember you, know your name and can help you. I also like trying to get discounts when I'm shopping, actually doing a deal with the assistants. I really enjoy shopping for shoes. I don't think it's something you can do on the Internet, although I know people do.

CD1 TRACK 28 (I = Interviewer, SL = Sue Leeson)
I: What does QVC do?

SL: QVC is a global multichannel retailer. We sell products across a wide variety of categories, from food through to fashion, through to accessories, through to beauty, to gardening and DIY. And we sell to consumers in Germany, Japan, USA, UK and Italy, and we sell both through our – the television and online.

CD1 TRACK 29 (I = Interviewer, SL = Sue Leeson)
I: What's the secret of a really good sales presentation?

SL: Firstly, having a product that you can easily demonstrate and a product that has a good story behind it. Secondly, that the person who's actually giving the sales presentation can engage with their audience in a credible fashion, can tell the story very clearly and can demonstrate the features and benefits of each product in a very clear and easy-to-understand way.

I: Can you give us an example of how you develop a sales pitch?

SL: First of all, it's all in the preparation, so it's all about knowing the product inside and out, what the product can do, what it can't do, when it is suitable, when the product isn't suitable, and then be able to demonstrate the product to its best advantage in a very clear and precise fashion, but also in an engaging way.

CD1 TRACK 30 (I = Interviewer, SL = Sue Leeson)
I: What was QVC's most successful product sale, and why?

SL: We have many successful product areas. One of our strongest is beauty. Beauty works so well on TV for two reasons. First of all, each beauty brand has a fantastic story behind it, and we can really bring life to the brand and to the product presentation through telling that story in a very engaging way.
And secondly, each product is very easy to demonstrate. So if it's a skincare product, like a moisturiser, we can show how to apply it, how much to apply in order to give the best effects. Finally, we add another layer to our sales presentation in that we may invite the expert behind that product to tell the story.

I: Are some types of product easier to sell than others?

SL: Yes, and in fact some products are very difficult to sell on our business model. So take fragrance, for example. Clearly the main, er, piece you want to communicate with a fragrance is how it smells, and that can be very challenging to do through a television environment.

CD1 TRACK 31 (I = Interviewer, SL = Sue Leeson)
I: How has online shopping altered the way you sell?

SL: It's given us a fantastic opportunity to sell in a different way to our consumers. So if a customer wants to buy a skincare product at 10 o'clock at night, and perhaps on air we're showing a gardening item, she can now go down to our website, she can browse through the range of products online that suit her at that moment in time, she can see an image of the product, she can see the product description, she can see what other customers think about the product through our ratings and review service, and as well she can see the video demonstration. So it opens up our range of 15,000 products to the customer at any time, day or night.

CD1 TRACK 32 (M = Martin, C = Chen)
M: So your plan is to provide electric cars in your town centre. People will rent them to do their shopping, go about their business and so on. Right?

C: Yes, pollution is a big problem here. We're trying all sorts of ideas to reduce it. We're interested in starting with 10 electric cars. If it works, we'll increase the number later on. I see from your price list that a standard two-seater car will cost about €12,000. Is that correct?

M: Yes, the price includes transport and insurance costs. If you order 10 vehicles, you'll be paying us about €100,000, minus the 2% discount we offer a new customer. But if you increased your order, we could offer a much higher discount.

C: OK, how much would that be?

M: Well, for an order of 20 or more vehicles, the discount would be 5%.

C: I see. Let me think about it. What about delivery? We'd like to start the programme in June if possible.

M: Mmm. To be honest, that's a bit early for us. We've got a lot of customers waiting for delivery. We could possibly deliver by late August, all being well.

C: Mmm, that might be OK, if you can guarantee delivery by then.

M: I'd have to discuss it with our production department. I'll get back to you on that.

C: Good. How about the warranty? We'd like a long period.

M: It's for two years – that's what we normally offer.

C: Only two years? You know, if you could offer us a longer warranty, we'd be delighted. How about five years?

M: Mmm, that's much longer than normal. It could be all right, as long as you pay more for the longer period. I don't know. I'll check with my colleagues, I can't give you a decision right away.

C: OK. What about payment? Do you offer credit terms?

M: I'm afraid not. It's company policy for a new customer. We need payment by bank transfer on receipt of the goods. Oh, and we ask for a down payment of 20% of the value of the order.

C: A down payment as well, I see … Right. Well, I think we've covered some of the main points. How about some lunch now? After lunch, I'd like to discuss after-sales service, it's important for us that you give us reliable sales support …

CD1 TRACK 33 (DE = Director EPJS, DM = Director Megaluxe)
DE: I suggest the first item should be the length of the agreement. We need to agree how many years we want it to be for, and after that let's talk about the number of rooms we want, and what types of rooms we'd like to reserve for our customers. OK?

DM: Yes, that makes sense to me. First the length of the contract, and then the number and type of rooms. After that, I suppose services come next. That item could take some time to discuss.

DE: Yes, I think it'll take the most time. So, services will be the third item on the agenda, and I'll allow quite a bit of time for that. Next, how about advertising?

DM: No, I think that should come later. We need to talk about the rates next and especially any discounts you can offer on your listed prices.

DE: OK, rates can come before advertising. We'll probably have quite a long discussion about discounts, so I'll make time for that. And then finally, we can talk about advertising costs. I hope that won't take too long. How's that?

DM: That's fine. I'm happy with the agenda. I think it covers all the main points we need to talk about.

DE: Good. See you next week, then. Goodbye.

DM: Bye.

WORKING ACROSS CULTURES 1

CD1 TRACK 34

Many of you will travel to foreign countries on business or go to international conferences and sales fairs. Some of you may end up living and working in a foreign country. For all of you, cultural and social awareness will be important if you want to become effective communicators when you're abroad. Today, I'm going to look at saying 'no' politely.

Whenever you say 'yes' to a request, you are doing so at a cost. That cost is usually your time. Sometimes you just have to say 'no'. I remember two embarrassing occasions when I had to say 'no'. One was in Finland, when a business friend invited me to a sauna. I just felt uncomfortable. The other was in Hungary, a country where it's sometimes OK to share private details. Someone asked me something rather personal. Again, I felt a bit uncomfortable.

In the first part of my talk, I'm going to look at five tips for saying 'no' politely. Firstly, pay attention. Listen carefully and make sure you don't say 'no' before the other person has even finished making their request. Listen to the request with an open mind.

Secondly, offer alternatives. You may even be able to recommend someone else who is more suitable.

Thirdly, show sympathy if someone asks you to do something that you can't do. Show that you genuinely wanted to help.

Next, be as clear as possible to avoid misunderstandings. Don't say 'maybe' when you really mean 'no'.

And finally, avoid long reasons and excuses. Sometimes the less you say, the better.

The times I have had to say 'no' the most is when customers have wanted huge discounts. As long as you can say 'no' politely with a smile, followed by a genuine 'I'm sorry', then you should be fine.

CD1 TRACK 35

In the second part of my talk, I'll look at saying 'no' in different countries. Japanese people hate saying 'no'. They don't even like using negative endings to verbs and they don't like any confrontation. So it's important to look at their non-verbal communication. They believe in harmony. They think that turning down someone's request causes embarrassment and loss of face to the other person. Many negotiators have come away from meetings in Japan thinking they have got agreement when in fact they haven't.

Indonesians can also communicate indirectly. They don't like to cause anyone embarrassment by giving a negative answer, so the listener has to work out what they really mean. In fact, Bahasa Indonesian has 12 ways of saying 'no' and also other ways of saying 'yes' when the real meaning is 'no'.

The Chinese will often avoid saying 'no'. They have an expression which means 'we'll do some research and discuss it later', which is a polite way of saying 'no'. Silence in China can also imply that there are problems. Silence in the Arab world is quite common, however, and does not necessarily mean 'no'. The Arab world does not find silence difficult. However, saying 'no' in the wrong situations can have bad consequences. An American business friend of mine once refused a cup of coffee from a Saudi businessman at the start of a meeting. In America, that wouldn't have been a problem. But this was seen as rather rude by the Saudi host and the meeting was unsuccessful. My friend should have accepted the coffee and just had a small cup. I'll now move on to …

CD1 TRACK 36

1
A: Would you like to go out for a meal later?
B: Thanks for the invitation, but I'm not feeling so well. Maybe some other time.

2
C: Would you like some more food?
D: Nothing more for me, thanks. It was delicious.

3
E: Shall we meet up next Tuesday?
F: I'm sorry. I'd love to, but I have other plans that evening.

4
G: Please stay a little bit longer.
H: I've had a wonderful time and I wish I could, but I really have to go.

5
I: Can you check that the fire-exit notices are all in the right place, please?
J: I'm afraid you've come to the wrong person. You'll have to ask Ingrid in Health and Safety.

UNIT 4 GREAT IDEAS

CD1 TRACK 37

Great ideas are generated in different ways. Sometimes an idea may simply be when a company takes advantage of an opportunity to extend its product range, to offer more choice to existing customers. Or a great idea could allow a company to enter a market which was closed to it before.

Companies which are prepared to spend a lot on R&D may make a breakthrough by having an original idea for a product which others later copy, for example Sony and the Walkman.

On the other hand, some products are developed in response to customer research. They come from customer ideas. These products are made to meet a need, to satisfy consumer demand. Or the product does something similar to another product, but faster, so it saves time. Some people will buy new products because the product raises their status – gives them a new, more upmarket image.

CD1 TRACK 38

Other people will buy any 'green' product which reduces waste or protects the environment, even if it is more expensive. If an idea is really good and the product fills a gap in the market, it may even win an award for innovation.

CD1 TRACK 39 (I = INTERVIEWER, KP = KATE PITTS)

I: In your opinion, what were the best business ideas of the last 15 years?
KP: I've thought about this for quite a long time and, in my opinion, it's a service and two products. The first is eBay, and this works for me because it provides individuals and small businesses with a channel to market that didn't exist before. It started in the dot-com boom and has been extremely successful, with a turnover in 2009 of $2.4 billion. It's not a new idea though – running an auction is almost as old as society. It's based on a model of traditional auctions. It's just transferred the model and the thinking to a different environment. My second is the product, and it's a USB stick for computers, or plug-and-play devices. This enabled data and pictures to be easily transportable and satisfied a demand for easy portability from computer to computer. The amount of data that can be transported now is enormous; and it had the huge benefit of meaning that you didn't have to take your portable computer with you everywhere. So it satisfied a basic customer need. The technology itself also enabled a lot of other devices.
The final one is the digital camera. I'm not sure it's – if it's strictly an invention of the last 15 years, or if it's just become a mass-market item, but it's revolutionised photography and it's now incorporated into many other devices as a free gift, like mobile phones or PCs. And again, it satisfied a customer demand to share pictures and images quickly and easily.

CD1 TRACK 40 (I = INTERVIEWER, KP = KATE PITTS)

I: Do companies spend enough time on research and development?
KP: I think this depends very much on the industry. There are some product-based companies, like pharmaceuticals and high-tech companies, that spend an enormous amount of time and money on research and development. Nearly 25 per cent of the cost of sale, for example, at Ericsson, the Finnish mobile-phone company, are on research and development.
I strongly believe that most companies can benefit from using information and relationships within their own company to actually develop new products and services. My definition of innovation is to look at what everybody else sees, and see something different. So that might mean looking at what you already do, and looking at where you can do it slightly differently to increase your product range, or extending your products into new markets. This can save time and money.

CD1 TRACK 41 (L = LINCOLN, M = MEI, C = CHENG, W = WAN)

L: OK everyone, let's begin, shall we? Our main purpose is to decide the date of the launch for our new product, DM 2000. After that, we've got to decide the recommended retail price for the phone and talk about our marketing plans, OK? Mei, what's your opinion? Should we launch in June or September?
M: Personally, I'm in favour of June. Let's get into the market early and surprise our competitors. It could give us a big advantage. It might even force them to bring out their new phones earlier. I mean, before they're really ready to do so.
L: Thanks, Mei. What do the rest of you think? Cheng, how do you feel about this?
C: Well, um, I'm not sure about June, really. Mm, I think it's too early – in fact, far too early. We need more time to plan our marketing. You know, a lot of people, potential buyers, will be away on holiday in June. It's not the best time to have a launch. We need to start with a

real bang.

L: Mm, thanks, Cheng. Wan, what's your view? I believe you'd prefer a later date for the launch. Is that correct?

W: Yeah, June's too early. I think September's the best time. We can promote the smartphone strongly then, with a multimedia campaign. The last three months of the year have always been the peak period for selling new electronic products. That's when we need to put the phone on the market.

L: Mm, I agree. I think there are good reasons for choosing September. What about the recommended retail price for the phone? Any thoughts on that?

M: Hold on a minute. I thought we were talking about the launch date, not the price.

L: OK, Mei, maybe we are moving a little too fast. Let's get back to the point. I get the feeling that most of us seem to prefer September, is that correct?

C/W: Yeah.

M: Mmm, maybe.

L: OK, we're agreed. The launch is in September. Now, what about price? Wan, I asked you to bring us ideas about this.

W: I know we've set a price, but we should think again. I think it should be about 900 Hong Kong dollars.

L: Ah. And your reasons?

W: Well, simply, our main competitor brought out a smartphone recently. It retails at just over 1,000 Hong Kong dollars. If we sell at 900, we'll be undercutting them by 10 per cent. So, we'll have a big price advantage at the start of our launch.

L: Good. We need to be sharp on pricing. Now, what sales outlets do you think we should target, Wan?

W: No problem there. We could start with the specialist mobile-phone stores and big department stores. After that, we could look at other distribution channels. You know, stations, airports – that sort of thing.

L: Right. Sounds OK to me. Everyone happy with Wan's suggestions?

M/C/W: Yeah. / Fine. / Great.

CD1 TRACK 42 (DS = DILIP SINGH, JF = JANE FERGUSON)

DS: You know, Jane, I'm really looking forward to choosing the winner of this competition. It seems to be creating enormous interest all over the world.

JF: Yes, a lot of people have asked for application forms. What are you looking for? I mean, how will you judge the projects?

DS: There are three things that are really important. They'll help me to make up my mind. The winner will have to come up with a great idea for an attraction. It'll have to be something different, a bit unusual, but linked in some way to the culture of the community or country. It could be anything, as long as it's exciting: a museum, an art gallery, a theme park or a research-study centre. The possibilities are endless. I want people to use their imagination, that's the idea of the competition.

JF: I see. What else will be important?

DS: Well, the new attraction must provide an enjoyable experience for visitors. They should really enjoy the visit and talk about it with their friends afterwards.

JF: Can you give an example?

DS: Well, I was very impressed with the Kennedy Museum in Boston. There was a replica of the Oval Office when John F. Kennedy was president. There are a lot of interesting exhibits, including the rocking chair he used to sit in.

JF: Sounds fascinating. I'll visit it if I ever get to that part of the world.

DS: One other thing that's important, Jane. I want the new attraction to make money. It must be self-financing. If it makes money, it can contribute financially to other facilities that the community needs. It shouldn't have to receive local government funds once it's been set up. The winner will have to come up with lots of ideas on how it can make money. I want it to be a commercial proposition.

UNIT 5 STRESS

CD1 TRACK 43 (I = INTERVIEWER, JC = JESSICA COLLING)

I: What are the usual causes of stress at work?

JC: There are lots of things that can make people feel under pressure at work – for example, having too much to do, not feeling in control, and also not having good relationships with the people that they work with. All of these things can build up, and when pressure gets too much, it spills over into feelings of stress.

I: How does your company help businesses to deal with stress?

JC: One of the things that we do is be able to help companies identify which areas of the bui— of the company are experiencing stress, and then we can work with those people to help build their resilience to stress. Now what that means is actually helping people to respond differently to stressful situations, so that they actually feel calmer when they're put in situations that they previously found stressful.

CD1 TRACK 44 (I = INTERVIEWER, JC = JESSICA COLLING)

I: How much stress at work can be considered normal?

JC: It's difficult to say really what's a normal level of stress for somebody to feel at work. Um, the problem with that is that what one person finds really motivating and it excites them to be able to do their job well, somebody else might find really, really stressful.
What do we see is that actually a high level of continued pressure can actually sometimes spill over into feelings of stress. So, although you might be quite, um … you're doing quite well at managing stress for a long period of time, actually if it continues without any break, then actually people sometimes tip over into feeling very stressed.

CD1 TRACK 45 (I = INTERVIEWER, JC = JESSICA COLLING)

I: How can companies help their staff to achieve a work–life balance?

JC: Work–life balance is an interesting question, um, because again, everybody has a different sense of what works for them. However, companies can really help by being flexible in how they expect staff to work. For example, if somebody doesn't like travelling in rush hour, you know, perhaps they could come in a little bit early and leave a little bit early. And other examples might be, just making sure that people don't feel that they have to stay late, just because their boss is working late.

CD1 TRACK 46 (I = INTERVIEWER, JC = JESSICA COLLING)

I: Do you find that men and women deal with stress differently?

JC: What we do see is that women tend to experience higher levels of stress, or at least report higher levels of stress. We're not sure exactly why this is. It could quite possibly be because women tend to have more responsibility in the home as well, so actually managing the home, looking after children. So they have many more sources of pressure in their life and therefore are more likely to feel stressed because of that.
The other possibility is that women are perhaps more open about their feelings and therefore feel more comfortable in reporting, you know, feeling under pressure and … or feeling stressed.

CD1 TRACK 47 (B = BRIDGET, D = DANIELLE, K = KEVIN)

B: OK, let's talk about the staff's health and fitness. Last year, days lost increased by over 15 per cent because of sickness and absenteeism. That can't go on. We've got to do something about it. Any suggestions, Danielle?

D: Well, I think we should carry out a survey, find out why staff are so stressed and unhealthy. That'd help. At least we'd know what the problems are. I have another idea. Why don't we encourage staff to keep fit? How about paying for their subscription to a gym if they go, say, twice or more a week?

B: Mmm, that's an interesting idea. But it could be a bit costly. What about staff who have a very heavy workload? What should we do to help them?

K: Um, we could hire more staff for them, give them an assistant. You know, some of them even work at the weekend. How about banning staff from working at weekends – that'd solve the problem. They'd have more time to relax then, wouldn't they?

B: I suppose we could do that. It's something to consider. You know, there's been a lot of complaints lately from staff who drive to work. They get really stressed when they get stuck in traffic jams. And mothers with young children find it difficult to get to work on time. What do we do about them, Kevin?

K: Why don't we introduce flexitime for parents with young children? I think we should offer it to our admin staff and maybe to some staff in other departments. Also, perhaps some staff could work from home.

B: Mmm, yes … interesting ideas.

D: I've got a good suggestion, Kevin.

K: Mm-hm. Go ahead.

D: Well, it might be a good idea to set up a counselling service, with a professional counsellor. Staff could go there and talk about their problems. Oh yes, and another idea I've just thought of, why not let staff change duties and roles from time to time? To give them a bit of variety in their work.

B: Mm, I think this needs further thought. Let's meet tomorrow, same time, and try and come up with a plan to improve the staff's health and fitness.

CD1 TRACK 48 (B = Bridget, D = Danielle, K = Kevin)

D: I think we should definitely pay staff's subscriptions to the sports centre. If they were fitter, they wouldn't be sick so often and take days off work. And they'd work harder if they were healthier.

B: Mm, I don't know, Danielle. It would be popular, but it could be expensive. What do you think, Kevin?

K: I think I agree with you, Bridget. It'd cost a lot, and attendance would be difficult to monitor. I mean, we couldn't check each week to see if the staff were attending the sports centre. We're not Big Brother, checking up on staff all the time.

D: Yes, but we could get over that problem somehow. The sports centre has great facilities – a big pool, a squash club, hairdressing salon …

B: Yeah, you're right. Its facilities are fantastic. Also, it has some rest rooms, with ergonomic furniture where people can just relax and chat to each other. It's very relaxing there. Our staff would get to know each other better.

D: Exactly. It would really help staff to be more healthy, um, improve communications and save the company money – in the long run, anyway.

K: I can't agree with you there, Danielle. I'm not sure it's a good idea. Surely, it's not our responsibility to encourage staff to go to a sports club? They should go there because they want to be fit and in good health. It's their responsibility, not ours. We don't want to run their lives for them.

D: Mm, I don't know, I still think it's a good idea. It's well worth trying. If it becomes too expensive or it isn't getting results, we can stop paying their subscriptions – it's as simple as that.

CD1 TRACK 49 (JP = Jessica Parker, SM = Sheila Murray)

SM: Hello, Sheila Murray speaking.

JP: Hi, it's Jessica. How are you, Sheila?

SM: Fine, thanks. You?

JP: I've got a big problem here, I don't know what to do. It's about James.

SM: Oh? What's happening?

JP: Well, you know, he's been very stressed lately. His wife wants to leave him, and he's been working day and night on this contract. It's really important for all of us.

SM: OK.

JP: Well, he got really drunk last Saturday with our clients. I didn't like the way he talked – very loudly, you know, always interrupting them. Making jokes that weren't funny, and stupid comments. The clients weren't at all impressed.

SM: Mm-hm?

JP: Then he didn't turn up for the meeting on Monday, and now he's just disappeared. It's two days now. No one seems to know where he is. Our clients aren't happy at all. I don't think they want to complete the deal now. I just don't know what to do.

SM: Can't you take James's place at the meeting? The contract's almost ready to sign, isn't it?

JP: Well, there are still a few points … but how can I take over? It would look really bad, wouldn't it? I'm just a junior account executive. James has been the main guy all along. I think he's had a breakdown, Sheila. He just can't cope any more.

SM: OK, Jessica. I'll talk to some of my colleagues and get back to you. We'll sort this out for you.

JP: Thanks, Sheila, I'd appreciate that. Bye.

UNIT 6 ENTERTAINING

CD1 TRACK 50 (E = Employee, C = Customer)

E: Hello, Flanagans. How can I help you?

C: Ah yes, hello. I'd like to book a table for tomorrow night for six people, please.

E: Yes, madam, and what sort of time?

C: About eight?

E: Let me see … er, yes, that's fine … and what's the name, please?

C: It's Branson.

E: That's fine, Ms Branson … so a table for six at eight o'clock. We'll see you tomorrow evening. Thank you.

C: Thank you very much. Goodbye.

E: Goodbye.

****

E: Good evening. Do you have a reservation?

C: Oh, hello, yes. It should be under the name of Branson.

E: Ah yes, here we are – a table for six. Your table will be just a couple of minutes. Would you like to have a drink at the bar first, and I can bring you some menus as well?

C: Yes, why not? / Yes, that sounds good.

****

C1: Well, it all looks very good, doesn't it?

C2: Yes, it does.

E: So, are you ready to order?

C: Yes, is there anything you recommend?

E: Well, the fish is very good today.

C: Well, as a starter, I'd like the soup, and then to follow, I'll have the salmon with …

****

C: Thank you very much. That was very good.

E: And would you like to see the dessert menu?

C: Er, no, I don't think so. Just some coffee, I think … and the bill, please.

E: Yes, certainly. Very good, sir.

****

C1: Well, that was really good. I'll leave a good tip.

C2: Yes, we should. It's excellent here. We must come again.

CD1 TRACK 51 (I = Interviewer, CB = Chris Bruton)

I: Can you tell us about your company?

CB: My company is the Cavendish Consultancy. It is a corporate entertainment and corporate event company, based in West London. It operates in all sports, show business and performing arts, mainly in the United Kingdom, but we also tender for overseas events, which gives us the opportunity to spread our knowledge and skills and expertise around the world.

I: What are the most popular events for corporate entertainment?

CB: The most popular events remain the major sports and the major events in those sports. Within sports it does vary. For example, those sports where the rules are fairly simple and straightforward are more popular. Thus cricket, which is a personal, um, like of mine, is not actually one of the most popular, because the rules are fairly complicated. Horse racing is very successful, football – *soccer* as it's called in many countries around the world, but *football* in England – is very popular.
Motor racing works well and then, moving onto the entertainment side, theatre, pop concerts, musicals – particularly, for a number of years, *Phantom of the Opera* has been very popular in New York and in London and in many other cities around the world where it has showed.

CD1 TRACK 52 (I = Interviewer, CB = Chris Bruton)

I: Is corporate entertainment changing as the economy changes?

CB: Cavendish has been in business 30 years, so we've seen two if not three recessions. In fact, we were founded in 1981, which was a recession in the UK, and it does change and it's also changed enormously over those 30 years.
The quality of the product that we develop, deliver now is vastly superior, much, much better than the product we delivered in 1981. The, the recent downturn and particularly because the downturn has affected the financial sector, and the financial sector was a very big entertainer, has changed quite significantly – not so much the product but people have reduced budgets. And when they reduce budgets, they have act—, perhaps surprisingly, not gone for a cheaper product, but just taken fewer people to the expensive product. So the top-of-the-range hospitality is holding up better than the less expensive alternatives.

CD1 TRACK 53 (I = Interviewer, CB = Chris Bruton)

I: What do you think makes a corporate event successful?

CB: First, you have to identify your aim, your purpose in entertaining people at this particular event. That's absolutely key. If you don't know why you're doing it, probably don't do it.
Um, then, having identified why you're doing it, it's all the planning and all the little things. You can have the very best sporting event, the very best pop concert, but if the little things go wrong, that's what people remember. So it's contingency planning. It's having ... back-ups. If it rains, have some umbrellas there.
The catering is absolutely vital. People now expect a very high standard of food and drink. And then, bear in mind that it is the staff on the day who will meet all the guests. It's not the overall event organiser. I can't meet every guest of every … at every Cavendish event. It's the quality and the training and the briefing of the staff that you employ on the day is absolutely key.
And the last thing I would say is, always follow up afterwards. And I think that gives the opportunity to cement the relationship. Did you enjoy the day, and what else would you like to go to and those sorts of things.

CD1 TRACK 54 (CB = Chris Bruton)

CB: The most extravagant event I ever heard of was in July 1998, when the British Grand Prix, the motor race at Silverstone, was on the same day as the FIFA Soccer World Cup Final in Paris. And it was then possible to get a helicopter from central London to Silverstone. Now Silverstone is about 60 miles, 100 kilometres, north-west of London, so you helicoptered to the ground, you watched Michael Schumacher win the race, you helicoptered back to London Heathrow, the big airport just to the west of London. And then you flew in an aeroplane that was then the best aeroplane in the world, Concorde, to Paris. It didn't go supersonic, that is above the speed of sound, um, but you did go to Paris in Concorde and flew back that night. So, in less than 24 hours, you had seen a Formula One motor race and the World Cup Final.

CD1 TRACK 55 (L = Liz, J = Jane)
CONVERSATION 1

L: Hello, I'm Liz.
J: Oh, hello again, Liz. How are you? It's Jane – we met in Paris last year.
L: Oh yes, I didn't recognise you! Your hair's a bit different. I'm fine, and what about you?
J: I'm very well, thanks.
L: And how's business?
J: It's going really well, especially in Italy.
L: Great.

CD1 TRACK 56
CONVERSATION 2

A: Ah, James, have you met Sam Clarke?
B: No. Hello, Sam. Good to meet you. I think we both know Mike Upton. We worked together in Turkey.
C: Oh, yes … Mike. He's in China now.
B: Really? I didn't know that. Give him my regards next time you see him.
C: Yes, I will.

CD1 TRACK 57
CONVERSATION 3

A: Julia, do you know Jürgen?
B: Yes, of course. Hello, Jürgen. Good to see you again. How are things?
C: Fine thanks, Julia. It's great to see you again.

CD1 TRACK 58 (J = John, L = Lisa)
CONVERSATION 4

J: Hi, I'm John.
L: Hello, John. Pleased to meet you. I'm Lisa, from the Amsterdam office.
J: Oh, Amsterdam. I've never been, but I hear it's a great city, very lively.
L: Yes, it is. It's great. You should come. The conference is going to be there next year.
J: Oh, I'd love to. I'll look forward to it.

CD1 TRACK 59
CONVERSATION 5

A: Carla, I'd like you to meet one of our best customers, Linda Eriksson from SRT in Sweden.
B: Hello, Linda. Great to meet you at last. I've heard a lot about you.
C: Not all bad, I hope!
B: Not at all. It's great to be able to put a face to a name.
C: Absolutely!

CD1 TRACK 60 (A = Ahmed, K = Kate)

A: It's not going to be easy to please everyone, Kate. What are the most important things, do you think?
K: Actually, I've made a list of things we'll need. Shall I go through it with you?
A: Yeah, go ahead.
K: Right, well, we're looking for a hotel that's good value for money. It's a priority for us, because we've got to keep costs down. The conference centre must have a really big room for, say, 100 people, because there will be some presentations that everyone must attend. And we'll need at least four meeting rooms. We're going to have quite a few workshops and training sessions, as we usually do.
A: Yes, and the meeting rooms will need to be quite big, Kate, with enough room for, say, 25 participants – even more if it's a popular session.
K: Yeah. Good point. We have to think carefully about the location for the conference. If possible, it shouldn't be too far away from an airport. Most people will be arriving by air. We don't want them to have problems finding the hotel, like they did last year. A shuttle service from the airport to the hotel would be a plus, don't you think?
A: Yeah, but not all hotels offer that facility.
K: True. One other thing, it's important that the centre has good leisure facilities. We want staff to enjoy themselves as well as take part in work sessions. Don't forget, they're free on Friday and they could also have some free time early on Monday as well.

A: Right. We certainly don't want them to go away complaining they didn't enjoy themselves or have enough time to buy presents for friends and relatives.
K: Yeah. There'll be a gala dinner on the Sunday evening. They should enjoy that. It'll be an opportunity for everyone to relax, do some networking and meet colleagues from all over the world.

WORKING ACROSS CULTURES 2

CD1 TRACK 61 (KM = Karim MAnsour, AM = Andrew Morgan)

KM: I am pleased you like our food, Mr Morgan. My son Ahmed will now bring us some cakes and pastries. Which would you like to try?
AM: I'm sorry, I just can't eat anything more.
KM: Oh, surely you could try just one?
AM: No, really, that's enough for me. I'm just not used to eating such big meals. Er … actually, I'm on a diet at the moment.
KM: Oh, I see. What a pity! You know, we're famous for our pastries.
AM: Really? I didn't know that.
KM: Well, as you know, my company has stores in all the major cities here. I'm sure you've heard about our business. Most of the stores sell household goods, and they're located in busy main streets.
AM: Ah, actually, I didn't know that. My colleague Hussein gave me your number and told me to contact you. I was very busy just before I left England, so I didn't have much time to prepare for this visit.
KM: I see, I see. Yes, Hussein e-mailed me to say you would be visiting us, so I expected to hear from you. Tell me, what's your main purpose in coming here?
AM: Well, we want to sell our products in Morocco – we're not doing that at the moment. And we plan to start by distributing our goods through large department stores. Eventually, I suppose, we'll set up a sales facility here. We've used this approach in other new markets, and it's worked well for us. It's a good formula.
KM: I see. I'm not sure if that approach will work well here in Morocco, using department stores … But I could give you some contacts if you like – people I know who have shops here, ones that sell a lot of household products.
AM: Thanks very much … but perhaps next time. I'm going to see the British Consulate tomorrow, they're going to give me some names of people to visit. I have to leave next Wednesday, so I don't have much time. I want to arrange as many visits as possible. It would be nice to take home some informal agreements with one or two companies, then later sign the written contracts. We want to have distribution agreements with some local businesspeople by the end of the year.
KM: The end of the year? In only three months? Look, maybe I can help you. Why don't you leave me some of your business cards? If I meet someone who could help you, I'll give them your card and ask them to get in touch.
AM: Yes, good idea. It could be very useful. Er, here are some of my cards, thanks very much.
KM: Mmm, they're very well designed. Everything's in English, I see …
AM: Yes. Most businesspeople speak English these days, don't they? Well, thanks very much, Mr Mansour. I've had a very … enjoyable meeting.
KM: It was a pleasure to meet you, Mr Morgan. Can I give you a word of advice? Try to learn as much as you can about the business culture here before your next visit. The more you know, the easier it is to do business here … Have a safe journey home.

CD1 TRACK 62
EXTRACT 1

I made a big mistake when I negotiated with a Korean team. There were four people in their team, and I talked mostly to a younger man who spoke excellent English. I thought he was the team leader. I didn't say much to the oldest man in the group. He sat silently for some time, because his English wasn't very good. But later in the meeting, the old man took control of the discussion with the help of an interpreter. He was the Chief Executive of the company and made all the big decisions. I learned a lot about Korean business culture from that meeting.

CD1 TRACK 63
EXTRACT 2

As soon as I got to Korea, everyone said to me, 'Print plenty of business cards and make sure they're translated into Korean.' They were right. Koreans want to know who they're dealing with and what your title is. Status is very important, and a business card tells them if you're of equal status to them. When you present your card, you should hold it in both hands. And when you receive a business card, accept it with both hands and read it carefully. It shows respect.

CD1 TRACK 64

EXTRACT 3

I was assistant to the Marketing Director. I had some ideas for improving the layout of our stores in Seoul. So I wrote my ideas on a sheet of paper and sent it to all the staff in the department. Everyone commented on my ideas and approved them. I then talked to the Marketing Director, and he announced that there would be a project to change the layout of the stores. You see, decisions come from the top in Korean companies, but everyone needs to have their say. They call it 'consensus' – everyone agreeing to a proposal.

CD1 TRACK 65

EXTRACT 4

I learned one thing pretty quickly about Korean business culture. There's often a lot of red tape. You'll need a lot of official documents before you can go ahead with a project. You may spend months trying to get permissions from ministries and government officials. But a bit of networking often helps. The right contacts are so important in that culture. You need to be patient.

UNIT 7 NEW BUSINESS

CD2 TRACK 1

The economy is stable following the problems of the past two years. By following a tight monetary policy, the government has reduced the inflation rate to two per cent. For borrowers, after going up dramatically, the interest rate is now down to eight per cent. The last six months have seen a slight improvement in the exchange rate against the dollar. For the country as a whole, the GDP has grown by point one five per cent. Exports are increasing, and the balance of trade is starting to look much healthier. In terms of jobs, the unemployment rate continues to be a problem, as it is still 16 per cent. In order to stimulate the economy and attract foreign investment from abroad, the government is offering new tax incentives, as well as making a renewed effort to reduce government bureaucracy and red tape. Finally, a large skilled labour force means there could be attractive investment opportunities over the next five years.

CD2 TRACK 2 (I = INTERVIEWER, AD = ABDIRASHID DUALE)

I: Can you tell us about your business?

AD: Our company name is Dahabshiil. We are a global money-transfer company. We transfer money to nearly 144 countries. We help students. We help business organisations. We help international organisations like World Bank and United Nations. We help migrant workers who are in Europe or other parts of the world who want to send money back home to their family.

CD2 TRACK 3 (I = INTERVIEWER, AD = ABDIRASHID DUALE)

I: What do all successful new businesses have in common?

AD: All successful business, I believe, my opinion, they have to have a plan, they have to have a vision of where they're going, how they're going to reach that vision. They have to motivate their staff, they have to keep their customer loyal. They have to maintain their relationship with their customer because, at the end of the day, the customer is the one who pays your salary, who pays your income. So you have to make sure that the customers are happy with your services. You have to maintain that relationship. So Dahabshiil, when the customers come to us and they send money globally, we have to think about their requirements and we have to make sure they're happy.

So it … and of course, you also have to maintain your costs. You know, if your income and your costs, there's a big difference, then you know, you have to manage that. Of course, you prefer to get more income than your expenditure. Otherwise, if your expenditure is more than your income, your business will ge— be bankrupt. You will have a problem. So you have to always think about how to make more profit, less cost.

CD2 TRACK 4 (I = INTERVIEWER, SB = SUSAN BARRATT)

I: What advice would you give to anyone starting their own business?

SB: I hope they've got lots of energy. I think it is difficult and quite hard work, and needs a significant level of commitment. I think it's really, really important to make sure you understand the marketplace and who your customers are going to be. And how you differentiate yourself, or make yourself different, from any of your competitors in that marketplace.

People will only go to you and buy your product or your service if they feel it is added value, over and above what they can get elsewhere, or something they can't get elsewhere. So, for me, understanding the market and the customer is absolutely critical, er, to, to the success of a business.

The other key thing is that you've got sufficient cash. Um, things will generally not go quite to plan, and it's really important that you've got access to enough cash to get the business going, to ensure you get some positive cashflow through the business.

CD2 TRACK 5 (BS = BIRGIT SCHEIDER)

BS: I remember when I first thought about quitting my job and you advised me to gain some experience before I started a new business. I need to earn some profit as soon as possible, as I don't have much spare cash. Or do I have to accept that I won't have much money while I'm starting up my new business? Do I need to have some savings while I get my new business off the ground? I'm just not sure how I'll survive until my company starts earning money. Please advise me as soon as you can.

CD2 TRACK 6

1 a) three hundred and sixty-two
b) one thousand, eight hundred and forty-one
c) thirty-six thousand, five hundred and three
d) six-hundred and eighty-four thousand, three hundred and twenty-one
e) four-million, five hundred and thirty-seven thousand, two hundred and ninety-five

2 a) three point five
b) two point eight nine
c) nine point eight seven five

3 a) three-quarters
b) an eighth
c) six-sevenths
d) a half
e) two-thirds

4 a) fifteen per cent
b) fifty per cent
c) ninety-seven per cent
d) a hundred per cent

5 a) eighty pounds
b) five thousand, eight hundred dollers
c) a hundred and fifty thousand euros
d) twenty thousand euros

CD2 TRACK 7

EXTRACT 1

And here is the business news. This month inflation is up by one point two per cent. The unemployment rate is now five per cent, giving an overall figure of one million, two hundred and fifty-eight thousand.

CD2 TRACK 8

EXTRACT 2

Laser plc, the supermarket giant, reports that profits rose twelve per cent to just over $ one point eight billion, with sales increasing a healthy eighteen per cent.

CD2 TRACK 9

EXTRACT 3

General Engineering said it would reduce its workforce by one-third over the next five years, resulting in the loss of five thousand jobs.

CD2 TRACK 10

EXTRACT 4

The Central Bank has reduced interest rates by nought point five per cent. Turning to the world economy, this will grow by two point eight per cent next year.

UNIT 8 MARKETING

CD2 TRACK 11

CONSUMER 1

I read about the launch and I really wanted it, but when I tried to buy it, I just couldn't get it anywhere. My friend heard that it was in one shop and he queued up for ages, but they'd run out by lunchtime.

CD2 TRACK 12

CONSUMER 2

The company held a party on a river boat to launch their new campaign. It was absolutely fantastic. We also got a free sample and a T-shirt with the logo on as a gift at the end.

CD2 TRACK 13

CONSUMER 3

These new boots were really expensive, but definitely worth it. I think the fact that they cost so much is what really makes them different from the rival brands.

CD2 TRACK 14

CONSUMER 4

I've had this wallet for over 20 years, and it still looks good. The leather is very high quality and very strong, but still soft. The colour is as good now as when it was new.

CD2 TRACK 15

'market re'search	'sales 'forecast
'market 'segment	'sales 'figures
'market 'share	'sales 'target
con'sumer be'haviour	'advertising cam'paign
con'sumer 'profile	'advertising 'budget
con'sumer 'goods	'advertising 'agency
'product 'launch	
'product 'lifecycle	
'product 'range	

CD2 TRACK 16 (I = INTERVIEWER, RT = RICHARD TURNER)

I: Which marketing methods work best when promoting your products?

RT: The core of all marketing to doctors is the need to spend quality time face to face with them. These are very busy people who have a busy day treating their patients, and we often find that we only have maybe five or 10 minutes within that busy day to sit down with them and take them through both the clinical, 'rational' advantages of our products – why we think they should use this product compared to the ones they've been using in the past – as well as the more traditional, 'emotional' advantages of the product. And by 'emotional advantages', I might mean how it would help their patients, help them understand the benefits for their patients, and how it will make them have easier lives.
And so we're still very much focused on how we can best present quite complicated data in a short period of time, face to face to the doctor.

CD2 TRACK 17 (I = INTERVIEWER, RT = RICHARD TURNER)

I: What problems can you face when marketing pharmaceuticals?

RT: I think the biggest challenge for us is the regulatory environment. The laws that we need to follow are quite strict – and quite rightly so. We in the pharmaceutical industry have the same interests as the doctor. We want to help patients lead better lives. We have to present the data in a fair and balanced way, not, not to overstate the advantages of our products. Because we're often trying to develop campaigns which are consistent across many different countries across Europe, and because the laws are different across these countries, it's often a challenge to work out exactly what we can say and the best way of saying it.

CD2 TRACK 18 (I = INTERVIEWER, RT = RICHARD TURNER)

I: Has the way you market your products changed much over the last few years?

RT: Unfortunately, um, because of the regulatory laws that we need to follow, we're not able to promote directly to patients. We can only talk to the doctor, because the doctor makes the decision about the medicine.
So, although we'd love to use all the benefits and opportunities that the Internet and the new communication methods offer, we're not able to use them as much as we'd like to do.
Having said that, we are beginning … I think many companies are beginning to look at the opportunities that new technologies such as the iPad may offer to present the data when we're face-to-face with the doctor, because it's a clearer and more involving way of presenting the data to the doctor than the traditional paper.

CD2 TRACK 19 (I = INTERVIEWER, RT = RICHARD TURNER)

I: What is a typical lifecycle for your products?

RT: The lifecycle for a pharmaceutical product is often very long. It can take anything up to 20 years from the scientist first coming up with the idea to it finally being widely used by physicians to help patients' lives.
The first 10 years of that life can be spent wholly on the clinical trials, to prove that it's safe and has effect and helps the patients. And then the next 10 years spending a lot of time and effort presenting this data to doctors, so they, they can begin to understand which patients, and in which situations, the drug can help them. And just as we're getting to those peak sales, we find the patent on the drug will go. Um, so there's a long, a long period from the first idea to finally getting it out there in doctors' and patients' hands.

CD2 TRACK 20

1 Yes, it's thirteen thousand, four hundred and fifty-six.
2 … and the number is double oh, double three, two, three, double nine, oh, three, two, four
3 … so the e-mail address is V dot altin at saws lan dot com.
4 … and her address is hundred and twenty-eight slash sixty Rattanatibeth Road

CD2 TRACK 21

Alpha, Bravo, Charlie, Delta, Echo, Foxtrot, Golf, Hotel, India, Juliet, Kilo, Lima, Mike, November, Oscar, Papa, Quebec, Romeo, Sierra, Tango, Uniform, Victor, Whisky, X-ray, Yankee, Zulu

CD2 TRACK 22 (F = FIONA, M = MARTIN)

F: Hello.
M: Hello, Fiona. This is Martin. How are things going?
F: Fine, thanks.
M: I haven't received your sales report yet for the quarter. Any problems?
F: Oh, no. Sorry, Martin. I've been really busy lately. But I can tell you, we've had excellent results.
M: Good.
F: Yeah. We've met our sales targets and increased our market share by two per cent. Our total sales were over £1.2 million.
M: Over 1.2 million. Great! Well done! What about the new range of shampoos?
F: Well, we had a very successful product launch. We spent 250,000 on advertising it and …
M: Sorry, did you say 215,000?
F: No, 250,000. We advertised it in the national press, took out space in trade magazines and did a number of presentations to our distributors. It was money well spent. We've had a lot of orders already and good comments from customers.
M: I'm really pleased to hear that.

CD2 TRACK 23 (F = FIONA, M = MARTIN)

M: Anything else to report?
F: Yes, there is one thing. One of my biggest customers will be visiting London next week. She'd like to have a meeting with you.
M: Fine. Could you give me a few details? What's her name?
F: It's Mrs Young Joo Chan.
M: Sorry, I didn't catch that.
F: Young Joo Chan. I'll spell that for you. Y for Yankee, O for Oscar, U for Uniform, N for November, G for Golf … then J for Juliet, O for Oscar, O for Oscar, then C for Charlie, H for Hotel, A for Alpha, N for November. She's Korean, actually. She's Chief Buyer for BHDS. Let me give you her telephone number: 82 20735 8879. Her e-mail address is y.joochan1@bhds.com … OK? Why not give her a ring or send her an e-mail? She's expecting to hear from you.
M: I'll do that. But first, let me read that back to you. It's Young Joo Chan from BHDS. Telephone number 82 2 0735 8875.
F: No, 82 20735 8879.
M: OK, I think I've got all that. Just one more thing. Did she say when she'd like to meet?
F: Yes, she said next Thursday or Friday – that's the 17th or 18th.
M: What about Friday the 18th? I'll give her a call and confirm by e-mail. Right, I think that's everything.
F: Fine. I'll get that report to you by the end of the week.
M: Right. Bye for now.

CD2 TRACK 24 (A = ASHLEY)

EXTRACT 1

A: It's a great jacket for cold weather. I wear it to college every day during the winter. But it's not good for the summer, you get too hot in it. And it's got too many pockets. It was really cheap – I liked that!

CD2 TRACK 25 (S = SCOTT)

EXTRACT 2

S: I'm sorry I bought it. I'm not very big, so it doesn't fit me very well. It certainly is warm and keeps me dry during the winter months, but I was really looking for something a bit more fashionable, in a bright colour – you know, bright blue or yellow. My jacket's black, it's a bit dull.

CD2 TRACK 26 (K = KAREN)

EXTRACT 3

K: I'm quite pleased with it. It's very warm, perfect for canoeing and snowboarding. But the zipper is awful. I always take a long time to zip up. And the hood is difficult to fold up after you use it. It's quite big, so it's difficult to pack in a bag or suitcase.

CD2 TRACK 27 (N = NAOMI)

EXTRACT 4

N: I saw an ad in a magazine and I liked the look of it. But it took me a long time to find out where I could buy it. I'd almost given up, then my husband spotted it in a camping store. It's very warm in winter, but I get too hot when I take the lining out and wear it in the summer.

CD2 TRACK 28 (H = HENRY)

AUDIO SCRIPTS

EXTRACT 5

H: I spotted an advert for the jacket in our local newspaper. I filled in the order form, then waited over a month for delivery. I almost cancelled my order because of the delay. I had to phone the supplier three times before it finally arrived. I love the jacket. It's warm, practical and keeps me dry in rainy weather.

UNIT 9 PLANNING

CD2 TRACK 29

Recently, we decided to open a new sales office in New York. First, I arranged a meeting with the finance department to discuss the project. We prepared a budget with details of the various costs involved. Then we collected information about possible locations for the new office. We considered two options – one in Greenwich Village and the other near Central Park. After doing some more research, I wrote a report for the Board of Directors.

Unfortunately, we made a mistake when we estimated the costs, as the exchange rate changed, so we didn't keep within our budget. We overspent by almost 20 per cent. We had to rearrange the schedule for moving into the building because the office was not redecorated in time. The Board of Directors was unhappy because we didn't meet the deadline for opening the office by December the 15th. It finally opened in January. However, we forecast sales of at least $1,000,000 in the first year.

CD2 TRACK 30 (I = Interviewer, IS = Ian Sanders)

I: How far ahead should businesses plan?

IS: I think that depends on the size of the business. If you're a business that has a commitment from a client for three years, you have a three-year contract, it makes sense to have a three-year plan, because you can project forward those revenues, you know that relationship will be in place, and you can make some assumptions about what you need to do as a business in order to deliver the requirements of that contract. But I think for a lot of other businesses, three years is a long time. For a lot of smaller businesses, new businesses entering the market, um, especially in technology for instance, when who knows what trends are going to come into play next month – new software, new platforms – you really can't have a three-year plan. For me personally, I like the idea of a three-month plan, because it feels very manageable. I'm not guessing. And I think that is the problem with business planning; it can sometimes be 'business guessing'.

CD2 TRACK 31 (I = Interviewer, IS = Ian Sanders)

I: What are the best business plans you know?

IS: I think the best business plans are ones that are simple and flexible enough to take into account changing markets and changing situations. Any plan that is too fixed or too set in stone becomes very unwieldy, because it can't accommodate economic changes, market changes, technology changes.

CD2 TRACK 32 (I = Interviewer, IS = Ian Sanders)

I: Can you think of a business plan that failed?

IS: Yes. I think there are thousands of business plans that have failed, because you're not always going to get it right. Entrepreneurs and business owners cannot predict the future, and I don't think that's a bad thing that the business plans fail. I think it's important that we as entrepreneurs learn lessons, and if something's not right, we can adapt it.

So I think, um, failure is not a bad thing. I mean, I can think of a business, an entrepreneur I met recently, who had set up a very successful international web-based business, where entrepreneurs and start-ups can create business cards very cost-effectively. Now, when he was planning that business, he planned a previous version of it, and the previous version failed. And it was his lessons that he learned in that failure that led him to create Version 2, if you like, which has been enormously successful. And I said to him, 'Well, could you ever have anticipated or planned for what is the success now?' And he said, 'Well, no, because I was focused very much on something else. I learned my lessons. It didn't work. And now we've created something else.' So great! He is a success because he failed, you know, that's … and that's fine.

CD2 TRACK 33

A: We need to decide exactly when we're going to move. Any suggestions?

B: Er, I think July would be the best time. It's very quiet then, isn't it?

A: You mean, we don't do too much business then.

B: Exactly. Our sales are always down that month, and quite a few staff are away on holiday. We could move all the office equipment at the weekend. Do everything at once. That's the best way …

C: Could I just say something?

B: Go ahead.

C: I think we should take longer to move. A weekend's too short. In my opinion, we should do it department by department.

B: How do you mean exactly?

C: Well, each week a different department can move. That way, there would always be people here who could handle customer enquiries, phone calls and so on.

B: Hmm, I see what you mean. Maybe it would be better to phase the move over several weeks. Of course, we'll have to keep our staff informed at every stage of the move. We can do that mainly by e-mail. Now, moving on to the question of transport. We've contacted two companies, National Transport and Fox Removals.

A: Sorry, could I just comment on that, Mark?

B: Certainly.

A: I don't think it would be a good idea to use National. I've heard one or two things about them – I don't think they're very reliable. But Fox would be fine. They've got an excellent reputation in the trade.

B: OK, perhaps it would be better to use Fox, then. You know, there's another possibility. We could get our own people to do the moving.

A: What? You think our transport department could do the job?

B: Why not? They're not too busy in July.

A: I don't think that's a good idea. This is a really big job. We need a specialised firm for that, like Fox. They've got the experience and will do a good job, even if it does cost us a bit more. Also, Fox offers a free consultation service.

B: Mmm, you're probably right. I'll call Fox and discuss the relocation with them. I'll see if I can persuade them to lower their price a little.

CD2 TRACK 34

A: You know, I think the magazine could do really well if we plan it carefully. There's a really big market for it, and I feel it's the right time to launch. The main thing will be to make it different from the other magazines out there.

B: Yes, it's got to have some unique features, but I'm sure we'll come up with some. OK, what about target consumers? I'd say we should be aiming at men and women in the 20 to 40 age range. Right?

A: That makes sense to me. I think the magazine will also need to have clear sections. I've looked at a lot of health-and-fitness publications in the last few weeks. Some are an absolute mess, you've no idea where to look for the topics you're interested in.

B: Yes, we must have well-organised content and really interesting features. Maybe a regular feature on a celebrity – a film star or top athlete talking about health and fitness?

A: Yeah, that'd be very popular. But pretty expensive …

B: It would really increase sales. People love reading about the lives of celebrities. Another thing, you know, once we get some readers, we need to keep their loyalty, so they go on buying the magazine. We must find ways of doing that.

A: Of course. The website can help us to stay closely in touch with readers and keep them buying the magazine. Do you think the online content should be free of charge?

B: Mmm, I suppose we could offer some free content. Then make readers pay a subscription for premium content – extra materials like DVD workout programmes – that sort of thing.

A: OK, let's see what the teams think about that. They'll have plenty of good ideas for the magazine and website.

WORKING ACROSS CULTURES 3

CD2 TRACK 35
call 1
A: It's the first time we have heard about this, and my view is that we should find out more about what the markets think, because—

B: No, I think this is—

A: —and then it will—

B: —because of the way that—

CD2 TRACK 36
call 2
It's the right time to think about the new marketing strategy for all the new ranges across all the markets, except for the Latin American region, where I think we should …

CD2 TRACK 37
call 3
A: Well, I don't think it will work here, but I like the idea in general …

B: Sorry, I don't know who said that ... where are you?

A: Yes, sorry, this is Carlos in Australia.

CD2 TRACK 38
call 4
Yes, about the marketing strategy ... well, this reminds me of the time when I was playing golf with Mr Takagi, and he told me about the best

way to hit the ball. There's an old Japanese proverb, which is a very good way of remembering the ...

CD2 TRACK 39
call 5
Yes … hello … is there anybody there? I'm a bit late, sorry. How does this microphone work again? Let's see … If I do this, then maybe ...

CD2 TRACK 40
call 6
A: Martin, what do you think?
B: Well, my suggestion is to look at the finance again to try and save ...

CD2 TRACK 41
Hello, everyone. Right, in this afternoon's session of the cultural training course, and before you go to your breakout groups, I'd like to talk a bit about international conference calls. These are becoming more and more common and cheaper, now that the Web is being used for phone calls. Firstly, I'd like to look at the most common problems, and then move on to a few tips and pieces of advice.

I suppose many things are common sense. However, it can all take some getting used to. The first thing to say is about technology. This is probably the most common problem I hear about. There are a lot of different systems and, as with all technology, it sometimes goes wrong. Systems can crash and people get cut off – so be prepared for that, as it can be very frustrating. Also, there are times when there are people taking part in a conference call who are not familiar with the technology and who don't know how the equipment works. This is a training issue.

The other thing is, background noise can be a big problem, especially if a mobile or cell phone is used, as these tend to pick up a lot of background noise. Finally, there may be problems with people not being sensitive and speaking very fast, maybe because of nerves, or just because they behave differently on the phone.

CD2 TRACK 42
... and now I'd like to look at a few solutions to the problems, and offer some tips for both participants and call leaders.

It may seem obvious, but when you are part of a conference call, make sure you are in a quiet place and not likely to be interrupted or disturbed. This follows on from what I said earlier. Actually, the 'mute' button is important to use when you are not speaking, so that you can reduce background noise. Personally, I use a headset for this type of call. Also try and avoid eating, drinking or chewing gum while on a conference call, as this can be noisy for others. If you really need to have a drink, remember to use the mute button.

Moving on to participants, a few quick pieces of advice.

Prepare for the call in advance. Think about and plan what you may need to say, and perhaps any questions you may have. Have any documents you may need close to hand, so that you don't need to look for them during the call. Being on time is also important.

When speaking, if it's not clear from the technology being used, it can be helpful to say who you are each time you speak. For example: 'This is Mike. I didn't catch the name of the marketing firm. Could you say it again, please?'

As in face-to-face meetings, when you speak, stay on topic. Short contributions will be more memorable, and a conference call is not really the place for long speeches. Another good tip is to signal or label what you say. For example, 'This is Mike, and my idea is …'

The other thing to say is, try not to interrupt people when they are speaking. Listen carefully and wait to be invited to comment by the call leader. Avoid taking notes on a computer, as typing will be noisy for the other participants. A pen and paper, although old fashioned, is still effective!

UNIT 10 MANAGING PEOPLE

CD2 TRACK 43 (I = Interviewer, LM = Laurie Mullins)
I: Which management styles have influenced or impressed you?
LM: I have been impressed by many different managers, but I would like to mention three managers, with a broadly similar style. I believe these three managers are pioneers in the effective management of people. Firstly, Lord Sieff, S-I-E-F-F, who for many years was Chairman of Marks and Spencer, Britain's foremost retail store. Lord Sieff placed emphasis on quality control, profit and staff welfare. An enduring feature of Lord Sieff's belief was that the effective management of the business organisation, particularly in the retail sector, and good human relations at work are two aspects of the same thing.

CD2 TRACK 44 (LM = Laurie Mullins)
LM: The two other managers I have selected both share a similar philosophy and managerial style. Second, Dame Anita Roddick, from 1976, founder of The Body Shop, which specialises in beauty and cosmetic features. Anita Roddick displayed a genuine caring attitude towards staff, but is perhaps best known in Britain because she had a strong belief in environmental and social issues, feminist principles and practical aid to Third-World countries.

A very interesting aspect of Anita Roddick's management style was she firmly believed that it's not possible to provide environmental and social support without making profit. Secondly, she was quite honest in saying that she was in business to make profit, including some profits for herself, as well as the substantial sums she gave to Third-World countries.

Third is Sir Richard Branson, founder since 1970 of the Virgin brand of over 360 companies. Sir Richard Branson is well known for combining a true entrepreneurial spirit with a genuine concern for people.

CD2 TRACK 45 (I = Interviewer, LM = Laurie Mullins)
I: What do those three managers have in common?
LM: All three managers have or had a genuine belief in effective communication; involvement and availability for their staff; visibility so that staff can see them, approach them; and they were able to have immediate contact with them. All either did or do engender a genuine commitment from members of their staff. All three had or have a genuine belief in creating a climate of mutual consideration, respect and trust with their staff.

CD2 TRACK 46 (C = Chair, A = Anna, K = Kurt, UR = Union Representative, B = Barbara)
C: OK, Anna, would you like to begin?
A: Well , the level of absenteeism has gone up over the month. We need to monitor sickness levels more closely.
C: Mm. What do you think, Kurt?
K: Motivation is the biggest issue. Staff feel that no one listens to them.
C: I see the union representative is here. Would you like to add anything?
UR: The unions want more days' holiday per year. This will lead to lower sickness levels.
C: How about you, Barbara?
B: Mm. Well, our staff have more days' holiday than any of our competitors. There is no excuse for the present level of absenteeism.

CD2 TRACK 47 (M = Mohammed, P = Paul)
M: What would you like to do this evening, Paul?
P: I don't know, I haven't planned anything.
M: Well, why don't you join me for dinner? I'm meeting a friend of mine tonight, Abdullah. He's got many business interests here. He could help you a lot while you're here. He's got a lot of contacts with carpet manufacturers.
P: Mmm, it's very kind of you to invite me, Mohammed, but I think I'd prefer to stay in the hotel if you don't mind. I'm really tired at the moment. It was a long flight and I feel a little jet-lagged. I need an early night.
M: OK, Paul, I quite understand. Perhaps we could meet Abdullah at the weekend?
P: I'd be delighted to. I want to make as many business contacts as possible while I'm here.

CD2 TRACK 48 (P = Paul, A = Abdullah, M = Mohammed)
P: I don't know too much about Syria, Abdullah. What do people like doing here in their spare time?
A: Well, we like the same things as Western people. We like to meet our friends in cafés and chat about business, sports – that sort of thing. And we like watching football in the evening on television. Women enjoy talking to their friends and, of course, going shopping. Everyone likes that! What about you, Paul, what do you usually do after work? How do you spend your evenings?
P: I generally watch TV with my wife. We often eat out at a restaurant, we enjoy that. And at the weekend, we play squash or tennis at a local club. How about you, Mohammed? What's your favourite pastime?
M: I like to go out to restaurants and meet my friends in coffee houses. We often go to a hammam, I love that. It's so relaxing after you've been working all day. Would you like to visit one?
P: Mmm, it sounds very interesting, but I don't think I have enough time. Thanks for the offer, though. Maybe on my next visit we could do that.

CD2 TRACK 49 (P = Paul, A = Abdullah)
A: So, what was your main purpose in coming to Damascus?
P: I'm looking for a company to supply carpets for my store. The carpets you make here are excellent quality and they're very popular in the UK. So far, I haven't had much luck. Can you recommend anyone, Abdullah?
A: I could make some enquiries for you if you like.

P: Ah, that's very kind of you.

A: Actually, I do know someone who might help you. It's a family business in the north of the city, run by Sharif Hamad. He specialises in traditional designs. I believe his prices are very reasonable. Hold on a minute, I've got his business card. Here you are.

P: Thanks very much. I'll give him a call tomorrow. Can I mention your name?

A: Please do. I've known him for years. Would you like me to give him a call first, to introduce you?

P: Thanks. That would be very helpful. I'd really appreciate it.

A: Now, let me recommend something else. Tomorrow evening, you must visit our famous mosque. It was built a long time ago, and everyone visits it when they're in Damascus. I'll take you there by car.

P: You're very kind. Thanks very much. I'd love to see it. Goodbye. All the best.

CD2 TRACK 50 (JD = Jim Driscoll, DB = Diana Bishop)

JD: Let me give you a bit of information about the two newest members of the team.

DB: OK, I'll make a few notes.

JD: Well, Adriana is the youngest member. She's been with us just over a year. She's an economics graduate, with a good head for figures. So far, she's doing pretty well. She met her sales target last year, she's come up with some good ideas for improving our website and she's added several clients to our database. She seems to know how to get new business for the company, so she's definitely got potential.

DB: Good.

JD: But she does have weaknesses. She lacks social skills. She doesn't get on very well with the other members of the team. And she's not comfortable when meeting clients for the first time. She never seems to be at ease with them. One other thing, her presentations to clients are not yet up to the standard we normally expect.

DB: Mmm, it sounds as if she's still got a lot to learn.

JD: Yes. Also, she doesn't like our payment system at all. She thinks it's very unfair.

DB: OK. What about Ahmed?

JD: Well, he's been with us just over two years – we hired him to improve our contacts with Arab clients. He's made a good start, his sales record's fine, and at the moment, he's searching for properties for several wealthy clients.

DB: Excellent.

JD: Yes, but there are some problems with him. He doesn't spend much time in the office, he's always out socialising with clients, so we don't see much of him. Well, not as much as we'd like. He doesn't come to many meetings, and he's made no contribution really to building up our database. He's not really a team player at all – very independent. Some consultants say he's actually un-cooperative.

DB: Mm, that's not good for team spirit. How does he feel about the payment system?

JD: He's very happy with it. He can't understand why some of the consultants complain about it.

UNIT 11 CONFLICT

CD2 TRACK 51

1	'patience	'patient
2	'calmness	'calm
3	'weakness	'weak
4	flexi'bility	'flexible
5	e'motion	e'motional
6	con'sistency	con'sistent
7	'sympathy	sympa'thetic
8	for'mality	'formal
9	en'thusiasm	enthusi'astic
10	crea'tivity	cre'ative

CD2 TRACK 52 (I = Interviewer, EC = Eileen Carroll)

I: Can you tell us about your organisation?

EC: Our organisation, the Centre for Effective Dispute Resolution, was founded, um, 20 years ago. Um, its base is in London, and, um, its main outputs are to, um, teach business and make business more aware of more effective ways of dealing with conflict. And our two primary areas of business are first, skills: so we've been involved in training up to 40,000 mediators around the world. Um, and we're also involved in providing services. So we have mediators who mediate, um, round the UK and round the world in business conflicts.

CD2 TRACK 53 (I = Interviewer, EC = Eileen Carroll)

I: What are the commonest causes of conflict at work?

EC: We actually surveyed this last year, and the findings are interesting. The key problem is inappropriate communication or no

communication. So I would say, avoidance; so that managers are not dealing with their employees as effectively as they might. There's a lot of European legislation now around the areas of sex discrimination and unfair work practices, and this does lead to a lot of controversy in the workplace. I think other areas, um, are: clash of personalities, culture, different belief systems, and interestingly, um, I think a lot of employees feel that their workloads can be very oppressive.

CD2 TRACK 54 (I = Interviewer, EC = Eileen Carroll)

I: How do you help to resolve business disputes?

EC: It's about trying to have an early dialogue and to recognise there is a problem, and then it's about having a good process, and that involves getting key decision-makers to, um, allow enough time. So typically, um, we would say they need to allow at least half a day, but in a bigger business problem, at least a day. And it's having a good agenda, and it's making sure that the difficult issues are talked about in the right kind of format with a mediator, both privately and in a group as well, and then private debriefs of the different protagonists in the conflict, and then bringing together parts of those groups to actually improve the levels of communication and to work on really constructive problem-solving, and a real focus on finding the solution.

CD2 TRACK 55

A: If I reduced the price by seven per cent, would you give me a firm order?

B: Mm, I don't know … Only seven per cent? I was hoping for a little more. If we increased our order, would you give us a bigger discount?

A: OK, how about this … If you increase your order to 1,000 units, we'll give you a 10 per cent discount. That's fair, isn't it?

B: A thousand units … mm … OK, 1,000 units, 10 per cent discount. Agreed.

A: Good.

B: What about spare parts? Can you supply them pretty quickly?

A: We can probably get them to you within a week. How about that?

B: That's fine. I think we've covered most things except terms of payment. If you give us 90 days' credit, we'll sign the order today.

A: Ninety days? Mm, er, we might find that a little difficult.

CD2 TRACK 56 (S = Scott, R = Rachel)

S: OK, Rachel, so you want to talk about your salary. I see you're currently earning about $60,000.

R: Yes, that's why I'm here. I think I'm worth a lot more than that to the company. My work's greatly undervalued at the moment. So I'm here to ask for a raise.

S: Right. What figure do you have in mind?

R: $120,000. I know it's double my present salary, but I'm worth it. I've done really well in the last two years. I've exceeded my targets by almost 40 per cent, and none of the sales staff has done better than that.

S: True, but a 100 per cent increase? It's not going to happen.

R: Look, I know for a fact that Sophie Legrand got a raise recently, and her salary's over $100,000. She's doing the same work as me and not getting such good results. It's not fair, is it? I should be getting the same salary as her.

S: Look, Rachel, I'm not going to discuss the salaries of the other staff with you. Put yourself in our shoes. We're facing a difficult economic situation, you know that. We've all got to cut costs. There's no way the directors would approve such a huge increase in salary for you. Well, not at the moment, anyway.

R: I understand what you're saying, but the fact is, I'm being underpaid for the results I'm getting. I'm not happy about it. Not happy at all. Other sales staff are being treated much better than me … You know, there are other companies I could work for, don't forget that.

S: I'm not sure I like the tone of what you're saying, Rachel. Threats won't get you anywhere.

R: I'm just trying to tell you how I feel, that's all.

S: OK, I understand what you're saying. I can see your point of view. Look, we do value your work, I can assure you. But times are very difficult at the moment. There's no way the directors would agree to pay you over $100,000 right away … Let me suggest a compromise. How about if we give you an increase to, say, $80,000 now, and promise to review your salary in six months' time?

R: $80,000 immediately and then a review … Hmm, I was hoping for a bit more … OK, if you guarantee I'll get a review later on, I guess I'd be happy with that.

S: I promise you we'll do that. I'm Chairman of the Review Committee and I'll make sure your salary is discussed.

R: OK, I suppose that's acceptable.

S: Right, I'm pleased to hear it. I think we've covered everything. I'll be writing to you to confirm the increase.

CD2 TRACK 57 (P = PRESENTER, JK = JOAN KNIGHT)

P: Good morning, Joan. What can you tell us about Herman & Corrie Teas?

JK: Well, they're well established, a very well-run company. They usually make a profit, but some analysts think they could be doing a lot better.

P: Uh-huh. What about their values, their principles?

JK: OK, they're what we'd call a 'green' company. Very green. For example, they won't buy tea from suppliers if chemicals have been used to grow the tea. And of course, they're against the use of any pesticides in the growing process.

P: Right.

JK: Another thing, they were one of the first tea companies to get a certificate as a fair-trade producer.

P: Mm, impressive.

JK: Yeah, they have very high standards indeed. They always invest part of their profits in the areas and communities which supply their tea, and they promote production methods that benefit local agriculture and the tea producers. You know, they even try to recycle the boxes used for packaging. So you see, they really care about the environment.

P: Yeah, there's no doubt about that. One other thing you could mention, Joan. The company's got very loyal staff, I believe. People say it's their biggest asset. They have a policy of keeping workers, even when economic conditions are really bad. They'd rather lose money than lay off workers.

JK: Yes, they really look after their workers, that's true.

P: Do you think the management will recommend accepting UCC's offer?

JK: Mm, I don't know, to be honest. But they'll be holding a meeting soon, and I suppose they'll make up their minds then. I understand the company's staff are strongly against the offer, so the meeting will be pretty lively.

PS: OK, well – when we know, we'll invite you back to comment on the decision, Joan.

UNIT 12 PRODUCTS

CD2 TRACK 58

speaker 1

I'm 20 years old and I've wanted a Ford Mustang since I was 10. I now have an eye-catching 1998 black Mustang coupé with leather seats. This car is fast and furious and is everything I have always dreamed of. It has been virtually maintenance-free. I give my friends a ride in it with the top down, and they think it's awesome. Overall, it's comfortable, reliable, gives great performance, has great interior and exterior design and is fun to drive.

CD2 TRACK 59

speaker 2

The best thing I've ever bought is a trampoline for my son and daughter. They've had hours and hours of fun playing on it with their friends … and it's been really good for parties. It's weather-proof and durable – it really has lasted a long time, over 12 years. I've even used it myself – it's a great form of exercise. It wasn't cheap, but we were happy to pay for safety and wanted a high-quality trampoline. Ours has a strong rigid frame and high-quality springs, so we get a really deep bounce. If you want to buy one, make sure it fits the space in your garden. And for safety, remember that all trampolines are designed for one jumper at a time.

CD2 TRACK 60

speaker 3

Well, I work from home and used to spend a lot of time propping myself up in bed with a laptop. But I recently bought this fantastic chair that copies the shape of your body when it's stretched out. It's made from an aluminum and plastic frame and has lots of pillows that support every part of the body. The computer monitor is cleverly suspended in front of me, to prevent neck strain. The keyboard and mouse are designed to be placed on the user's lap. I really can relax whilst using the Internet and I haven't had any neck problems since I started using it. Also, the curved frame provides support for my back. It's also eye-catching and quite popular with my design-conscious friends!

CD2 TRACK 61

speaker 4

I'm an experienced backpacker and I've been to four continents, up mountains, through deserts and jungles, and slept in smart hotels and on train station benches. Obviously everyone needs a good rucksack when travelling. But to answer your question: a large Arab scarf. That was the best thing I ever bought. It's a sarong, a scarf, a turban, a beach towel, a bath towel … Tie the corners together and you've got a bag. Hang it from a window for 15 minutes and it's dry. All backpackers should get one.

CD2 TRACK 62 (I = INTERVIEWER, JW = JAMES WALLMAN)

I: What makes a product great?

JW: The three or four things I would look for in a product, and what makes a great product, is that it's … firstly, that it's easy to use. That you don't need to think about what you need to do, you don't have to spend time reading a manual, that it's intuitive and simple and obvious how you should use that. The other thing is, at its heart, a product should solve a problem or fulfil a need. So, for example, the, um, the electric cars that are coming out today, they solve an essential problem in the world, which is that we are running out of oil, and at the same time there is a problem with global warming, caused by burning fossil fuels. So that's a great example, an electric car is something that solves a problem. And the third point is simply that it should be functional, that it should be helpful, that it should make your life easier and make things better in some way.

CD2 TRACK 63 (JW = JAMES WALLMAN)

JW: It's the Tesla Roadster. It's the new electric vehicle, which goes from nought to 60 miles per hour in 3.4 seconds. I drove one in France in, from, from Nice to Cannes, about a month ago, and I've never driven a car as exciting as this.

Driving it is like a cross between driving a Scalextric car, a bumper car that you used to have at the old fun fairs – and probably still do have at funfairs – and a rocket ship. The response that you have from the accelerator is instant. So it's not like with a turbo lag, it's not driving a petrol-driven car, where there's some gap between when you push the pedal and it goes, it's absolutely instant. And as you release your foot from the accelerator, the car slows down in the same way a Scalextric car does, when you pull on the trigger. So the Tesla is very exciting.

CD2 TRACK 64 (I = INTERVIEWER, JW = JAMES WALLMAN)

I: What product do you expect to see in the near future?

JW: There's a number of innovations that I think are happening at the moment that will give us new and exciting products. Possibly one of the most exciting is the driverless car, not because I don't like driving, but sometimes driving can be very boring, driving in cities is a pain as opposed to driving in the countryside. Driverless cars will be with us certainly by 2020. General Motors plan to have a driverless car on the road by 2018. Google has put money into this, Audi is putting money into this. We're in a position at the moment where cars are shifting from completely driver-controlled to some control by the car itself, by the computer within the car. And what we'll see over the next years is the shift so that, just as with a 747 aeroplane, you can either drive it yourself or hand it over to the machine to drive.

CD2 TRACK 65 (I = INTERVIEWER, JW = JAMES WALLMAN)

I: What's your favourite product, and why?

JW: My favourite product is my Mac computer. It's a black Mac, so it looks good. And the reason I like it is because I'm a journalist, it's the thing that I use to write my work on. I'm writing a novel, it's the thing I use to write my novel on. It connects me to e-mail, because obviously I have Wi-Fi at home. When I go to a café, I have Wi-Fi, I take it with me when I go on holiday and I go to places that have Wi-Fi. I can Skype video and talk to friends in New York. I can Skype video and talk to friends in Australia. I'm in constant contact with my parentsthrough the machine, and it has the wealth of the Internet, the information that is there and all the people that that can connect me to.

So for me, my computer and its connection to the Internet, and its connection to people around the world, makes it invaluable and makes my life more connected and more fun.

CD2 TRACK 66

I'm going tell you about our new product, a fast ice-cube maker for use in the kitchen.

It was designed by Paolo Rossi and launched last month. We're promoting it at the moment on TV shopping channels and using a lot of point-of-sale advertising. We're distributing it to upmarket department stores and specialist kitchenware shops.

Now, about the product. It comes in three colours: white, black and silver. It has several special features. As you can see, it's stylish, well designed and elegant, as you would expect from a Paolo Rossi product. We think it'll be extremely popular with people who like giving parties. It's made of stainless steel and is very sturdy. It's a bit larger and heavier than some other ice-making machines. It weighs approximately 12 kilos, but it's very strong and reliable. It was tested for months before we put it on the market and it never broke down. You can check its dimensions in the handout I'll be giving you. What about its main selling points? Well, it's very economical in terms of power and exceptionally quiet when you're using it to make ice. Also, it's easy to use. You just put water in and press a button. Nothing could be simpler. What about its performance? Well, that's one of the ice maker's outstanding features. It produces faster and bigger quantities of ice than any other model. It can produce 15 ice cubes in eight minutes, two kilos of ice in an hour or 18 kilos in 24 hours. Incredible! Now, a word or two about its benefits for the user. Firstly, it'll save party givers a lot of time making ice cubes. And because the machine's so versatile, it can make cubes of different sizes. It's fairly expensive compared with other models. The retail price is around 320 euros, but it's great value for money because it comes with a full five-year guarantee on parts and labour. We think the ice maker is a real winner. From now on, when people give parties, there won't be any embarrassing moments when they run out of ice and have to wait hours for a few more cubes. Those days are over. It simply won't happen if they have our ice maker in their kitchen.

Thanks very much, everyone. Are there any questions?

CD2 TRACK 67 (CN = CHIKA NAKAMURA, HD = HUGH DAVIS)

CN: OK, Hugh, I think we're ready now to put everything in writing on the website. Shall I summarise what we've agreed?

HD: Sure. Go ahead.

CN: OK, first point. We're looking for products that show originality and creativity. If they're really unique, so much the better.

HD: Absolutely. Our awards are meant to encourage innovation. It's the most important point, so it's got to come first in the list of criteria.

CN: OK. Next, I think this point is important, too: we're looking for things that improve consumers' lifestyle, that give them a better quality of life or a wider choice of a product, maybe.

HD: Yes, we want products that really benefit consumers in some way.

CN: OK, and I think we also agreed the winning products will need to be, um, environmentally friendly. Is that right?

HD: Well, all we actually said was that they shouldn't be bad for the environment, not harmful to it in some way.

CN: Right. We had three other points for the list. Um, the winning companies will have to explain to us their plans for marketing their products, tell us how they'll advertise and promote them. And they get bonus points if they have creative plans – if their marketing is a bit different in some way. Now, let's see, what else …

HD: We want the products to make plenty of money for the company. They've got to be profitable. So the question we'll be asking them is, will it make money, or is it just a fad – here today, gone tomorrow?

CN: Exactly. And the last point: is the product advanced in terms of technology?

HD: I think we can put that another way, Chika. The question is, has the company used technology in a new way, in an interesting or exciting way? That's what we're looking for.

WORKING ACROSS CULTURES 4

CD2 TRACK 68 (S = SPEAKER, A = AUDIENCE MEMBER)

S: Today, we're going to be talking about culture – what it is, and how knowledge of it can help when doing business internationally. I've divided my talk into two parts. Firstly, I'd like to talk about the visible aspects of culture – the things we can see – and secondly the invisible aspects – the parts we can't see.
OK, so firstly the visible aspects. Earlier I asked you to think about this. What did you come up with?

A1: The weather!

S: Yes, you laugh, but it does have an effect on culture and behaviour. Anything else?

A2: We came up with food, written language, the way people drive and, er, the style of buildings.

S: Yes, very good. The point is that these are easy to see and may be different to what you are used to. In business terms, this will also include the way people greet each other, and how close they stand when talking – what we call 'personal space'. This may also extend to the use of gestures with the hands or face – in other words, body language. There may also be differences between the roles of men and women.

CD2 TRACK 69

Moving on, I'd now like to take a quick look at the other aspects of culture which we cannot see – the invisible parts. These are things such as beliefs and attitudes, which are important because they help us to understand how people in other cultures think and operate. This will depend on the whole structure of society – how important things like the individual, the family, the team or group is.

Building relationships and developing trust over a period of time are much more important in certain cultures than getting instant results. Risk-taking may be seen in a different way, so it may take longer to make decisions. Attitudes to time are also important, not only in relation to things like deadlines, but how long- or short-term the thinking is. Business deals could take a very long time. One further point is about the status of a person. Remember, status may be linked to age or connections rather than simply talent or ability.

Overall, it's clear to me that when people talk about cultural problems, they are usually in these areas. They're not language problems. They are to do with misunderstandings of behaviour caused by attitudes and values which are different and may be difficult to understand.

To sum up, the most important thing when doing business with other cultures is to be more aware of your own culture. What is normal for you may seem strange to people from other cultures. As well as thinking about your own culture, the final tips I can give are to be sensitive, to try and notice things and be flexible in your approach. You can't hope to cover everything, but with a little bit of research, an open mind and an awareness of your own culture, you can go far. Thank you and good luck!

Market Leader Extra: Business skills
Audio script Pre-intermediate

1.1 INTERVIEWS

BSA1.1.1

Hello there, Mr Soni. My name's Jennifer Daniels and I was given your details by Dino Patel. I believe that you worked with him on the Indi-Accounts project last year? We have a client who is looking for someone with your skills and experience. I'd like to discuss the possibility of you coming in for a chat about that position. If you're interested, can you please call me to discuss this further on 09892293875? Many thanks.

BSA1.1.2 (J = Jennifer, A = Arjun)

J: Hello, Mr Soni. Nice to meet you.
A: Nice to meet you, too.
J: Now, we have your profile here from your Total Staff account. You're a project manager.
A: Yes, that's right. I've worked in project management for eleven years.
J: And you're working for Dynamic Business Solutions.
A: Yes, I am. I've worked with them for the last three years.
J: And what are some of your responsibilities there?
A: Well, I have to manage a range of different projects, from start to finish. My biggest challenge was a two-year project to introduce a new telecommunications system, with a budget of twenty million US dollars. That project's coming to an end now.
J: And were you in charge of that project?
A: Yes, I was. I had a small team of four people working with me directly, and at the moment we're working with a larger team of around thirty staff at the client's offices.
J: And you've worked with companies abroad.
A: Well, yes and no. I haven't worked in other countries, but I did one project with an international company that had offices here in India and in the UK. That's where I worked with Dino Patel.
J: You worked with Dino Patel at METS.
A: No, actually, it was Danford Management. I enjoyed that experience and it was an important opportunity to learn about cultural differences. I worked with the UK team and I really enjoyed it. That's why I'm looking for more international work now.

1.2 PRESENTATIONS

BSA1.2.3

OK, thank you for coming. Let's get started, shall we? As you know, the health and fitness of our members of staff is important. Regular exercise means less stress, fewer illnesses and generally better work. What's more, studies show that the best professional staff say they prefer to work for a company with free gym membership. For these reasons, we have decided to team up with a local gym to offer our members of staff free gym membership and make it easy for them to make healthy lifestyle choices. Let's look at the reasons why we think gym membership will be good for our staff and for the company.

BSA1.2.4

We began to look at the problem of workplace stress in 2015. Slide A shows the reasons people gave for leaving our company in 2015. As you can see from this slide, thirty-two per cent said that stress was one of the reasons they decided to go. That's a large number. This means that many of our current employees probably suffer from stress on the job.

BSA1.2.5

So, as you can see from my presentation, there are many good things about the Fit Now gym: the convenient location near our office, the great facilities and the low cost to staff. To conclude today's presentation, I believe that for the company, this partnership with Fit Now means that we can make health and fitness choices easy for our staff. It's good for managers because this should mean fewer absences for illness, and happier, healthier, more productive staff. And for Human Resources, it will give us a competitive edge over other companies when recruiting new staff. For these reasons, we have decided to go into partnership with Fit Now. So, are there any questions?

2.1 SMALL TALK

BSA2.1.6 (S = Susan, M = Mike, Ma = Massimo)

S: Hello, I'm Susan Vine.
M: Oh hello, Susan. I'm Mike Veneto. I think we've spoken on the phone before.
S: Oh yes, we have. I remember now. You work for Cannini Construction, don't you?
M: That's right. So you must be with SPT Supplies?
S: Yes, I am. And how's business?
M: It's going very well at the moment, thanks. We didn't have such a good year last year, but this year's been very good.
S: That's good to hear. We've had a few problems, too, but business has been steady.
M: Excuse me. Hey Massimo, come over here. Susan, do you know Massimo Farina? He works with me in Italy.
S: No, I don't think I do. Hello, Mr Farina, nice to meet you.
Ma: Nice to meet you, too. And please call me Massimo, Susan.
S: Thanks, Massimo.
Ma: And, who do you work for?
S: SPT Building Supplies. I'm the Sales Manager.
Ma: Oh yes, we get some of our supplies from you, don't we?
S: Yes, you do. Oh, please excuse me, I need to speak to my boss. He's over there.
M: Hey Susan, how about having dinner with us this evening?
S: Oh, I'd love to, thanks. That would be very nice.

BSA2.1.7 (S = Susan, M = Mike, D = Davina)

S: Hi, Mike.
M: Hi again. Susan, this is our new boss, Davina Hoffen.
S: Sorry, I didn't catch your name.
D: Davina, Davina Hoffen.
S: Hello, Davina, pleased to meet you. You're not Italian, are you?
D: No, I'm American. I've just taken over from Paolo Spiteri.
M: She speaks fluent Italian, you know.
S: Really?
D: Yes, my mother's Italian. She met my father at university in Italy, they got married and he took her back to live in the States.
S: How do you like working in Italy?
D: It's great. And I just love being in Europe. What about you? Have you worked abroad before?

S: Yes, I have, actually. I worked in our German branch for two years.

D: Did you like it?

S: Yes, I enjoyed working there.

D: Tell me, how much do you get paid at SPT.

S: Er, mm … I'd rather not answer that.

M: Excuse me, I think Susan is ready for a drink. Can I get you something, Susan?

S: Oh, yes, thank you. I'll have a mineral water, please.

BSA2.1.8 (S = Susan, M = Mike, Ma = Massimo, D = Davina)

M: Ah, here's Massimo now. Let's look at the menu.

Ma: Hi, everyone. Sorry I'm late. Had to take a client call.

D: Everything all right?

Ma: Yes, fine. No problems.

S: When are you all flying back to Italy?

M: Davina's leaving tonight, but Massimo and I are staying for another day. We thought we'd do some sightseeing.

S: Would you like me to show you around tomorrow?

M: Oh, that would be great.

Ma: I'm really sorry, I'd love to, but I'm visiting a client tomorrow. But I'll be free for dinner.

M: That's settled then. We'll all have dinner together again.

Ma: You should come and visit us in Italy, Susan.

S: I'd love to. I've never been there.

M: Well, let us know when you want to come and we'll arrange everything.

S: Wow, that'd be wonderful!

Ma: Right, are we all ready to order?

M: We haven't looked at the menu yet – been too busy chatting! I recommend the steaks here. They're very good.

2.2 MEETINGS

BSA2.2.9 (L = Leonora, S = Sam, T = Tanya, LC = Lok Chen)

L: OK, team. Thanks for being on time. Let's begin. As you all know, the other day I went to a Health At Work seminar. I must say, it was really interesting. I've been a bit concerned about the working culture in this company for some time. The only topic of conversation seems to be 'work, work, work'. Some people are working very long hours, which is not good for stress levels and long-term health. Anyway, at this seminar, another HR manager presented a case study from her company. Their working culture was very similar to ours – that is, until her company's employees changed it. It all started two years ago, when one of their engineers organised a weekend walk to a local historical beauty spot. He invited other employees and their families to join him. Quite a few people went. They had a picnic lunch and he gave a short talk about the site. What happened next was interesting. A visiting group of Korean engineers and their wives enjoyed the day so much that they organised a Korean culture evening as a thank you; delicious food and a talk about Korean culture. They showed short clips of beautiful Korean scenery and traditional dance. It grew from there. These days there is at least one weekend event a month and a choice of several clubs most evenings. Families join in and there is one golden rule: nobody talks about work. Now that's what I call a work–life balance! Really inspiring! Maybe we could follow their example? So, what do you think?

S: Well, I think it's a great idea. I can think of loads of clubs we could start up.

L: What do you think, Lok Chen?

LC: Well, I'm not sure it would be very popular, actually. People seem too busy in their jobs to have time to organise lots of social activities. I don't think the bosses will be too happy if they work less.

L: Mmm … I can see your point, but companies actually benefit when they encourage a good work–life balance. We would certainly have to make sure that everyone understands the downsides of workplace stress. Workaholics always cause problems sooner or later.

T: I totally agree there. We have all read the surveys showing that employees who take fewer holidays feel more stressed. I think it's exactly the same for employees who work fourteen hours a day without a change of scene. Maybe we should do a company stress test?

L: Sorry, Tanya?

T: Well, at least if we did an employee satisfaction survey first, it might help the bosses to see the benefit. They might even encourage our idea.

S: Exactly! Managers are responsible for managing the business. And managing workers' stress levels is an important part.

L: OK, Sam and Tanya, could you create a short employee satisfaction survey in the next couple of days? We can meet again on Thursday to check it over. Friday is always a good day to send out surveys.

S: Yes, sure. We'll make sure we put in a good question about work stress and overwork, etc.

L: When we get the results back, we can meet to brainstorm some ideas for clubs and events, so it would be great if you could think of some good ideas in the meantime.

T: Absolutely. We could ask a few people, too. You know, when we meet them at the coffee machine.

L: Great! Good work, team. Well, I'll look forward to reading your survey questions. See you on Thursday.

3.1 TELEPHONING

BSA3.1.10 (ER = Ewan Riley, JB = Janice Bell)

JB: ExtractaJuice, how can I help you?

ER: Hello, can I speak to Harold Taylor, please?

JB: Who's calling, please?

ER: This is Ewan Riley, from the UK office.

JB: Hi, Ewan. I'm Janice Bell, Harold's assistant. He's not in the office right now, but would you like to tell me what it's about?

ER: Certainly. My line manager, Ella Bright, asked me to call you and give you this month's sales figures.

JB: OK, let me get a pen. Right, I'm ready.

ER: Well, the figures are good – sales are up by fourteen per cent this month.

JB: Up forty per cent – that's fantastic!

ER: Sorry, not forty, fourteen. One, four.

JB: Oh, I see. Fourteen per cent. Well, that's still good. So that means total sales of how many units this month?

ER: Fifty-seven units. That's from stores in two cities – London and Birmingham. So we're thinking of hiring demonstrators for stores in some other big cities.

JB: Well, those are good results for a new market. Which other cities are you thinking about?

ER: Glasgow and Manchester.

JB: Manchester and … oh sorry, I didn't catch the name of the first place.

ER: Glasgow.

JB: OK, got it. So I'll tell Harold. He will be pleased. And I have some news for you.

ER: Oh, what's that?

JB: We think you are doing well – really well. But we want to help you do even better.

ER: Yes, how?

JB: We are sending one of our top trainers to give your demonstrators on-the-job training. Is the fifteenth and sixteenth of next month OK for you?

ER: Well, I have to check with my boss. Can you give me some details?

JB: Yes, sure. The trainer's name is Shona Thompson.

ER: Can you spell her first name, please?

JB: It's Shona. S-H-O-N-A.

ER: And Thomson is T-H-O-M-S-O-N, I suppose.

JB: No, there's a P in the middle.

ER: B for Bravo?

JB: No, P for Papa. T-H-O-M-P-S-O-N.

ER: OK, I've got it.

JB: So, she will need a hotel room for three nights, and a training room in the same hotel on the fifteenth and sixteenth of October.

ER: So the accommodation is for the fourteenth, fifteenth and sixteenth. Is that right?

JB: Correct.

ER: OK, I'll tell Ella. She'll write back and confirm.

JB: Great. Nice talking to you, Ewan. Goodbye.

ER: Goodbye.

3.2 E-MAIL

BSA3.2.11 (B = Bob, M = Maribel)

B: Morning, Maribel. You're in early today.

M: Morning. Yes, I need to send an e-mail to Jan Hansen about the project. He wants a sponsor update.

B: Aha. An e-mail to senior management. Good luck! I know what Jan is like.

M: Yes, I know, too. That's the point. I hate writing to senior management like him – always wanting things perfect. I don't want to make any mistakes. That's why I'm here so early. It's taking ages.

B: Hey, sorry. Look, just keep it short and simple. Let me see. OK, that's good. He'll like that.

M: I'm just worried about my English. I don't want to write with lots of mistakes; it just looks so bad.

B: Don't worry about language mistakes. Just make sure the project information is correct.

M: Yes, but …

B: Look, if you want, I can check over the e-mail before you send it.

M: Yes! Thanks, Bob. I'm nearly finished. Five minutes?

B: Can we make it nine thirty? I have a meeting with Jean Luc – in his office.

M: OK, see you then. Thanks.

BSA3.2.12 (B = Bob, C = Maribel)

M: Oh Bob, before you go, can I just check with you?

B: Yes, sure.

M: Should I start *Dear Jan* or *Dear Mr Hansen*? I've never written to him before.

B: *Dear Jan*. Just use the first name. I use *Hi Jan* and *Hey Jan*, but I know him. Mr Hansen is too formal in this company.

M: OK, thanks. And is *please find enclosed* OK? I'm sending him a copy of the latest project planner.

B: Erm, no, you need to say *please find attached*. If you say *enclosed*, it's when you send by post – a letter.

M: Ah, OK, good. So I need to change that. And I finish *If you want more information, let me know*, is it OK?

B: Let me see. It's OK, but I guess the standard is more something like *If you need any more information, don't hesitate to let me know*. *Yours* is a bit … maybe a bit direct. Sorry, but I'm late for Jean Luc. Can you finish it up and I'll look through after my meeting. Nine thirty?

M: OK. Sorry, Bob. Thanks for helping.

B: Just one thing: make sure the subject of the e-mail is clear. You've got *Project update* – can you make it more detailed? It's easier to find.

M: OK.

B: Got to run. Bye.

M: Bye.

BSA3.2.13 (B = Bob, M = Maribel)

M: Hi, Bob. Is now a good time?

B: Sure, come in.

M: Did you have time to look at my e-mail?

B: Yes, absolutely. I underlined a few things. Shall we take a look together?

M: Yes, thanks. If you have time.

B: No problem, of course. So, first thing is the date. I would write this in full, so *5th June 2015*, or just *5 June 2015*. US and British English are different. So it's always really important to write dates in full.

M: OK, thanks.

B: Then, forget the first sentence. Too informal. I wouldn't use that. And then, after that, it's just a few words. Here it's *brief*, here *on time*, *Peter is* and not *Peter's*, that style. I think short forms are too informal for this e-mail, so use full forms, as you did – I think – everywhere else. Yep, good. OK?

M: Yes, OK.

B: Then, *some important information, he told me* or just *he said* – without *me*. And I wasn't sure: what do you mean *actual*?

M: Er, I mean now, at the moment.

B: OK, then I would say *current*. And I think that's it.

M: So, not too bad.

B: No, I think the main thing is to be careful with style. Don't mix formal and informal, and don't use the informal with more senior managers – people you don't know very well. It can look a bit unprofessional.

M: OK. Thank you so much, Bob. Really.

4.1 NEGOTIATIONS

BSA4.1.14 (M = Miguel, P = Pete)

M: It's been a long time, Pete.

P: That's right Miguel. Nearly six months.

M: So, how was your journey?

P: Not bad, thanks. There was a storm last night, but nothing serious.

M: And how's your job going?

P: Great. When you travel, you meet interesting people. And you? Any plans to retire?

M: Oh no! Not yet. So, what can I get you? We've got sugar, coffee, bananas or pineapples.

P: It depends on the price. Maybe pineapples.

M: We have the best prices on the coast!

P: Can I try one before I buy?

M: Of course! This one is very sweet. Here you are. What do you think?

P: Mmm, very sweet. Will they last the journey to England?

M: Don't worry. They'll last six weeks.

P: I don't want a boat full of bad fruit when I get back to Portsmouth! How much for a hundred?

M: Two pesos for one, that's two hundred pesos.

P: Two pesos for one pineapple!

M: Aah! They're top quality, Pete, and they don't grow in England! Would you like anything else?

BSA4.1.15 (M = Miguel, P = Pete)

M: Can I interest you in some premium coconuts or delicious bananas?

P: How much are the bananas?

M: They're a bargain. This week we're selling them at just two and a half pesos per kilo. Here, try one.

P: Mmm, it tastes good. All right, I'll take two hundred kilos at four hundred pesos.

M: But it's two and a half pesos per kilo. That's five hundred pesos for two hundred kilos of bananas.

P: Yes, but I usually get a discount when I order large quantities. Four hundred pesos.

M: Let's see ... I'll give you two hundred kilos of bananas for four hundred and fifty pesos.

P: Four hundred and fifty?

M: Yes. And the pineapples cost two hundred pesos. I can't lower that price.

P: Well, if you can't lower the price, why don't you give me an extra twenty pineapples?

M: That's an extra ten per cent!

P: What's ten per cent for a regular client?

M: Regular? I haven't seen you in six months!

P: I've been busy, Miguel. And then I had some trouble with my business partner, Harry, in Barbados.

M: What happened?

P: He lost his eye. Unfortunate accident, at sea.

M: I see. Anyway, I didn't trust that man. He never gave me eye contact.

P: You know what they say: keep your friends close, but your enemies closer!

M: That's very true. Look, for you, Pete, let's say four hundred and fifty pesos for two hundred kilos of bananas and two hundred pesos for a hundred pineapples, and I'll give you an extra five.

P: Can I go over that again? Two hundred kilos of bananas at four hundred and fifty pesos and two hundred pesos for one hundred pineapples, plus five extra ones.

M: So, that's six hundred and fifty pesos.

P: We've got a deal! Let's go for a drink in the Green Parrot tavern!

BSA4.1.16 (M = MIGUEL, P = PETE, H = HARRY)

M: Can I get you something? Pineapple juice?

P: Thanks. Can I tell you something, Miguel? I'm too old for travelling. I'm looking for a partner, someone I can trust, who can help me with some business.

M: What kind of business?

P: Do you know Grey Rock Island?

M: Grey Rock Island? Yes, I've heard there's gold there but the waters are very difficult to navigate.

P: I know. If I didn't have this bad leg and if I were younger, I would go on my own. But I'm offering you an opportunity, Miguel.

M: I don't see what you mean.

P: I'd like to make a suggestion. What if we go into business together? If we go together, I'll show you the treasure map. You do a little manual labour and when we find the treasure, we'll share it.

M: If we find the gold.

P: I'm not stupid, Miguel. Look, I'll show you the exact location later. Seventy–thirty. Seventy per cent for me, thirty for you. How does that sound?

M: I'm not sure. I won't be your partner unless the deal is fifty–fifty. You know I've got an excellent record sailing these waters. You can't do this without me.

P: That's true. But I know where the money is. Think about it. If you came with me, you would never have to sell another banana or pineapple again! We'd be rich!

M: Yes, but I think I should be paid more, Pete. Sixty for you, forty for me. I'll have to take you because you don't know the area. And you've got one bad leg. Sixty–forty. That's my final offer.

P: Fine. Partners! Well, I must go now. Need to see a man about buying a little boat.

M: Why don't you come back later, at night? Bring the map and we'll talk about the plan in more detail, OK?

P: Sure. It's always a pleasure doing business with you, Miguel! Excuse me, sir ...

M: Another pineapple juice, Harry?

H: No, thanks.

M: What do you think then?

H: As we agreed: fifty–fifty. Fifty for you, fifty for me. It's a win–win situation. When he comes back, we'll steal that map!

4.2 PRESENTATIONS

BSA4.2.17 (A = ALAN, M = MARIA)

A: OK, so the single-walled shipping box is slower to assemble than the new Rapid Packing Box. Forty seconds, compared with under five seconds for the new box.

M: And the single-walled shipping box is heavier than the new box, too. The new one's only 100 g.

A: The brown shipping box costs about the same per unit as the new box.

M: Yes, but the single-walled shipping box is less environmentally friendly – the customer can return and reuse the new box.

BSA4.2.18

Good morning. Thank you all for coming today. This is my first time here visiting the Madrid office and I hope it won't be my last. It's a beautiful city. So, as you know, we design and produce cardboard packing boxes. I want to talk to you today about a new type of box we're introducing. We want to change our box design for two reasons. The first is cost. For some of our customers, over thirty per cent of their costs are on packaging. Cheaper boxes can make a big difference. Another reason is the new European regulations. These mean that companies need to produce less waste. We hope this new box will help.

So, let's start by comparing it with our old box. First, I'll explain the problems with the old box and then I'll talk about solutions to those problems.

BSA4.2.19

There are three main problems with the current box.

Firstly, assembly time. Assembling the single-walled box takes about forty seconds per box, so paying someone to assemble a thousand boxes is expensive.

The second problem is that customers need to use plastic tape to close their boxes. This mixed plastic and paper waste is difficult to recycle or dispose of.

The final thing we need to think about is that the end user, the shop or business, can't return the boxes. Some customers here in Spain pay up to a hundred Euros a month to a waste management company to remove the empty boxes.

To solve these problems, we're introducing a new company box called the Rapid Packing Box. The box is quicker to assemble. It costs the same as the single-walled box, but the labour costs are lower. It'll be much cheaper for most of our customers.

The Rapid Packing Box uses no plastic tape. It closes with a thin line of glue. It uses less cardboard, too – between fifteen and twenty per cent less, reducing waste. So it's more environmentally friendly – no problems with mixed plastic and cardboard waste. It's better than the old box for European regulations.

Finally, the box is easy to return. When the customer empties the box, it goes back to the flat shape it had before. Customers can return it to the factory to be used a second time.

So, to recap, the three key benefits are: it's cheaper because it's quicker to assemble, it's more environmentally friendly, to meet EU laws, and it's easier to return and reuse. So, we're sure that the Rapid Packing Box is going to be a new best seller. Do you have any questions?

BSA4.2.20 (A = ALAN, S1 = SPEAKER 1, S2 = SPEAKER 2)

A: So we're sure that the Rapid Packing Box is going to be a new best seller. Do you have any questions?

S1: Do we need special equipment to assemble the boxes?

A: No, you don't need special equipment. The boxes are quick and easy to assemble.

S2: Is the glue as strong as the plastic tape?

A: Yes, the glue is very strong. But the main advantage is that the glue comes off the box easily when you open it, so the box isn't damaged.

S2: Will it be expensive to send the boxes back?

A: No, it won't be expensive. The savings we make from reusing the boxes will balance the cost of returning them, so at the moment it shouldn't make any difference to our budget. We believe this is going to be a very popular product. OK, any more questions? No? Thank you. So, my colleague ...

1.1 Interviews

Ⓓ SPEAKING 2

Student A

1 **Interview Student B. Find out the information below.**

   1 The company he/she works for. You've heard he/she works for Dalby Money Management.

   2 Their responsibilities in that job. You believe he/she is an investment manager.

   3 Their educational background. You've heard he/she studied in Texas.

2 **Answer Student B's question. Use the information below.**

   1 employer: Instep, a technology company that supplies equipment to industry; job title: Development Engineer

   2 your responsibilities: carry out research, test products, inform sales and management about new products, manage budgets, lead a team of three researchers

   3 your education: degree from your own country, PhD in Engineering, Manchester, UK

PRE-TASK Exercise 1

❶ Job posting

❷ Company information

Sales Manager

Expanding gym group requires a dynamic sales manager.

Our client is looking for a strong, focused sales manager to join their sports and leisure company. They have locations around London and the rest of the UK.

You must be able to work alone to find new business and also be able to lead your team to success. Ideally, currently working as a Gym Sales Manager or in Hotel or Restaurant Management.

2 days ago

About Gym Now

Gym Now launched in 2010 and operates 42 gyms across the UK, with 24 sites in London. Its members pay a low fee monthly, with no contract commitment. Gym Now gyms offer fitness and weight-training equipment. There are around 80 additional classes at a small extra cost. They operate a low-cost business model, the fastest growing sector in the gym business. The 24-hour model has allowed people who have never owned gym membership before to join – police officers, restaurant workers, etc. All memberships are managed online to reduce costs. Gym Now have recently secured a £3-million investment to meet the growing consumer demand for gym membership, and are looking to expand outside of the capital. They are looking for a dynamic individual to take the company forward in the next few years.

1.2 Presentations

C SPEAKING 2 Exercise 3

Student A

1 Present the information below on another possibility Priyanka considered to improve the health and fitness of staff. Make positive points with *so ...* and explain more negative points with *but ...*

> ### The 10 k Run training programme
> Join a team for the Adventure Run in May
> - Training sessions at Beginner, Intermediate and Advanced / suitable for all staff if interested
> - Want to be sure participants are fit / pre-training medical check offered
> - Free training 7.00 p.m. Mondays / extra training Thursdays 8.30 p.m. costs £7.50

2 Listen to your partner's presentation. Take notes on the main information.

TASK Part 1

Group A

1 **Proudways Foods**

Catering services for top businesses

6 a.m. – 7 p.m. coffee and light refreshments available

Quality drinks and a range of fresh smoothies at discount prices

All food made fresh on the premises

Five-a-day specials

Chef's theatre, where the chef cooks your meal fresh in front of you

Catering for meetings and outdoor events optional

Re-heating facilities for those bringing their own food

Group B

2 **Catering Now**

Range of healthy food

All food made fresh on the premises

Talks and meet the chef sessions twice a month

Weekly themes (e.g. Asian Week, Texan Week)

The balanced meal guide to help make healthy choices easy

Outside catering for 10–200 guests

Self-service drinks available 24 hours

Desk delivery service

PRE-TASK Role cards

Person A

You would like the company to start up the following clubs:

- martial arts club – we have a lot of Japanese colleagues
- international cookery club – to exchange exotic recipes with overseas colleagues

You think that potholing is for crazy people and very few employees would do it.

Person B

You would like the company to start up the following clubs:

- football club – it's a universally loved sport
- sailing club – there is a beautiful lake nearby

You think that cookery only appeals to women and there are plenty of good restaurants. Why cook?

Person C

You would like the company to start up the following clubs:

- landscape painting club – it would be a great way to show overseas colleagues our countryside
- choir – singing music from all over the world together

You think that football is too male-oriented and there are plenty of football clubs in the area.

Person D

You would like the company to start up the following clubs:

- potholing – great for adventure and team-building
- tennis club – both men and women would like this

You would rather walk the landscape than paint it. Painting isn't really a team activity.

2.2 Meetings

PRE-TASK

Useful Language

Making suggestions	Agreeing	Disagreeing
I think we should …	I think that's a great idea.	I don't know about that.
We could …	I really like that idea.	I'm not sure about that idea.
I'd like to …	I totally agree.	I really don't like that idea.

3.1 Telephoning

C PRONUNCIATION

INTERNATIONAL SPELLING ALPHABET			
A	Alpha	**N**	November
B	Bravo	**O**	Oscar
C	Charlie	**P**	Papa
D	Delta	**Q**	Quebec
E	Echo	**R**	Romeo
F	Foxtrot	**S**	Sierra
G	Golf	**T**	Tango
H	Hotel	**U**	Uniform
I	India	**V**	Victor
J	Juliet	**W**	Whisky
K	Kilo	**X**	X-ray
L	Lima	**Y**	Yankee
M	Mike	**Z**	Zulu

TASK Part 1

Group B Context:

You work for a company who designs and sells jewellery to fashion shops all over the world. One of your customers who buys from you is going to call to make an appointment for his/her manager to visit.

You will then call the customer back to give further details about your current special offers and new ranges you are designing.

Before you make the call, you need to create a profile for your jewellery design company. Complete the notes below.

The name of your jewellery design company:

Your name:

Your role in the company:

Where your jewellery design company is based:

Information about your business:

The style of jewellery you make:

Special offers:

New ranges you are designing:

1.1 Interviews

D SPEAKING 2

Student B

1 **Answer Student A's question. Use the information below.**

1 employer: Dalby Money Management, a company that looks after the wealth of high-income individuals; job title: Investment Director

2 your responsibilities: manage large investment funds, speak to clients, produce reports for investors, increase clients' wealth

3 your education: degree from your own country, Masters Degree from University of Texas, Dallas

2 **Interview Student A. Find out the information below.**

1 The company he/she works for. You've heard he/she works for Instep.

2 Their responsibilities in that job. You believe he/she works in research.

3 Their educational background. You've heard he/she has a PhD.

1.2 Presentations

C SPEAKING 2 Exercise 3

Student B

1 **Listen to your partner's presentation. Take notes on the main information.**

2 **Present the information below on another possibility Priyanka considered to improve the health and fitness of staff. Make positive points with *so ...* and explain more negative points with *but ...* .**

The Yoga Centre

Sign up today

• Learn relaxation techniques / great for improving mind and body

• Yoga and relaxation sessions 12:30p.m. to 1:30p.m. daily / classes not free, 50% discount on normal fees

• No registration needed / just come along

4.1 Negotiations

TASK Parts 1 and 2

Group A

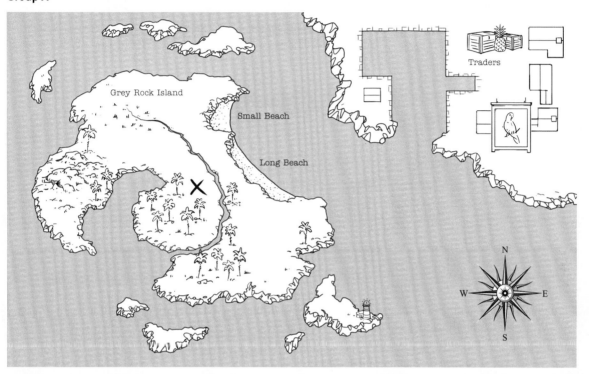

4.1 Negotiations

TASK Parts 1, 2 and 3

Group A

You represent the pirate, one-legged Pete. Look at the things that you have. What else will you need to find the treasure?

- You know where the treasure is – see the cross on your map. Don't show your map to the others!

- You have one spade for digging. You have a wooden leg.

- You don't have a boat. You have water but no food.

- You need someone to help you sail to the island and dig for the treasure.

- You have heard that the treasure is valued at 150,000 pesos.

- You don't trust Harry, although he has worked for you before.

- You have 175 pesos to buy things you need to find the treasure.

You can choose to work with only one partner or two but remember you will have to share the treasure!

4.2 Presentations

C SPEAKING 2

Student B

Present the product below using the following phrases to structure your presentation.

I want to talk to you today about
a new type of …

The dental industry is …

A common problem is that …

We're introducing a new …

(Describe the new product and
its benefits.)

So, to recap …

Product name:	The two way toothpaste tube
Problem:	A lot of toothpaste is wasted because of the bad design of a normal toothpaste tube
Toothpaste industry:	Currently worth $12.6 billion annually around the world. Growth is coming from Europe and Asia
Size:	Small, medium and large
Material:	Recyclable plastic
Selling points:	Good value for money, environmentally friendly, reduces waste

4.1 Negotiations

TASK Parts 1, 2 and 3

Group C

You represent the pirate, one-eyed Harry. Look at the things that you have. What else will you need to find the treasure?

- You have a boat, a compass and one spade for digging.

- You don't know where the treasure is and you don't have any food or water.

- You only have one eye and need someone to help you navigate and sail the boat.

- You have been to the island before. There are crocodiles in the river around the palm trees. But you have a sword to defend yourself.

- You don't trust Pete, although you have worked for him before.

- You have 175 pesos to buy things you need to find the treasure.

You can choose to work with only one partner or two but remember you will have to share the treasure!

4.1 Negotiations

TASK Parts 1 and 2

Group B and C

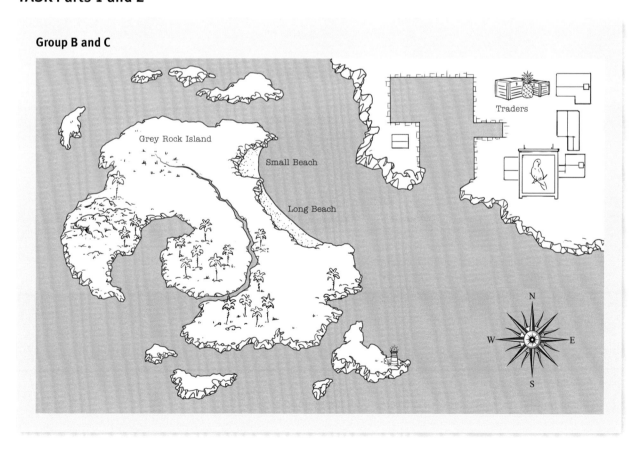

4.1 Negotiations

TASK Parts 1, 2 and 3

Group B

You represent the trader, Miguel. Look at the things that you have. What else will you need to find the treasure?

- You have food and water for the journey: fish, bread, fruit and water.

- You don't know where the treasure is and you have never looked for treasure before.

- You need a boat and two spades. A boat costs between 825–1,000 pesos. A spade costs about 75–100 pesos.

- You know how to sail around the difficult waters near Grey Rock Island.

- You haven't worked with Pete or Harry before.

- You have 650 pesos to buy things you need to find the treasure. You also have a talking parrot.

You can choose to work with only one partner or two but remember you will have to share the treasure!

4.2 Presentations

🅒 SPEAKING 2

Student A

Present the product below using the following phrases to structure your presentation.

I want to talk to you today about a new type of ...

The pet industry is ...

A common problem is that ...

We're introducing a new ...

(Describe the new product and its benefits.)

So, to recap ...

Product name:	The slow feed dog bowl
Problem:	Many dogs eat too quickly, causing health problems and over-eating
Pet industry:	Currently worth £2.7 billion annually in the UK 400% growth in the last year
Size:	Small, medium and large
Material:	Plastic
Selling points:	Cheap, light, easy to clean, recommended by vets

Glossary

- **adjective** *(adj.)* Headwords for adjectives followed by information in square brackets, e.g. *[only before a noun]* and *[not before a noun]*, show any restrictions on where they can be used.
- **noun** *(n.)* The codes *[C]* and *[U]* show whether a noun, or a particular sense of a noun, is countable *(an agenda, two agendas)* or uncountable *(awareness, branding)*. Note that some nouns in the examples are used as part of a noun phrase.
- **verb** *(v.)* The forms of irregular verbs are given after the headword. The codes *[I]* (intransitive) and *[T]* (transitive) show whether a verb, or a particular sense of a verb, has or does not have an object. Phrasal verbs *(phr.v.)* are shown after the verb they are related to where applicable.

accident *n. [C]* If something happens *by accident*, no one planned it or expected it to happen.
Most of the best ideas are discovered by accident.

achieve *v.* to succeed in doing or getting something you want
The jacket could achieve its sales target with a new marketing approach.

advertising *n. [U]* the business of advertising things on television, in newspapers, etc.
I'll explain how we can communicate with people through our advertising and promotion.

advice *n. [U]* when you suggest what someone should do
What advice would you give to someone starting their own business in your country?

agency *n. [C]* a business that arranges services for people
An advertising agency is a business which advises companies on advertising and makes ads.

agree *v.* to have the same opinion as someone else
I agreed with her that we need to change our marketing strategy.

aim *n. [C]* something that you want to do or get
What are the aims of the new magazine?

ambitious *adj.* determined to be successful or powerful
Luke is ambitious and does not want to be a sales assistant all his life.

appeal *n. [C]* the quality of something that makes you like it or want it
Create an event with universal appeal to a potentially highly diverse audience.

appeal *v.* If something *appeals* to you, you like it.
It needs to appeal to people living and working in cities, as well as to outdoor enthusiasts.

appear *v.* to become widely available or known about
How often will the magazine appear?

argument *n. [C]* **1** If you have an *argument* with someone, you shout or say angry things to them because you do not agree with them.
What would you do if you saw two colleagues having an argument?
2 the reasons that you give to show that something is right or wrong
I want to hear all the arguments for and against the offer before we make a decision.

arrange *v.* to make plans so that something can happen
I arranged a meeting with the finance department to discuss the project.

attendance *n. [U]* when you go to a meeting, school, church, etc.
She was warned about her poor attendance and time-keeping.

attractive *adj.* If something is *attractive*, people want to see it, go to it or have it.
There could be attractive investment opportunities over the next five years.

available *adj.* If something is *available*, you can buy it, use it or have it.
The collar is available in many different styles and fabrics.

balance *n. [C] singular* when you give the right amount of attention to two different things, rather than giving too much attention to one of them
What is a good work–life balance for you?

behave *v.* to do or say things in a particular way
Behave as though nothing has happened.

behaviour *n. [U]* Your *behaviour* is the way that you act or do things.
Certain standards of behaviour are expected at work.

behind *prep., adv.* responsible for something that has happened
Thomas Geissler is the German businessman behind the machines.

best-selling *adj.* bought by many people
Nestlé makes many of the world's best-selling food products.

bill *n. [C]* a list of things that you have bought or that someone has done for you, showing how much you have to pay for them
Ask for the bill.

body language *n. [U]* changes in your body position and movements that show what you are feeling or thinking
Pay attention to the other side's body language.

GLOSSARY

bonus *n. [C]* money that is added to someone's usual pay
We are willing to reward staff with attractive performance-based bonuses.

boost *v.* to increase the value or amount of something
The badge boosts sales of the product.

brand *n. [C]* a product that a particular company makes
Its brand is well known in Japan and in the United States.

break *n. [C]* If you take a *break*, you stop what you are doing for a short time in order to rest or eat.
Some people take a career break to do something adventurous.

budget *n. [C]* an amount of money that is available, or a careful plan of how to spend an amount of money
If you had an unlimited budget, what would be included in your dream corporate-hospitality package?

bully *v.* to frighten or threaten to hurt someone who is smaller or weaker than you
What would you do if you saw a colleague bullying another colleague?

bureaucracy *n. [U]* an official system that annoys and confuses people because it has too many rules
The government is making a renewed effort to reduce bureaucracy.

call *n. [C]* a telephone conversation
Would you like me to give him a call first?

campaign *n. [C]* a number of things that people do in order to get a particular result, especially people in business or government
Tell your partner about a marketing campaign that impressed you.

career *n. [C]* a job or profession that you do for a long time, especially one in which you can move to a higher position
Do you have a career plan? Where do you want to be in 10 years' time?

carry out *phr.v.* to do something that has been planned and organised, or that someone has told you to do
I think we should carry out a survey.

cashflow *n. [U]* the movement of money coming into a business as income and going out as wages, materials, etc.
Increased production and strong demand have had a positive effect on our cashflow.

catch *v.* to not hear or understand what someone says
Sorry, I didn't catch that.

CEO *n. [C] Chief Executive Officer:* the person with the most authority in a large company
It has set up a special committee to look for a new CEO.

client *n. [C]* someone who pays a person or organisation for a service or advice
The job involves dealing with clients and their needs.

comment *v.* to give your opinion about someone or something
Could I just comment on that?

commission *n. [C]* money that a person or organisation is paid when they sell something
The average sales executive expects to earn between £25–35k, including bonuses and commission, in their first year of work.

communication *n. [U]* when people talk to each other or give each other information using letters, telephones, etc.
Communication was better in Geraldine's company than Ruby's.

company *n. [C]* an organisation that makes or sells things
Would you prefer to work for several different companies?

competition *n. [C]* a situation in which people or organisations compete with each other
There is very strong competition in the US advertising industry.

competitive *adj.* determined to be more successful than other people
We are a highly competitive business.

confidence *n. [U]* belief in your ability to do things well
This confidence in his products is typical of Mr Kashio.

confident *adj.* sure that you can do something well
You must sound and appear confident.

conflict *n. [C]* a disagreement or fighting
How good are you at managing conflict?

consider *v.* to think about something carefully, especially before deciding what to do
The business owner has additional pressures to consider.

consumer *n. [C]* someone who buys things or uses a service that a company provides
Dino Conti manufactures and distributes ice cream to consumers in the state of California.

contact *n. [C]* someone whose name or e-mail address is stored on your phone, computer, etc.
Do you have any contacts in …?

contract *n. [C]* a formal written agreement between two people, companies, etc.
We'll sign the contract now.

cover *v.* to include something
Good, I think we've covered everything.

credit *n. [U]* a system in which you receive things and pay for them later
We'll give you 90 days' credit.

customer *n. [C]* someone who buys things from a shop or company
The customer database does not produce reliable results.

deadline *n. [C]* a date or time by which you must finish something
What deadlines do you have to meet in your daily life?

deal *v.* If you *deal* with a problem, you do something to make sure the problem no longer exists.
How would you deal with these problems?

delegate *v.* to give part of your power or work to someone in a lower position than you
Delegate to a deputy as often as possible.

deliver *v.* to take something such as a letter or a package to a place
We could possibly deliver by late August.

demand *n. [U]* If there is a *demand* for something, people want to buy it.
These products are made to satisfy consumer demand.

design *v.* to be made for a particular type of person or a particular purpose
It's designed to be used with any type of material.

discount *n. [C]* a lower price than usual
We must not offer any further discounts.

discrimination *n. [U]* unfair treatment of someone because of the group they belong to
There's a lot of European legislation now around the areas of sex discrimination.

dish *n. [C]* food cooked or prepared in a particular way
It's a vegetarian dish.

distribute *v.* to give something to each person or organisation
It produces 15 flavours, which it distributes mainly to supermarkets and company-owned stores.

dominate *v.* to be the most important or most noticeable person or thing
The professional photography market is dominated by Canon and Nikon.

download *n. [C]* something that you download from the Internet, for example software, a computer game or a song
It isn't available as a download.

electronics *n. [U]* the process of making electronic equipment, such as computers or televisions, or the study of this
problems for the Japanese consumer electronics industry

employer *n. [C]* Your *employer* is a person or company that pays you to work for them.
Employer–employee relations at John Lewis are completely different.

exchange rate *n. [C]* the value of the money of one country when you change it for the money of another country
The last six months have seen a slight improvement in the exchange rate.

expand *v.* to become bigger
Dino Conti has expanded rapidly in recent years.

expect *v.* to think that something will happen
We are expecting to sell more televisions, food and drink.

face *v.* If you *face* a bad situation or problem, you have to accept it or deal with it.
It is facing strong competition from other charter airlines.

facilities *n. [C] (plural)* rooms, equipment or services that are available in a place
The sports centre has great facilities.

fall *n. [C] singular* when an amount or level becomes less or lower
A recent fall in profits has disappointed the management.

favour *n. [C]* **be in favour of** to support a plan or idea
Personally, I'm in favour of June.

feature *n. [C]* an important or interesting part of something
Will the magazine have any special design features?

feel *v.* to have an opinion about something, based on your feelings
How do you feel about this?

figure *n. [C]* a number that shows an amount
According to new figures, checks on Facebook and Twitter are now as important in the job-selection process as a CV or interview.

finance *n. [U]* activities connected with the spending or saving of large amounts of money
What is the key difference between people who work in finance and those who work in research?

finance *v.* to provide money for something
The winner(s) will receive $20 million to finance and develop their project.

finish *v.* to come to the end of doing or making something
If you'll just let me finish …

flexible *adj.* able to change or be changed easily
The secret is to be flexible – although this often takes a lot of courage.

flexitime *n. [U]* a system in which people work a particular number of hours, but can change the times at which they start and finish
The company is changing to flexitime.

focus *v.* to give all or most of your attention to a particular thing
To be a good manager you need to focus on tasks, not people.

forecast *n. [C]* a description of what is likely to happen
A sales forecast is how much a company thinks it will sell in a period.

fortune *n. [C]* a lot of money
In banking, you can make a fortune with the big bonuses and retire at 35.

found *v.* to start an organisation
Anita Roddick founded The Body Shop.

GDP *n. [C] singular Gross Domestic Product:* the total value of all goods and services produced in a country, in one year, except for income received from abroad
The GDP has grown by 0.15%.

get *v.* to bring someone or something
Can I get you a drink?

go over *phr.v.* repeat something in order to explain it or in order to make sure it is correct
Let's go over the main points again.

grow *v.* to get bigger in size or amount
We are changing, growing and doing well at a difficult time for the industry.

growth *n. [U]* when something gets bigger or develops
Now its growth is slowing down.

high-performance *adj.* cars, computers, etc. that are able to go faster, do more work, etc. than normal ones
Ferrari make high-performance sports cars.

high-tech *adj. High-tech* equipment is very modern and uses the most advanced electronic parts.
IBM manufactures high-tech computer products.

hold *v.* to have a meeting, party, election, etc.
We normally hold our sales conference in Mumbai.

hold on *phr.v.* to tell someone to wait or stop doing something
Hold on a minute.

hope *v.* to want something to happen
Coca-Cola is hoping to more than double its number of bottling plants in China.

hospitality *n. [U]* when you behave in a friendly way towards visitors and make them feel welcome
What corporate-hospitality event would you like to be invited to?

human resources *n. [U]* in a company, the department that deals with employing, training and helping people
In 2010, Mukherjee, the Head of Human Resources, recruited 70,000 people.

ignore *v.* to know that someone or something is there, but to deliberately not do anything to show that you know
If managers ignore unacceptable behaviour, problems will get worse.

image *n. [C] singular* the way that someone or something seems to the public
How does entertaining affect a company's image?

impatient *adj.* Someone who is *impatient* becomes angry because they have to wait.
He gets very angry if people are late – he is very impatient.

impression *n. [C]* the feeling you have about something or someone because of the way they seem
You want to make a good impression on them.

improve *v.* to make something better
Decide what the company must do to improve the sales of the Wincote XWS.

in advance *adv.* before a particular time or event starts
You need to make your reservation 180 days in advance.

income *n. [C]* money that you receive, for example from your job
The company would be targeting consumers with average disposable income of Rmb5,000 a month.

inflation *n. [U]* a continuing increase in prices
The government has reduced the inflation rate to 2%.

influence *v.* to change how someone or something develops, behaves or thinks
Which of the four Ps influenced your decision to buy?

innovative *adj.* An *innovative* idea or way of doing something is new, different and better than those that existed before.
A competition is held each year to find the most innovative new consumer products.

interest rate *n. [C]* the percentage amount charged by a bank, etc. when you borrow money, or paid to you by a bank when you keep money in an account there
As soon as interest rates rise, the economy will slow down.

interrupt *v.* to say something at the same time as someone else is speaking
Sorry to interrupt, but …

inventor *n. [C]* someone who thinks of or makes something completely new
The inventor plans to build a global network.

investment *n. [C, U]* when you put money in a bank or buy something in order to get more money back later
Gold is a safe investment at a time of financial instability.

invite *v.* to ask someone to go somewhere, or to do something with you
Ruby and Geraldine were both invited to a meeting.

involved *adj.* If you are *involved* in an activity or event, you take part in it.
Why should managers get involved as soon as conflict develops?

issue *n. [C]* an important subject or problem that people discuss
Focus on the issues, not on personalities.

key *adj.* very important and necessary
Here are some key facts about our company.

kind *n. [C]* a type of person or thing
It's a kind of seafood.

kind *adj.* Someone who is *kind* cares about other people and treats them well.
It's very kind of you, but another time perhaps.

labour force *n. [C] singular* all the people who work for a company or in a country
The Netherlands took action to get the unemployed back into the labour force.

launch *v.* to make a new product available
The collar will be launched in new fashion collections.

link *n. [C]* a relationship or connection between different situations, events or people
There appears to be a link between stress levels and GDP.

look after *phr.v.* to do things to make sure that someone or something is safe and well
Who's going to look after our guests tonight?

manufacture *v.* to make large quantities of goods, using machines
Multinationals which manufacture in developing countries help the world economy.

manufacturer *n.* [C] a company that makes large quantities of goods, using machines
Boeing is a well-known aircraft manufacturer.

manufacturing *n.* [U] the process or business of producing goods in factories
Would you like to work in manufacturing?

market *v.* to try to persuade people to buy something by advertising it
If you want to market a product successfully, you need to get the marketing mix right.

marketing *n.* [U] the job of deciding how to advertise and sell a product
There are three candidates for the position of Sales and Marketing Director.

meet *v.* If something *meets* someone's standards or needs, it is good enough.
I've always met my sales targets.

meeting *n.* [C] an organised event where people discuss something. You organise, arrange or call a *meeting*. Then you have or hold it somewhere. You cancel a *meeting* if you decide not to have it
Managers should attend all meetings.

memorable *adj.* very good and likely to be remembered
Make sure the event is memorable.

message *n.* [C] a piece of information that you send or give to another person
Can I leave a message, please?

mind *v.* You say this to politely ask if you can do something.
Do you mind if I take one of these maps?

mission *n.* [C] the purpose or the most important aim of an organisation
I'll tell you about our mission statement. This describes what we're all about, why we're in business.

mix *n.* [C] *singular* all the different people or things that are in a place
The product mix in smaller cities will be chosen so that the entry price for consumers would be 15 per cent less than in Adidas's existing shops in larger cities.

model *n.* [C] one type of car or machine that a company makes
The company sells four models of bicycle.

monitor *v.* to watch or measure something carefully for a period of time to see how it changes
She said we needed to monitor sickness levels more closely.

move on *phr.v.* to start talking about a new subject in a discussion
Let's move on now.

multinational *n.* [C] a large company that has offices, factories, etc. in many different countries
Employees in large multinationals have excellent career opportunities if they are willing to travel.

multinational *adj.* A *multinational* company has factories, offices and business activities in many different countries.
GFDC is a multinational company based in Dubai.

need *n.* [C] something that is necessary
These products are made to meet a need.

negotiate *v.* to discuss something in order to reach an agreement
They are currently negotiating an important contract with an agency.

occasion *n.* [C] an important event or ceremony
We're getting together next week for a special family occasion.

offer *n.* [C] when you say that you will do something for someone or give them something if they want it
Never be the first to make an offer.

offer *v.* to say that you will do something for someone if they want you to
It's very kind of you to offer.

opening *n.* [C] when the public can start using a new place
We attended the opening of a new store.

opportunity *n.* [C] If you have an *opportunity* to do something, you get a chance to do it.
He never failed to take advantage of an opportunity.

order *n.* [C] something that a customer asks a company to make or send them
Place an order today.

organic *adj.* *Organic* food is grown or produced without using artificial chemicals.
Organic products are overpriced and often not as good as the alternatives.

outlet *n.* [C] a shop, company or organisation through which products are sold
Which sales outlets does Wan want to target?

participant *n.* [C] someone who is involved in an activity with other people
Participants arrive on Thursday evening.

participate *v.* to do an activity with other people
They feel they have no control over their work and they don't participate in decisions.

percentage *n.* [C] an amount that is part of a larger amount, expressed as part of a total which is 100
What percentage of your income do you spend on transport?

perform *v.* If something or someone *performs* well, they work well. If they *perform* badly, they work badly.
The company has been performing badly.

perform *v.* to do a job or a piece of work
Some of the operations are performed by robots.

place *n. [C]* a particular area or town, or a particular building, shop, restaurant, etc.
The conference will take place in July.

pollution *n. [U]* harmful chemicals and waste, and the damage they cause to the environment
Pollution is a big problem here.

potential *n. [U]* natural qualities which could make someone very successful in the future
The jacket was considered to have great sales potential.

prefer *v.* to like one thing or person more than another
Read the two theories and say which you prefer.

prepare *v.* to make something ready, so that it can be used
We prepared a budget with details of the various costs involved.

presentation *n. [C]* an event at which someone explains an idea to a group of people
After all the presentations, discuss which product is the most exciting and innovative.

pressure *n. [C]* when something makes you feel anxious or unhappy, for example because you have too much to do
Do you like working under pressure?

pretend *v.* to behave in a particular way in order to make people believe something is true, although it is not
They are often sick or pretend they are sick and take days off work.

privatise *v.* If a government *privatises* an organisation that it owns, it sells it.
Many companies in the UK have been privatised.

product *n. [C]* something that is made and sold by a company
A rep's job is selling products or services.

profile *n. [C]* a short description that gives important details about a person, a group of people or a place
What is a typical consumer profile for the brand?

profit *n. [C]* If you make a *profit* when you sell something, you get more money for it than you spent on it.
The money a company makes after taking away its costs and tax is its net profit.

profit margin *n. [C]* the difference between the cost of producing something and the price at which you sell it
Our profit margin is low.

profitable *adj.* producing a profit
Which idea do you think will be the most profitable?

qualification *n. [C]* an official examination that you have passed, which shows what level of education you have reached or what training you have had
Study for extra qualifications in your free time.

quality *n. [C]* something that a person or thing has as part of their character or nature, especially something good
Talk about the good or bad qualities of managers/ bosses you have had.

quit *v.* to leave a place or job permanently
I thought about quitting my job.

range *v.* to be between two limits
Prices range from US$1,000 upwards.

range *n. [C]* a number of different things that are all the same type of thing
The product range includes cars, vans and trucks.

reasonable *adj.* a reasonable amount or number is not too much or too big
That's very reasonable, don't you think?

receipt *n.* when someone receives something
We need payment on receipt of the goods.

recommend *v.* to tell someone that something is good or enjoyable
Can you recommend anyone?

redundant *adj.* to stop employing someone because there is not enough work for them any more
It is very likely that Diana Bishop may soon be asked by head office to make one consultant redundant, in order to cut costs.

refund *n. [C]* money that is given back to you in a shop, restaurant, etc., for example because you are not satisfied with what you bought
In order to get a full refund, customers must send back goods in the original packaging.

relaunch *n. [C]* a new effort to sell a product that is already on sale
The management decided to relaunch the product and change their approach to marketing it.

remind *v.* to make someone remember something that they must do
Ask someone (e.g. your PA) to remind you.

report *v.* to tell people about something that has happened
It was reported that he turned down a $2 billion offer from Yahoo.

report *n. [C]* something that gives facts about a situation or event
I wrote a report for the board of directors.

respond *v.* to answer
A good manager should respond to employees' concerns promptly.

response *n. [C]* a reply or reaction to something
On the other hand, some products are developed in response to customer research.

result *v.* to happen because of something
It results in an increase in sales and profit.

retirement *n. [U]* the time when or after you stop working at the end of your working life
You should plan your retirement from an early age.

return *v.* to give or send something back to someone
We will return your money if you are not happy.

rise *n. [C]* an increase
The boss has just given her a pay rise.

rival *n. [C]* a person or group that you compete with
Rivals are not only racing to launch new products but also cutting prices.

running *v.* managing or controlling a business, organisation, etc.
The job involves being in charge of people and running the organisation.

salary *n. [C]* the pay you receive from the organisation you work for
It's the percentage of their salary that each John Lewis employee takes home as that year's bonus.

sales *n. [U]* the total number of products that are sold during a particular period of time
Overall, sales revenue was 35% below target.

salesperson *n. [C]* someone whose job is to sell things for a company
It questioned sales professionals on what they considered to be the most important qualities for a salesperson.

say *n. [C] singular* If you have a *say* in something, you can give your opinion about it and help decide it.
Its employees – or partners – have a say in how it is run.

segment *n. [C]* one of the parts that something is divided into
Which market segment is the product aimed at in your country?

sell *v.* to be bought by people
The boots sold well.

serve *v.* If you *serve* food or drink, you give it to people.
It's served with rice.

set up *phr.v.* to start a company or organisation
The 29-year-old decided to set up an Internet business.

share *n. [C]* a part of something which each person in a group has received
Among UK supermarkets, Tesco has the highest market share.

sharply *adv.* suddenly and by a large amount
Sales have fallen sharply in the last three years.

shrink *v.* to become smaller
In Ireland, the economy is shrinking, and business owners are worried about how they will keep their business alive.

side *n. [C]* one person, group or team in a fight, sport or negotiation
He let the other side have everything they wanted in the negotiation.

sight *n. [C]* places that are interesting to see, and which many people visit
I'd love to see some of the sights.

skill *n. [C]* an ability to do something well, especially because you have practised it
What qualities and skills should a good manager have?

slight *adj.* small and not very important
The last six months have seen a slight improvement.

source *n. [C]* the place that something comes from
Some potential sources of conflict at work are obvious.

specialise *v.* to study only one subject or do only one activity
He specialises in traditional designs.

spend *v.* to use time doing something
What types of company spend a lot of time on research and development?

stable *adj.* not likely to move or change
The economy is stable following the problems of the past two years.

staff *n. [U]* the people who work for an organisation
More and more staff are taking medicine because they feel highly stressed at work.

strategy *n. [C]* a set of plans to achieve something
Our strategy is to make sure as many of our products as possible are new.

stressful *adj.* making you worried and unable to relax
Which of the situations is the most stressful for you?

summarise *v.* to give only the main information about something without all the details
OK, let's summarise.

superior *n. [C]* someone who has a higher position than you at work
Use charm with your superiors.

supply *v.* to provide people with something that they need
Cisco Systems is an American company which supplies Internet equipment.

suppose *v.* to think that something is probably true
I suppose we could do that.

survey *n. [C]* a set of questions that you ask a lot of people in order to find out about their opinions
The survey was carried out for Pareto Law, a recruitment and training company.

target *v.* to try to sell a product or give information about something to a particular group of people
Many consumer-goods multinationals have recently decided to target smaller cities and less wealthy consumers.

target *n. [C]* an amount or level that you are trying to achieve
Did they meet their sales targets?

test *v.* to use something to find out whether it works
All Casio products are tested before shipping.

tip *n. [C]* an additional amount of money that you give to someone who has done a job for you as a way of thanking them
Leave a tip.

top *adj.* best or most successful
The top five companies receive a badge from the Foundation.

trend *n. [C]* the way that a situation is changing or developing
What are the trends in your country?

turn *n. [C]* the time when you can or should do something, used when different people do something at different times
At a formal meeting, each person should speak in turn.

turn down *phr.v.* to say 'no' when someone offers you something
As we had another engagement, we had to turn down their invitation.

turnover *n. [C]* the amount of business done during a particular period
The amount of money a company receives from sales in a particular period is called its turnover.

unemployment *n. [U]* when people do not have jobs, or the number of people who do not have jobs
The unemployment rate is 8.25%.

value for money used to say that something is worth what you pay for it or not what you pay for it
It's great value for money.

venue *n. [C]* a place where a public event takes place
The marketing team sent out a questionnaire to find out what type of venue the participants preferred.

voice mail *n. [U]* a system that records telephone calls so that you can listen to them later
I'm sorry, there's no answer. I can transfer you to his/her voice mail.

waste of time not worth the time that you use because there is little or no result
Making lists of things to do is a waste of time.

wholesaler *n. [C]* a person or company that buys things in large quantities and sells them to shops
Suppliers often sell large quantities of goods to wholesalers.

WiFi *n. [U]* a way of connecting computers and other electronic equipment to a computer network using radio signals instead of wires
I go to places that have Wi-Fi.

workaholic *n. [C]* someone who spends all their time working
Why do people become workaholics?

working *adj.* relating to work
It was an ordinary working day.

workload *n. [C]* the amount of work that a person has to do
My workload keeps increasing.

worth be interesting or useful to do
I think it's a good idea. It's well worth trying.

Pearson Education Limited

Edinburgh Gate, Harlow, Essex CM20 2JE, England
and Associated Companies throughout the world.

www.pearsonelt.com

First Edition first published 2002

Third Edition first published 2012

Third Edition Extra first published 2016

Third impression 2018

ISBN: 978-1-292-13478-9

Set in Meta OT 9.5/12pt

Printed in Slovakia by Neografia

Acknowledgements
The publishers would like to thank the following authors for writing
the Business Skills lessons: Margaret O'Keefe, Clare Walsh, Iwona
Dubicka, Lizzie Wright, Bob Dignan, Sara Helm and Fiona Scott-Barrett.

The authors would like to thank the following for their invaluable help
during the project: Melanie Bryant, Peter Falvey, Sarah Falvey, Gisele
Cotton, Mark Cotton, Jason Hewitt and Richard Falvey. Thanks also to
Lewis Lansford for writing the Review units and Jonathan Marks for the
Glossary.

The authors and publishers are very grateful to the following people
who agreed to be interviewed for some of the recorded material in this
book: Susan Barratt, Dr Chris Bruton, Eileen Carroll, Jessica Colling,
Abdirashid Duale, Melissa Foux, Sue Leeson, Laurie Mullins, Dr Kate
Pitts, Ian Sanders, Richard Turner, James Wallman.

The publishers and authors are very grateful to the following advisers
and teachers who commented on versions of this material and
contributed to the initial research: Aukjen Bosma, Anna Culleton,
Carla D'Elia, Ian Duncan, Hazel Flack, Tim Kotowich, Malgorzata
Nowak, Nancy Pietragalla Dorfman, David Kadas, Hans Leijenaar,
Sabine Prochel, Ulrich Schuh.

Logos
Logo on p.8 from Twitter, copyright © 2011 Twitter; Logo on p.8 from
Facebook, copyright © Facebook, 2011; Logo on p.8 from LinkedIn.
Reproduced with permission. LinkedIn and the LinkedIn logo are
registered trademarks of LinkedIn Corporation, Inc. in the United
States and/or other countries. All rights reserved; Logo on p.39 from
www.google.com. Reproduced with permission.

Text
Extract on p.8 from "Facebook profile could 'damage job prospects'"
by Andy Bloxham, *The Telegraph,* 29/01/2010, copyright © Telegraph
Media Group Limited 2010; Extract on p.17 adapted from "Is John
Lewis the best company in Britain to work for?" by Jon Henley, *The
Guardian*, 16/03/2010, copyright © Guardian News & Media Ltd
2010; Extract on p.39 adapted from "Google leaps language barrier
with translator phone" by Chris Gourlay, *The Times*, 07/02/2010,
copyright © NI Syndication, 2010; Extract on p.39 from "Perfect
for a Boris bike... 'invisible' cycling collar with a built-in airbag" by
Mark Prigg, *This is London*, 21/10/2010, copyright © The Evening
Standard, 2010; Extract on p.39 from "Gold bullion – coming soon
to a vending machine near you" by Kate Connolly, *The Guardian*,
22/10/2010, copyright © Guardian News & Media Ltd 2010;
Extract on p.47 adapted from "Over half of business owners feeling
increasingly stressed" Grant Thornton Press Release 17/03/2010,
www.grantthorntonibos.com, copyright © Grant Thornton; Extract on
p.55 from "Corporate hospitality club interviews", *Event Magazine*,
16/10/2009. Reproduced with permission of the copyright owner,
Haymarket Media Group Limited; Extract on p.77 from "Adidas
targets the Chinese interior" by Patti Waldmeir, *The Financial Times*,
16/11/2010, copyright © The Financial Times Ltd, 2010. All rights
reserved; Extract on p.107 adapted from "Managing conflict at work:
A guide for line managers", pp.4, 6, Chartered Institute of Personnel
and Development, 2008. Reproduced with permission of the
publisher, the Chartered Institute of Personnel and Development,
London, www.cipd.co.uk.

In some instances we have been unable to trace the owners of
copyright material, and we would appreciate any information that
would enable us to do so.

Photos
The publisher would like to thank the following for their kind
permission to reproduce their photographs:
(Key: b-bottom; c-centre; l-left; r-right; t-top)

Alamy Images: Bill Bachman 131, Ellen Isaacs 36t, Glow Images 51tr,
Jeff Morgan 85, Kevin Foy 17cr, Paul Hakimata 102cr, PhotoAlto 103tr,
Westend61 / GMBH 103tc; **Corbis:** 28t, Aflo 104t, Andre Kosters
Pool / EPA 96t, Bob Krist 29c, Imagine China 77br, Justin Guariglia
58br, Michael Falzone / JAI 110bl, Rainier Ehrhardt / Zuma Press 72,
Roulier / Turiot / Photo Cuisine 21, Sergio Pitamit 59bl, Tibor Bognar
22t; **Fotolia.com:** Chungking 82, fotografiche.eu 66t, R Caucino 78cl,
Syda Productions A7br, Viorel Sima 102, Yuri Arcurs 11; **Getty Images:**
Adam Brown / Uppercut Images 39cl, AFP 17tr, 74t, AFP 17tr, 74t,
Andreas Rentz / Bongarts 55tr, Barcroft Media 43t, Bloomberg 39bl,
69tr, Bloomberg 39bl, 69tr, BLOOMimage 27, Mark Daffey 112, Daniel
& Les Jacobs / Cultura 56, Dave & Les Jacobs / Blend Images 99,
db2Stock 103, Doug Menuez / Photodisc 101, Dream Pictures / The
Image Bank 13tr, Dreamlight / The Image Bank 60b, Geber86 A7bl,
George Doyle / Stockbyte 121, Hero Images A15-A16, Image Source
107, Indeed 137tr, Javier Pierini 80-81, Joe Lasky / Gallo Images 55tc,
Junior Gonzalez / fstop 51br, Justin Pumfry / Stone 58-59, Kurita
Kaku / Gamma Rapho 115, Nicole Waring / The Agency Collection
25tr, PBNJ Productions / Blend Images 51tl, PBNJ Productions /
Photodisc 60br, Purestock 117, Robert Churchill / Vetta 110-111,
Studio Box / Photographers Choice 13br, Terry Vine / Blend Images
47, The Image Bank / Reza Estakhrian 89, Thomas Barwick / Stone
60-61, Tom Schierlitz / The Image Bank 20bl, Visions of America / Joe
Sohm / Digital Vision 58bl, Zia Soleil / Iconica 102b; **iStockphoto:**
Neustockimages 118-119, Sherry Perry 13tl; **John Carter Tramper:**
42; **Pearson Education Ltd:** Rob Maidment 9, 16, 24, 37, 46, 54, 68,
68bl, 76, 84, 98, 106, 114, **Pearson Education Ltd:** Sozaijiten A15c;
PhotoDisc: Keith Brofsky 49, 87, Keith Brofsky 49, 87; **Photolibrary.
com:** Asia Images 41, Bios 44t, Britain On View 52t, Image Broker 14t,
Nordic Photos 59br, Oliver Eltinger 91, Randy Faris / Flirt Collection
12, Robert Harding Travel 73; **Plainpicture Ltd:** Cultura 13tc, A1-A2;
Rex Shutterstock: BPI / Ben Queenborough 55tl, Picture Perfect 6t;
Sandra Felsenstein: 69br; **Shutterstock.com:** Africa Studio A3-A4,
Alexander Raths 81, Ben Jeayes 71, Goodluz 103tl, Joe Klune 29t,
Monkey Business Images A5-A6, Myimagine A11-A12, Pressmaster
A7-A8, A13-A14, Sport Graphic 86, Szefei A1cl, Wavebreakmedia
19, 88, A9-A10, Yuri Arcurs 79; **SuperStock:** Axiom Photographic 50,
Blend Images 30, 51cl, Blend Images 30, 51cl, Image Source 109,
Moodboard 31; **TopFoto:** 40

All other images © Pearson Education

Video
© Pearson Education

Illustrations
Martin Sanders (Beehive Illustration)